ALSO BY LOUP DURAND
DADDY

J·A·G·U·A·R

J·A·G·U·A·R

LOUP DURAND

Villard Books New York 1991

Translation copyright © 1990 by J. Maxwell Brownjohn

All rights reserved
under International and
Pan-American Copyright Conventions.
Published in the United States by Villard Books,
a division of Random House, Inc., New York. Originally
published in France as *Le Jaguar* by Olivier Orban in 1989.
Copyright © 1989 by Olivier Orban. This translation
first published in Great Britain by Century
Hutchinson Publishing Group
Limited in 1990. Villard Books is
a registered trademark of
Random House, Inc.

Library of Congress Cataloging-in-Publication Data
Durand, Loup.
[Jaguar. English]
Jaguar/by Loup Durand.
p. cm.
Translation of the French work with same title.
ISBN 0-394-58825-8
I. Title.
PQ2664.U6734J2813 1991
320.973—dc20   90-50220

Manufactured in the United States of America

9 8 7 6 5 4 3 2

First American Edition

Designed by Michael Ian Kaye

THE ULTIMATE TRUTH OF THE JIGSAW PUZZLE IS THIS: ALL APPEARANCES TO THE CONTRARY, IT ISN'T A SOLITARY GAME. THE PUZZLER'S EVERY MOVE HAS BEEN MADE BEFORE HIM BY THE PUZZLE-MAKER. EVERY PIECE HE PICKS UP, EXAMINES AND FINGERS, EVERY COMBINATION HE TRIES AND TRIES AGAIN, EVERY TENTATIVE EXPERI-MENT, EVERY STROKE OF INTUITION, EVERY MOMENT OF HOPE OR DISCOURAGE-MENT HAS BEEN PREDETERMINED . . . BY THE OTHER.

—GEORGES PEREC, *LA VIE, MODE D'EMPLOI*

IT'S A VERY LONG TIME SINCE I CEASED TO BE PREOCCUPIED WITH REALISM.

—ALFRED HITCHCOCK

I

IF CAPTURED VERY YOUNG,
THE JAGUAR CAN BE DOMESTICATED
WITHOUT DIFFICULTY. IT SOON RECOGNIZES
ITS KEEPER, ACTIVELY SEEKS HIS COMPANY
AND EVINCES GREAT PLEASURE
AT HIS APPROACH.

II

THE JAGUAR WILL EAT ALL
THE LARGE MAMMALS IT CAN CATCH.
IT WILL ALSO CHASE WATERFOWL THROUGH
REEDS AND IS ADEPT AT CATCHING FISH
IN THE SHALLOWS. IT DOES NOT
SEEM DETERRED BY SNAKES
OR CAYMANS.

III

PROVIDED IT CAN FIND
SUFFICIENT FOOD AND IS
UNDISTURBED, THE JAGUAR WILL KEEP
TO A FIXED TERRITORY. IT ALWAYS MOVES
AT NIGHT. BEING AN EXCELLENT SWIMMER,
IT WILL IF NECESSARY CROSS THE
WIDEST OF RIVERS.

IV

THE JAGUAR'S CALL BEARS
NO RESEMBLANCE TO THE CONVENTIONAL
ROAR OF THE WILD BEAST. IT IS, IN FACT, A
SILENT CREATURE. A LOW GROWL IS THE MOST IT
EVER UTTERS, THOUGH MANY TRAVELERS CLAIM
IT CAN BE LOCATED BY THE DIN MADE
BY HOWLER MONKEYS WHEN IT
COMES THEIR WAY.

V

THE JAGUAR AVOIDS MAN
WHEN IT MEETS HIM AND SELDOM
RETALIATES EVEN WHEN WOUNDED. IT BECOMES
A MAN-EATER ONLY IN VERY EXCEPTIONAL
CIRCUMSTANCES.

VI

THE JAGUAR HAS ALWAYS BEEN
HUNTED BY MAN. SOUTH AMERICAN INDIANS
USE CURARE-TIPPED ARROWS FOR THIS PURPOSE. IT
CAN ALSO, THOUGH THIS IS MORE DANGEROUS, BE
FLUSHED OUT AND BROUGHT TO BAY WITH DOGS. ALL
THAT REMAINS IS TO WRAP A SHEEPSKIN AROUND
ONE'S ARM AND STAB THE ANIMAL WITH A SPECIAL
TYPE OF DOUBLE-EDGED KNIFE. THE DOGS
ARE THEN LEFT TO FINISH IT OFF.

VII

WHEN A JAGUAR DISPLAYS
EXCEPTIONAL FEROCITY, THE NATIVES
BELIEVE IT TO BE A MAGICAL OR IMAGINARY
BEING, NOT A REAL ANIMAL. THEY MAY ALSO
REGARD IT AS THE INCARNATION OF SOME
LONG-DEAD AND PARTICULARLY
EVIL MAN.

The descriptions of the jaguar and its habits are taken from *Beautés du Monde* (Librairie Larousse).

Prologue

amantha?

Where are you, Samantha?

I'll never give up, you know. Never.

Candido, alias Jaguar, was a prisoner in the Great Silence. Some time ago, while awaiting execution in an ordinary jail, he'd been given an injection. His memory was a blank—he could remember nothing, not even being transferred here. Then consciousness slowly returned. He opened his eyes, looked around . . . and heard it.

A silence strong enough to shatter the eardrums.

To drive a man insane.

He stopped pacing to and fro, sat down cross-legged in the middle of the white cube, unclenched his fists and forced his fingers to relax.

That's what THEY want, Candido, to drive you insane, just as THEY wanted you to become a jaguar—the *Jaguar.*

Good, you're getting a grip on yourself.

Go over the whole story in your head, from the beginning. Not starting with your birth, but nineteen or twenty years later, when you got to the Mato Grosso— well before you knew Samantha. Before you knew Aliochka Alekhin, the diabolical puzzle-maker. Before Afonka Tchadayev and the other Jaguar's Claws.

When you were home, in Brazil, and the whole thing really began.

Four years ago.

◆ ◆ ◆

Candido was nineteen years and a few months old, and he was walking. He'd kept up a reasonable turn of speed for the first few weeks after escaping from the Indian village where the military patrol had almost captured him. Now he was toiling along, step by agonizing step. Later on, in the Great Silence, he would be amazed by his own extraordinary, almost animal powers of endurance.

He headed as nearly due north as he could, guiding himself by the sun—when there was any—and by the moss on the tree trunks. When the few supplies he'd been given by the Indians ran out he ate fruit, leaves, the occasional root, snakes, worms—even baby caymans, which he decapitated with his machete and devoured raw. But hour after hour of every day he sank up to his thighs in the ever-deepening mud.

Rain fell incessantly on the Mato Grosso, those millions of acres of wild and almost uncharted Brazil. It was swelling the Rio Guaporé, a tributary of the Amazon whose farther bank is Bolivian, not Brazilian. The heavy, viscous downpour was typical of summer in those southern latitudes (Christmas had probably occurred some days earlier). It scoured craters in the red mud and transformed the Pantanal into a vast swamp covering an area of some ten thousand square miles between the basin of the Paraguay River in the south and the Guaporé in the north. At this rate, everything but the flat-topped mounds of basalt known as *trombas* would soon be nine or ten feet under water.

He'd lost his boots and his officer's tunic. His bare feet were being devoured by huge chiggers that encrusted his flesh and left oozing sores that looked like shelled oysters. Dozens of leeches clung to his chest and back. The sea of mud rose steadily until it was waist-deep. Apart from his machete, which was providentially attached to his wrist by a leather thong (he'd long since lost his service revolver and jettisoned the holster), he carried nothing but the rubberized poncho with which he had deserted from the garrison some months ago. He didn't use the poncho to protect himself from the rain: instead it was wrapped around his copy of *Der Abenteuerliche Simplicissimus Teutsch* by Hans Jakob Christoffel von Grimmelshausen. Candido held this precious bundle high above his head whenever he sank into a pothole.

That way, when he was finally engulfed—an hour or a day from now—his bedside book would survive him for a little while.

◆   ◆   ◆

Candido Stevenson Cavalcanti de Noronha was five feet four inches tall, with nice green eyes and no experience of life. Sole heir to the huge financial empire of the Cavalcanti de Noronhas of São Paulo, he had two half sisters from his father Dom Trajano's second marriage. (His mother, from whom he had inherited his small stature and slender build, had died giving birth to him.)

Last July the sky had fallen in on him. He awoke one afternoon and lazily rang for breakfast in the usual way, but no valet appeared. Instead, two of Dom Trajano's attorneys stormed into his bedroom. With minimal ceremony they announced that enough was enough: Dom Trajano regarded his fling with the daughter of the minister of war as the last straw. Three hours later, equipped with a brand-new second lieutenant's commission and a uniform to match, Candido found himself on board a northbound train, bemused but incapable of resentment toward Dom Trajano. It wasn't in his nature to be angry with anything or anyone, least of all his father. It hurt him, of course, that Dom Trajano hadn't spoken a word to him for over four years, but innate optimism led him to hope that his sire's ill humor would soon evaporate. Candido was almost alone in his ignorance of certain rumors concerning himself and Dom Trajano. In his scheme of things, a father could no more loathe his son than a son could detest his father.

The officers and NCOs of the small backwoods garrison to which Candido was assigned—professional soldiers doomed to a dreary existence by their own mediocrity and lack of connections—took only a few days to grasp that they had acquired a perfect target for their sadistic tendencies. Not only was Candido the son and heir of one of São Paulo's wealthiest men—and everyone in Brazil resented the Paulistas' wealth and arrogance—but he had been sent up-country, as the colonel carefully explained, for them to make a man of him.

◆　◆　◆

He'd covered only a few hundred yards in the last few hours. The impenetrable curtain of rain reduced visibility to a hundred feet. To attempt a crossing here in the rainy season was sheer madness.

I'm going to die, Candido told himself. *What a shame. Dom Trajano will be sad, I'm sure, and so will Herr Doktor, but it's all my own fault. I've never been the son Papa expected. . . .*

As for the colonel and his officers, my death will suit them perfectly. Why did they christen me "Jaguar"? I'm not a wild beast. If I must be an animal I'd sooner be a cuddly little kitten—one the ladies like to stroke. The war minister's daughter, for instance. She was nice. . . .

Night was falling and the water still rising. Even at the most optimistic estimate, dry land and the nearest human habitation must be upwards of a hundred miles away.

Twice already, when he'd plunged into an unexpected dip, the poncho-wrapped Grimmelshausen had disappeared beneath the surface. Both times, he wept.

The light was almost gone, not that it mattered. His eyes were so clogged with mud he couldn't see anyway. And that was how he came to scramble up the *trombas* without knowing it—without realizing that he'd hauled himself onto an islet that might just possibly remain unsubmerged.

He collapsed in a heap and curled up around the Grimmelshausen.

◆   ◆   ◆

He'd written to Dom Trajano, four times in all, a couple of months after joining the garrison. He made no mention of the treatment to which he'd been subjected: the countless humiliations; the forced marches during which he alone marched while the men of his detachment ambled along on horseback; the thirty-hour drills he was compelled to undergo; the insolence he had to endure from private soldiers egged on by his brother officers; the two thrashings he'd received; the attempted homosexual rape to which he'd almost succumbed; the theft of his watch, signet ring and clothes; the smashing of his guitar and the burning of all his books except the Grimmelshausen, which he'd managed to hide. Not a word about any of those things—no, he simply asked, with the rather awestruck courtesy he'd always shown his father, if Dom Trajano would care to secure him another posting, no matter where. He received no reply. The colonel commanding the Mato Grosso garrison showed him the four letters, all of which had been returned to the military authorities unopened, and sentenced him to two weeks' detention on bread and water in a corrugated-iron shed where the temperature hit 130 degrees in the shade.

Early in October he tried to hang himself, having previously failed to escape southward to São Paulo. He was cut down just in time. Far from taking pity on him, the military authorities were infuriated by what they regarded as two separate cases of desertion and intensified their brutal treatment. Everything conduced to this: Candido's gentle and submissive temperament, the return of his letters, which proved that he could expect no paternal protection, and a stream of directives from the vengeful minister of war.

At the beginning of the second week in November he deserted again. This time he headed north and took refuge for a while with the Juruna Indians, only to be tracked down once more by his colonel, who considered it a point of honor to recapture him.

Finally he fled westward and was swallowed up by the Pantanal.

◆   ◆   ◆

In the greyish light of dawn his position looked quite hopeless. As far as the eye could see, almost everything was submerged. Apart from the treetops that jutted above the surface here and there, the forest itself had disappeared. The only patch of terra firma in sight was an inlet more or less the size of the *trombas* on which chance had stranded him, and even that was at least a couple of miles away. There was no point in trying to reach it.

He stretched out with the poncho over him and read some *Simplicissimus,* of which he knew hundreds of pages by heart. Herr Doktor used to be irritated by his mania for rereading the same book when there were so many other literary treasures to discover, but Taxile Grüssgott (to give the German tutor his full if rarely used name) was the only person to have shown Candido the slightest affection since his infancy. Even now, Candido would have rejected—not with anger, of which he was incapable, but with surprise and sorrow—any suggestion that the education lavished on him by Herr Doktor had been bizarre in the extreme.

He managed to read after a fashion, though he dozed off at intervals. Weak with hunger, overcome by alternate spells of dizziness and torpor, he was hazily aware of the passing days and nights, of the rain that sometimes ceased, only to descend on him again with redoubled ferocity.

And then he felt the touch of a hand and heard a human voice. He struggled feebly as he was picked up, convinced that he'd been found by one of the colonel's patrols. He was struggling to grasp his machete. He wanted to use it to cut his own throat.

Some time later he came to, drank the mug of sweet, lukewarm coffee that was held to his lips, ate, passed out, came to again, ate and drank some more, discovered that his body had been washed and tended and that he was now lying in a hammock on the deck of a boat.

"Only the Jaguar could have done what you did," said a voice.

There they go again with their Jaguar nonsense, Candido thought vaguely as sleep reclaimed him. *So the colonel's patrols have recaptured me after all. . . .*

The following dawn proved him wrong. Now able to stand and walk unaided, he was astonished by the look of admiration on the faces of the men surrounding him. They announced that he was traveling down the rain-swollen Paraguay River bound for the River Plate and Buenos Aires, and had been rescued by one of the five boats that had scoured the Pantanal for him at Herr Doktor's insistence. The search had lasted nearly two weeks. Meantime, the Brazilian military authorities, who considered him a deserter and a dangerous subversive, had tried and sentenced him to death *in absentia.*

"My name is Policarpo Moravec." The speaker was a man with extraordinarily deep-set eyes and the feverish air of a fanatic, if not a sufferer from some terrible wasting disease. He smiled at Candido's obvious bewilderment. "We're going to do great things together, Jaguar," he added, and produced a letter in which Herr Doktor urged Candido to trust him implicitly.

"How soon do we get to Buenos Aires?"

Herr Doktor explained in his handwritten letter that he thought this the ideal moment to undertake the trip to Germany they'd been planning for so long. Candido must go on ahead and he would join him later, "after pacifying your father and persuading him to overlook your escapades."

Candido's mind was immediately made up: he would leave for Europe, the land of his dreams. The Mato Grosso receded into the distance, the rain stopped. A nightmare had ended.

Policarpo Moravec asked if he would be willing to sail for Germany on the first ship available.

"Yes," he said.

Once he was in Germany there would be flaxen-braided young ladies to pursue. No one *there* would go on about the Jaguar.

The right bank of the river was now Paraguayan. On the left, wreathed in blue clouds, loomed the crests of the Serra de Amambaí.

It was the true beginning of his story.

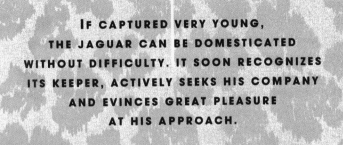

If captured very young, the jaguar can be domesticated without difficulty. It soon recognizes its keeper, actively seeks his company and evinces great pleasure at his approach.

heka," said Alexis Mikhailovich Alekhin.

He thrust his ID through the window of the car, which slowed but didn't stop, and the soldiers promptly stepped aside. "Aliochka," Dzerzhinsky had told him in Moscow, "we must see to it that the very word Cheka inspires terror—Red terror. No one must think himself exempt from our omnipresent and merciless severity. Our peasants believe in Baba Yaga the witch. We too must become Baba Yagas—mythical beings on a national scale. And don't be afraid of making mistakes. One dead innocent will contribute more to our myth than the most well-deserved execution."

It was January 1920, and Alekhin had now been in Petrograd, formerly St. Petersburg, for two months. He was back in his birthplace, the city where his father's elegant shoe shop on Konyushennaya Street had been patronized by such luminaries as the composer Rimsky-Korsakov, the writer Turgenev and the dancer Nijinsky.

The car, a backfiring Mathis of French manufacture, with Alphonse Tchadayev at the wheel, picked up speed again and was soon bowling along the Fontanka embankment. The Nevsky Prospekt loomed ahead. They drove along it past Kazan Cathedral, the glass-domed Singer Company building, now disused, and the Stroganov mansion with its white and bottle-green facade.

It was sixty-five days since Alekhin's recall from the Ukrainian front, where the Red cavalry had succeeded in smashing the White armies commanded by Denikin and Wrangel. A political commissar, Alekhin had been interviewed in turn by Yagoda himself, then by young Lavrenti Beria and finally by no less a person than the creator of the Cheka and his supreme boss, Felix Dzerzhinsky. The same questions each time: what subjects had he studied, what languages did he speak, what countries had he spent time in prior to 1917 and, of course, what service had he seen with the Red Army? His interrogators doubtless had all this information on file, but the way in which they put their questions spoke volumes.

Alekhin gathered that he was to be given a special assignment of some kind. "Lavrenti Pavlovich thinks you could be useful to us," Dzerzhinsky told him. "So do I. You leave for Petrograd at once. Then we'll see."

Alekhin set off the same day, having obtained permission to take the inseparable Tchadayev with him. There followed twenty hours by train in a *tiepluchka,* a crude cattle car equipped with wooden benches and a small cast-iron stove. At Petrograd he made the acquaintance of his immediate superior, Yury Naumov, the former capital's Cheka boss, a stocky, redheaded little man, almost illiterate but cunning and fanatical. More importantly, he also encountered Grigory Evseyevich Zinoviev. A repellently obese and dirty man in a grey astrakhan pelisse, Zinoviev had for two years been chairman of the Petrograd Soviet, which surpassed even that of Moscow in importance. He also headed the Communist International and was thus responsible for spreading revolution throughout the world.

So Alekhin's instinct had been right: the mission for which he was being considered by Dzerzhinsky and the other Moscow bigwigs would take him beyond the borders of Russia. Dzerzhinsky, often mentioned as a possible successor to Vladimir Ilyich Lenin, had eyed him curiously. "You're tall, Aliochka. How tall? Six feet three? I'd have bet you were taller. According to Genrik Yagoda you're the best-looking man in Russia—and not without brains, either. How's your English? Not bad at all—almost no accent. What about your German? Hmm, it says here you speak it perfectly—you could pass for a Berliner born and bred. . . ."

The Mathis, driving along the bank of the Neva almost at walking pace, passed the Winter Palace on its left. Petrograd was frozen solid, and the huge, unheated rooms of the former imperial residence now housed a shivering multitude of refugees. Visible across the river in spite of the heavy snow were the massive fortress of SS. Peter and Paul and the university on Vassilievsky Island.

"I was a student there, Afonka. So was Lenin, but not at the same time."

Now thirty years old, Alekhin had wavered between one side and the other in 1917. He almost threw in his lot with Kornilov, then with Denikin. When the Whites, with French and British support, got to within two hundred miles of Moscow, he took it into his head to rejoin Bukharin and his cutthroats. He thought he was done for and doomed to exile, but the establishment of Lenin's regime in April 1918 set his mind at rest. Not that he'd been afraid. He was as immune to fear as to any other emotion. He'd even lost the ability to surprise himself. He was what he aspired to be, a universally insensitive robot guided solely by self-interest. "There's something monstrous about you," Dzerzhinsky had told him, and Dzerzhinsky was a shrewd judge of character.

So they were going to send him abroad. Excellent. He even thought he knew why. If this mission was the one he had in mind, and if he were to execute it successfully, he would have to devise a plan. His one passion, if he could be said to have one at all, was a fondness for careful and unhurried planning. He was far more interested in devising puzzles than in solving them.

"That's far enough, Afonka. Take me back to Shpalernaya."

He had one or two prisoners to interrogate there. Cruelty bored him, nothing more. Either it served a purpose or it didn't.

He neither knew nor had ever heard of Candido Cavalcanti.

Nor of Samantha Franck.

◆ ◆ ◆

The house on Chicago's Schiller Street was filling up with mourners just back from the cemetery and eager for their funeral lunch. Samantha waited for them to get settled. Then, satisfied that no one would disturb her, she sneaked downstairs to what had, until only a few weeks ago, been her father's consulting room. Nothing had been touched: the shelves laden with innumerable books in German and English, the pair of pen-and-ink drawings he liked so much, one of the Alexanderplatz in Berlin, the other of a Black Forest landscape, the polished oak desk with its Tiffany lampshade, the pipe rack, the fountain pen he used for writing prescriptions, his stethoscope, his framed diplomas, the first awarded in Berlin, the second in Chicago and dated 1889, three years after he emigrated to the United States.

She sat down in one of the two armchairs facing the desk.

"Don't be angry with me for doing this, Papa. *You* wouldn't have reproached me, I know. *You'd* have understood."

A hum of conversation drifted up from below. Things were warming up—she could even hear laughter.

Going over to a bookshelf, Samantha picked out the complete works of Bakunin, a three-volume set printed on Bible paper. She made it back to her bedroom just in time and was strapping up her bags when someone knocked on the door.

"You should have come downstairs and had lunch with us, Sam. Your mother's furious."

It was Cousin Herbie, looking his usual idiotic self.

"Help me with these," she said.

She reached the bottom of the stairs and crossed the hallway without even turning her head. Uncle Moritz tried to intercept her, but she was outside and into the Chevy almost before he knew it.

They drove along the Loop in silence.

"Do you really have to be back in college by tonight?" Herbie asked eventually.

"Yes."

"Look, Sam, we all know how close to him you were. . . ."

"I'd rather not talk about it."

He insisted on parking his car, carrying her bags, escorting her first to the ticket office, then to the train, then into the train itself.

"Don't wait, Herbie, please. And thanks."

He went at long last. As the train started to move, she grabbed her bags and jumped down onto the platform without losing sight of him in case he turned around. She even followed him at a safe distance and lurked in the crowd until he got into his car and drove off.

An hour later she boarded the long-distance bus for New York. She managed to sleep a little during the interminable trip. The letter she'd written her mother in advance she entrusted to the old woman sitting beside her. It disclosed almost everything about her plans, but it would arrive too late for anyone to interfere. In New York she took a room at the YWCA on Lexington Avenue. It was only her second visit to New York. The first had been in 1917, when she and her father went there to demonstrate against sending American soldiers to fight in Europe. Her father was arrested and thrown into jail for having emptied a pot of yellow paint over a colonel, and Uncle Moritz had to bail him out.

Uncle Moritz was the only member of the family she could stand, and even he had his off days. She supposed Cousin Herbie was all right too, except that he tended to cling like a limpet.

Next morning she checked her ticket and her passport. Fortunately, no one noticed that her date of birth had been altered to credit her with two years more than the nineteen to which she was really entitled.

That afternoon she called at the Brooklyn address given to her by Walter Lingg. There was no one home. Having hung around on the landing for three hours she returned to her room in Manhattan, where she spent the evening and part of the night reading. She almost delved into the Bakunin, which her father used to read aloud to her, but decided against it. She had time—she would save it for the boat. In the end she went back to *The Crisis of Social Democracy* and *The Russian Revolution* by her beloved Rosa.

It was her last night in America. She felt tempted to go out and walk the streets but decided against it. Not that she was perturbed by the thought of roaming around at night in a city even bigger than Chicago. What she dreaded was her impending leap into the unknown, her separation from all that had made up her life till now. Added to that was the sorrow she felt at her father's death and the memory of those final weeks during which he'd lain dying of cancer, rendered less and less lucid by pain.

But she would have left for Europe even if he'd still been alive. He would have understood. As for Rosa, she wouldn't have hesitated.

The next morning she returned to Brooklyn, and this time someone answered the door.

"Emma Goldman?" said the man with the sleep-crumpled face. "She isn't home. She's away someplace, no idea where."

"When will she be back?"

He shrugged.

He's lying, that's obvious. He must be suspicious of me. Genuine anarchists never trust anyone, being hunted the way they are. How exciting, I'm in the underworld at last!

"Werner sent you?" said the man. "Werner who? I don't know any Lingg in Chicago or anyplace else. Come inside, though. I was just fixing myself some coffee."

He spoke English with a German accent.

Samantha hesitated. Something about the look in his eye made her feel uneasy—panic-stricken, in fact. For a start he was much taller than her, and few men were. He was also naked, or as good as. He'd pulled on a pair of pants, but his fly was open and you could see things. What was more, he was hairy all over—his chest would have done credit to a bear. OK, so he probably was a genuine anarchist (since Emma let him sleep with her), but just the same . . . Werner Lingg had told her all about the sexual freedom on which anarchists ought to pride themselves, but Werner was seventy years old and so blind he couldn't see his own hands without glasses.

She blurted out some stupid excuse and beat a retreat.

Back in Manhattan she wrote to Werner, whose brother had been one of the five anarchists (the other four were Engle, Fischer, Parsons and Spies) charged, rightly or wrongly, with throwing bombs on May 3, 1886. *Werner's brother had committed suicide the night before the other four were executed.* "I'm leaving tonight, Werner," she wrote. "I called twice at E.G.'s, but she isn't in New York so I won't meet her. I'm very disappointed. You may condemn what I'm doing, but I want you to know you're not responsible. The very fact that I didn't tell you proves I was afraid you'd disapprove. . . ."

Another ten hours to wait. She rearranged the books in her two suitcases: Pierre Joseph Proudhon's *La Justice,* Piotr Kropotkin's memoirs, Henry George's *Progess and Poverty,* Bakunin's oeuvre and—of course—her beloved Rosa's five tracts. Nestling in their midst was a real blot on the political landscape: Louisa May Alcott's *Little Women. You think Rosa would have taken a thing like that along? You ought to be ashamed!*

She removed *Little Women* and hid it behind the lavatory—abandoned it, albeit reluctantly. Either you were an anarchist or you weren't.

She counted her worldly wealth: two hundred and eleven dollars.

Eight hours to go. She spent them touring the Metropolitan Museum of Art until politely ejected at closing time. Museums, capitalist or not, had always been a love of hers.

She went aboard that evening, well in advance of sailing time. The trio of women sharing her third-class cabin were maidservants whose employers were traveling first class. They, too, were bound for Germany. After several hours of sustained but fruitless attempts to convince them of the imminence of the proletarian revolution that would abolish the class system altogether—on board ship as elsewhere—Samantha severed all contact with them. It was impossible to communicate with empty-headed flibbertigibbets whose only topics of conversation were clothes and men.

◆　◆　◆

"It must have been around the middle of August," Candido said. "I'd been in the Mato Grosso a month when a salesman called at the garrison. He sold lottery tickets. I didn't want to buy any, but I had no choice—the others forced me to give him all my pay. It wasn't even me who chose the tickets with a jaguar on them. They bullied me into buying the whole series."

"And you won?"

Yes, he'd won a major prize. The others shared out the proceeds among them and left him nothing. Except a mocking nickname: "Jaguar."

Policarpo Moravec nodded. He was standing on deck as they chugged down the Paraguay River, an emaciated man with a hoarse voice and a hurried, breathless way of speaking. He never kept still for a moment, never really listened to what was said. His feverish gaze was forever scanning the riverbanks. He regarded everything and everyone with suspicion. From time to time he scribbled notes on scraps of paper, only to burn them immediately afterward and scatter the crumbled ashes overboard.

Moravec was crazy.

Crazy, maybe, but a friend of Herr Doktor's. If it weren't for him I'd be lying dead on my trombas *in the middle of the Pantanal.*

Candido lounged in his hammock and dozed as he continued his south-ward journey. He dreamed of Germany more and more between two bouts of fever, the second of which confined him to bed when he reached Buenos Aires. Awaiting him in the Argentinian capital was another letter from Herr Doktor enclosing a sum of money sufficient to cover his transatlantic passage, his expenses on board ship and the journey by train from Le Havre, via Paris, to Berlin. There he was to lodge with Herr Doktor's sister while waiting for Herr Doktor himself to arrive. "What-ever happens," wrote his tutor, "you may put your trust in Herr Moravec and, consequently, in any person whose help he suggests you enlist while in Europe."

"His name is Kuppelweiser," Policarpo Moravec said in his hoarse, breathless voice, "—Oskar Kuppelweiser. Memorize the address, don't write it down. He'll be informed of your presence in Berlin and will be requested to help you. Have you got that?"

Candido spent four days only at Buenos Aires. He very nearly crossed the River Plate and took the first train to São Paulo to see his father, but everything happened too quickly. Besides, he was still a little weak. His legs were less swollen and his cuts were healing, but he wasn't too fit yet.

Moravec got him a berth on a French steamship, which suited him perfectly. In addition to his native Portuguese he spoke perfect French, English, German, Spanish and several Indian dialects. He had a gift for languages, as even Herr Doktor, who spoke at least a dozen, was pre-pared to concede. His knowledge of other subjects was limited, however. He knew, for example, that a war had recently been fought in Europe, but he had no idea who had taken part or who had won or lost.

He went aboard with no baggage other than the Grimmelshausen.

◆ ◆ ◆

At Petrograd the temperature had dropped during the night to fifty below. Within a few hours nine hundred people froze to death. All along the route taken by the Mathis, with Afonka Tchadayev once more at the wheel, soldiers were dumping corpses on the piles of snow beside the road to await removal by trucks that seldom turned up. It wasn't uncom-mon for the dead to lie abandoned for days.

Aliochka Alekhin congratulated himself yet again on his intuition. They were going to give him a foreign assignment—he guessed it as soon as he entered Zinoviev's luxurious suite in the First House of the Soviets. Built in 1912 and situated between the Church of St. Isaac and the Admiralty, the First House had been the Hotel Astoria before the revolu-tion. It was requisitioned in 1914, being German-owned, and became a military hotel reserved for high-ups in the Kerensky government. Zinoviev had renovated it for his personal use and that of his cronies. It was the only building in Petrograd whose central heating still functioned, and its restaurant regaled a select few with a range of delicacies unobtainable elsewhere in the city: caviar, smoked salmon, *zakuski,* grilled steaks, French wines and cheeses, Scotch whiskey. Alekhin had been officially summoned there, but he was still made to spend several minutes kicking his heels in the lobby while the Lettish guards manning the kommandatura obtained confirmation that he was expected.

Grigory Zinoviev was flanked by two men. Alekhin recognized one of them as the Hungarian revolutionary Béla Kun, a Party member only since 1917 (like Alekhin himself) but a personal friend of Zinoviev's and appointed by Lenin to head the international propaganda machine.

As for the other . . .

"You've lived in Berlin, I gather?" Béla Kun was the first to speak.

Alekhin answered with cold, characteristic brevity. The other man was introduced as Karl Radek (real name Karl Sobelsohn—Alekhin's memory instantly turned up his file, which confirmed his hunch that they were sending him to Germany).

"Karl did a magnificent job in Berlin," Zinoviev said. "He was imprisoned in the Moabit only because someone else blundered. He's just been released."

And I'm to replace Radek? thought Alekhin. *That's more than I'd hoped for.*

"What we need in Germany," Zinoviev went on, "is a man without emotions, a coolheaded analyst. Felix Dzerzhinsky and I think you could be that man, Aliochka. You leave tonight."

It was an open secret that the Comintern expected, or fervently hoped, that Germany would be the next country to succumb to the delights of proletarian revolution. Alekhin's task was to predict the timing and manner of this German revolution and suggest ways of hastening it.

"Do you have any family ties, here or abroad?" That was Radek.

"No, none at all." Alekhin had no need to risk a lie. His parents were dead and his younger brother had been killed during the German offensive of 1914. He led a solitary life except when consorting with the occasional mistress, and that didn't count.

Radek kept him there for another three hours and gave him a list of men and women he might come across in Germany—people on whom he could more or less rely—together with a large file of situation reports.

Alekhin rejoined Tchadayev in the Mathis feeling mildly elated, a surprising phenomenon in one who seldom felt anything at all. Was it the prospect of leaving Russian soil for the first time in six long years? No, it was something else: the imminence of danger and the thought of a challenge to be met, a long-awaited opportunity to exercise all the Machiavellian cunning he knew he possessed.

"Am I going with you, Aliochka?"

If there was one human being in whom Alekhin had a modicum of faith, it was Afonka Tchadayev, the one-time bear hunter he'd known since the outbreak of the war with Germany. Afonka had been his orderly, and they'd remained together ever since.

"No," he said tersely.

Once back in his requisitioned apartment on Sennaya Square (the Cheka had shot the owner by mistake) Alekhin examined the file given him by Karl Radek.

"Want me to light the stove?" Afonka asked.

"No."

Quite indifferent to the cold, Alekhin was busy memorizing the hundreds of names on the list compiled for his exclusive use. Among them— not that he had any particular reason at present for taking more interest in it than in any other—was that of a certain Oskar Kuppelweiser.

◆　◆　◆

After five days in Berlin Samantha was cold and furious. Nothing had gone as she'd hoped since she disembarked at Hamburg. To begin with, she hadn't been arrested or thrown into jail. It would only have meant three or four days inside—a mere fleabite compared to the months of imprisonment inflicted on Rosa—but even a modest beginning would have been better than nothing. The customs officers who searched her baggage spotted her Rosas, Kropotkins, Proudhons and Bakunins, but what did they do, the knuckleheads? Precisely nothing! One of them had actually chuckled. "An anarchist, eh? My brother-in-law's an anarchist too, and he's a foreman at the gasworks." That was all. They might at least have conducted a body search and found the revolver she carried beneath her skirt, secured to her thigh with a garter, but no such luck. "Enjoy your stay in Germany, Fräulein," was all they could think of to say.

Idiots!

Another disappointment awaited her when she got to Berlin. She'd memorized the name and address of a man—obviously an anarchist—of whom her father had often spoken in affectionate terms: Reinhold Plattnik, a cabinetmaker living near Biesenthal, a small town some thirty miles north of Berlin. Accordingly, she took a train there.

After trudging interminably through the countryside, lugging her bags, all the while counting on Plattnik's hospitality, she came to a dismal canal. The cottage beside it was shuttered and deserted. She waited on the canal bank for hours until her hopes were revived by the appearance of a mustachioed roadmender with a pick and shovel on his shoulder. An agent of the secret police in disguise?

"Does Reinhold Plattnik live here?" she inquired.

The roadmender laughed. "Yes, when he isn't in jail, like now. They usually send him to Tegel Prison."

"Where's his workshop?"

"Same place. He goes inside so often they've converted his cell. It suits everyone. The prison authorities know where to find him whenever they need a piece of furniture—in fact they rearrest him every time a job comes up."

Samantha returned to Berlin. That left only her great-uncle and great-aunt Plück, who lived on Rosenthalstrasse and owned three small cinemas permanently devoted to the showing of pornographic films.

They gave her a lukewarm reception, partly because of the expense her stay would entail but also because of her political opinions. "Let's get one thing straight," said Great-uncle Plück. "We don't meddle in politics, but if we ever did it would be in the hope of seeing Germany run by a strong man—one who'll rid us of all these Jewish socio-anarcho-communist scum."

The Plücks finally agreed to take her in on two conditions: that she keep quiet politically and work for a living. Work at what? They had the answer at their fingertips: it so happened that they were short of a cashier for their Münzstrasse cinema. Take it or leave it.

That was how she found herself selling tickets for a wage that exactly covered the cost of her board and lodging.

There was worse to come. She'd just gone to bed after finishing a late-night stint at the cashier's desk and was reading *Paroles d'un Révolté* when she heard footsteps. She hurriedly switched off the light to escape accusations of extravagance. Then, sensing someone in her room, she switched it on again. Great-uncle Emil Plück was advancing on her wearing nothing but a smile and preceded by a protuberance of such monstrous dimensions it was a wonder his trousers managed to house it under normal circumstances. He wasn't alone, either. Great-aunt Roswitha Plück, also stark naked and grinning lasciviously, was following two paces behind.

"No need to be coy," said Great-uncle Plück. "Everyone knows you anarchists are in favor of free love. You must have had dozens of lovers already, thanks to all the ideas your father put into your head."

With an outraged yell, Samantha dashed out of the bedroom and locked herself in the lavatory, bracing her back against the door and her feet against the base of the bowl. When silence fell she perched on the seat, which had a candlewick cover adorned with pink bobbles. She remained there, shivering and pondering, till daybreak.

It was clear, first, that she must quit the house and her cashier's job, but she didn't know where to go. Her fellow anarchists certainly didn't advertise their whereabouts in the press.

Secondly, she was a virgin. That was a handicap. At nineteen Rosa had already had one official lover, Léo Jogiches, and had even contracted an unconsummated marriage. She herself had a lot of catching up to do.

Third and last, her ideal course of action would be to take an anarchist lover. That would kill two birds with one stone, but how and where was she to find such a man—one who wasn't covered with hair or wrinkled all over like Great-uncle Plück? What she needed was a gentle, decent lover with whom she could have a nice, uncomplicated relationship.

She contemplated her frozen feet with a wry chuckle. Honestly, what a size! Papa had taken twelves, and she was every inch his daughter.

He would have to be a regular hero, her lover.

◆ ◆ ◆

Alekhin had just emerged from Stockholm Cathedral and was heading for the Storkyrkobrinken, a steep, narrow street flanked by medieval houses. Accompanying him was a man named Tieck. It was on Tieck's account that he'd made for the cathedral immediately after disembarking at dawn from the small Finnish freighter that had brought him across the cold, grey, sluggish waters of the Gulf of Finland and the Baltic Sea to Sweden. They had rendezvoused in front of a carved St. George and the Dragon and identified themselves by exchanging prearranged code words. A little man with the air of a frightened mouse, Tieck had just arrived from Germany, where he'd been imprisoned twice, once at Berlin-Moabit and once in Munich.

"At Bremen I got away by jumping out of the window."

Yes, thought Alekhin, *but three of your associates were gunned down, two more are behind bars and you yourself are on the run.*

"This won't be any picnic, comrade. You'll be lucky to be treated as well as Radek if they catch you. They handled him gently because they thought it would be useful to keep a line open to Russia—and also, so rumor has it, because he did a deal with them. I hope our comrades in Moscow don't trust him too implicitly."

The street debouched into a pretty square dominated by the immaculate, white hall of justice. Farther on it crossed a canal and a single railway track before ending at a red brick church with a pierced spire.

Tieck's first trip to Germany had been in December 1917, when Lenin had personally assigned him to observe and report on the situation without becoming actively involved. He was intelligent and fanatical, a combination that never failed to surprise Alekhin, who found it odd that any intelligent man could be an ideological or religious fanatic. Tieck had come to two conclusions: that the German proletariat was not yet prepared to embrace any form of Marxist revolution, but that the revolution was bound to triumph in the end.

"It's a historical inevitability," he declared.

Alekhin smiled. At Petrograd he'd sent hundreds of people to the firing squad on the Cheka's behalf. One of them was a student convicted of having nailed a sign to the wall of his room in such a way that it could be swiveled in any direction. On it, underlined with an arrow, were the words: "The future course of history."

"Our task will take a long time to accomplish," Tieck added. "Conceivably, a generation or two. It may even be that neither of us will see it completed, but I'm as ready as you are to die for its sake."

"That's quite obvious," said Alekhin.

Tieck concluded his report. Alekhin smiled at him. _I could break his neck with two fingers,_ he reflected.

"Good luck, comrade," Tieck said, and hurried off, glancing cautiously about him as he went.

No, I'll let him live. He'll soon be back in Russia. In Moscow he'll be interviewed by Dzerzhinsky and Beria—perhaps by Vladimir Ilyich himself. He'll present his report and they'll have him shot for blighting their hopes.

There never would be a German revolution. The mission that was taking him to the land of Goethe was doomed to failure from the outset.

He could always take off—emigrate to America, for instance. He'd even considered it until he found that he was suffering from a kind of incurable disease: an affection for his native land.

No, I'll think up something between now and my return—something that'll not only save my neck but render me indispensable. I want to manufacture puzzles instead of merely solving them.

He embarked the same evening and landed on the German coast during the night.

◆   ◆   ◆

Candido strolled gaily down Unter den Linden, whose twin rows of linden trees were white with frost. He'd reached Berlin in excellent shape. The long voyage from Buenos Aires had eliminated the last traces of his ordeal in the Mato Grosso. Two or three friendly ladies had made a great fuss over him on board ship. Indeed, one of them had gone so far as to invite him to remain in Paris and share her bed, but he'd heroically journeyed on and atoned for his desertion of her by sending her a huge bouquet of hothouse flowers. He didn't have a bean left, but who cared? He wasn't used to carrying money anyway. In Brazil, some minion of Dom Trajano's had always been there to follow him around and pay his bills, however exorbitant, and here in Germany things would be taken care of by Herr Doktor, with whom he would soon be reunited.

In short, Candido had regained the *joie de vivre* of his pre-army days. He was feeling thoroughly content.

Hungry but content.

The Brandenburg Gate showed up ahead, at the very end of the avenue. Candido was quite at home in Berlin. He'd so often studied the layout of the city under Herr Doktor's guidance that he could almost have found his way around blindfolded. The next street he came to would be Kanonierstrasse—he made a bet with himself.

It was.

He drew level with the red-and-white-striped awning of the Hotel Adlon. Had Herr Doktor Taxile Grüssgott of São Paulo, Brazil, left a message for him?

No, no message. Herr Doktor must not have arrived yet—either that, or he was waiting for him at his sister's place in Wilmersdorf. Candido set off again. He walked through the Tiergarten, bore left across the big park to the Kurfürstendamm, and turned off down Uhlandstrasse. The woman who answered the door of the pretty, two-storied house was munching a pretzel.

But she wasn't Herr Doktor's sister. Oh yes, she said, Frau Feingold *used* to live here, but she moved out two months ago. To Bavaria. A letter from Brazil? Yes, there had been one, but she'd returned it to the post office. Would the nice *junger Herr* care to come in for a bite or a drop of something?

Candido turned and fled. He hankered after blond fräuleins, true, but not after specimens built on such a Wagnerian scale. Maybe he should have accepted her invitation for the sake of a pretzel or two, but still. It shouldn't take him too long to find a suitably proportioned Berlin female prepared to welcome him with open arms.

Besides, in a pinch he could always go and seek help from the man whose particulars had been given him by Policarpo Moravec. What was his name again? Oskar Kuppelweiser, Andreasstrasse 39, near the Schlesischer Bahnhof.

For that matter, he could go there right now. He hesitated, then walked on. Still trying to make up his mind, he retraced his steps and found himself back in the Tiergarten with its paths, canals, miniature bridges, ornamental lakes and stretches of frost-encrusted grass. Few other people were out walking in such icy weather.

Which was why the girl's lone figure caught his eye. Her head was bowed and her face set in an earnest, almost prayerful expression. Furthermore, she was standing near enough to the edge of a canal to suggest that she meant to throw herself in.

Candido stepped over the low metal barrier separating the path from the grass, walked up to the girl and halted two or three paces behind her. He now saw that she topped him by at least a head. *Puxa vida,* she was a regular giantess! He was about to say something like "Please don't jump into that icy water, I'm a strong swimmer and I'd feel duty-bound to jump in after you" when she swung round and regarded him with a look of vague melancholy in her wild, beautiful eyes.

"This is where they killed her," she said.

Candido inspected the waters of the canal but could see no sign of a body.

"They worked her over on the way here by car. They smashed her pelvis and her ribs with their pistol butts, and then, when they got here, they beat her brains out the same way. Finally, they dumped her body in the canal. At this very spot."

The girl's voice trembled with that mixture of outrage and pent-up fury from which Candido would, when he knew her better, infer that it was time to take cover. Her head was bare, though a black straw boater adorned with a flimsy blue chiffon scarf was thrust into the belt of her coat. Her hair was cut in a fringe surmounted by a funny little topknot. Her straight nose was on the large side but slightly tip-tilted. Her mouth was just as oversized, and so were her hands and feet. As for her eyes, they were simply enormous.

She was an absolute knockout.

"A member of your family?" Candido inquired politely.

She stared at him as if he'd just uttered the century's most asinine remark. He watched her, entranced, as she unhooked the boater and perched it on her head, and when she set off he followed.

Side by side, they headed for the Brandenburg Gate and Unter den Linden.

"Rosa Luxemburg," the girl said. "That was her name."

It had all come about quite naturally. She'd begun by talking about this Rosa Luxemburg, who meant absolutely nothing to Candido but appeared to have been some kind of revolutionary. He took care not to interrupt her; she was talking more to herself than to him anyway. They were almost at the end of Unter den Linden by the time she dried up. Anxious not to see the last of her, he told her—for want of anything better to say—that he was a hungry Brazilian who wouldn't mind something to eat. She didn't seem to have heard, but suddenly, having made some incomprehensible reference to a couple named Plück and the bean soup they'd fed her on for most of the previous week, she veered off into a café. Here she sat down and ordered sausages, sauerkraut and hot chocolate for two.

They dug in.

"I don't have a bean, by the way," Candido told her.

No reaction. She had a prodigious appetite.

"But I'll pay you back. I'll be getting some money tomorrow."

The girl might have been deaf. She continued to wolf her sausages and sauerkraut, so he launched into an account of his experiences in the Mato Grosso, the caymans, the snakes, the Pantanal, the *trombas*, the chiggers embedded in his flesh.

Still no reaction, though her eyes occasionally strayed to his face with a look of utter indifference. A glance at the street revealed that darkness had fallen. The temperature was also falling fast and he'd nowhere to sleep. In despair, he proceeded to embroider his story. Improvising, he explained that he'd been banished to the depths of the jungle for political reasons. His poor father *(Dom Trajano would kill me if he could hear)* was a liberal fervently devoted to the workers' cause, so they'd both incurred the wrath of a government minister, an appalling type. . . .

"*Political* reasons?"

It was a miracle. Without knowing why or how, he'd aroused her interest at last.

"Yes," he said firmly.

She put her fork down and eyed him.

"You mean you're a revolutionary?"

What should he say, yes or no? He allowed himself to be guided by instinct.

"In a way," he replied in a disarmingly modest tone.

The girl gazed at him with such sudden intensity, he wondered if he'd gone too far. Then, carried along by his own momentum, he added the final touch.

"The Brazilian authorities are so scared of me, they call me the Jaguar."

She paid the bill. They left together and headed, as near as Candido could judge, for Alexanderplatz. It was snowing a little, but not enough to stick. The girl seemed thoughtful—she hadn't said a word since his Jaguar brainstorm.

She's impressed. At least, I think she is.

They turned down a side street and came to a sudden stop. Candido looked up. They were outside a small cinema showing a film entitled *Das Mädchen und die Männer.*

"You can come in. At least you'll be warm."

"What about a ticket?"

She got in behind the cash desk, opened the drawer with a key from her purse and tore off a ticket, which she handed him.

"I'll pay you back for that too," he told her.

She simply nodded. Without taking any more notice of him, she settled herself at the desk, slid the window shut and draped a hideous green blanket over her shoulders. Some customers turned up. Candido went inside and sat down. He was tired. He hadn't slept at all in the train, and the lady who'd wanted him to stay with her in Paris had been very demanding.

He saw almost nothing of the film. What, he wondered, would the girl do when the show was over? Take him home with her?

She gave him a really strange feeling: a kind of stitch in the chest accompanied by a touch of shyness, which surprised him. It wasn't as if he'd had nothing to do with women in the past five or six years; he'd known plenty, both younger and older than himself. He'd never been backward in coming forward, not with them, but this girl . . .

She was tall—absurdly tall: around six inches taller than himself. A pity he wasn't built like his father, who was over six feet.

Which reminds me, I must write to him. Or should I wait till Herr Doktor gets here? Herr Doktor will be here any day, bringing the latest news. Better wait till then.

He ended by falling asleep in the soupy warmth of the auditorium. When he opened his eyes again the screen was dark and the cinema deserted. The girl was standing in front of him, gently prodding his leg with a broomstick.

"I've been thinking," she said. "I don't have enough money to lend you any, but you can sleep here. There's a camp bed in the projection booth. I'll leave you my blanket."

No one would disturb him until the performance tomorrow night. She herself would return late tomorrow morning, but he could get out of the building betweentimes if he wanted.

"Use the emergency exit over there at the back. The key's in the lock."

"Thanks."

She stared at him again with the meditative expression he'd noticed when they left the café. Then she abruptly turned and walked off. All the lights went out except the one in the projection booth. He heard her lock the main doors behind her.

Am I disappointed she went off like that?

Yes. Yes and no.

It's really odd, this funny feeling in my chest.

Anyway, he would go and see Oskar Kuppelweiser tomorrow. Maybe Kuppelweiser would lend him some money.

◆ ◆ ◆

A dinghy had just put Alekhin ashore on the German coast. The Finnish freighter that had brought him from Sweden was invisible in the darkness now, two or three miles out in the Bay of Pomerania and sailing without lights. The silence was absolute. The clouds that had been gathering at Stockholm now formed an unbroken overcast. Alekhin squatted down and gave his eyes time to become accustomed to the gloom. He made out a row of juniper bushes and beyond them some pine trees, but the vegetation was sparse. It was raining. He shielded the flashlight beneath his oilskin coat and briefly flipped the switch. His watch said twenty-three minutes past midnight. He took a compass reading and set off in a south-southeasterly direction.

The road showed up two miles farther on, as expected. A signpost informed him that Peenemünde lay five kilometers away to his right, Karlshagen six hundred meters to his left.

Left.

The voice hailed him just as he was leaving the outskirts of the village. A man's voice backed up by the glow of a lantern.

"Werner?"

Alekhin came to a halt and waited.

"Is that you, Werner?"

The man approached, the beam of the dark lantern widened.

"Who are you?"

Alekhin, with the light shining full in his face, smiled. He'd identified the man as a customs officer. A lone customs officer.

"You'll never believe it," he said, "but I'm a Soviet agent sent here by the Comintern to spread Red revolution."

The knife blade went in beneath the man's chin, pinning his tongue to the roof of his mouth and penetrating the brain. Supporting the limp body with his left hand, Alekhin dragged it over to the side of the road, where he crushed the cervical vertebrae for safety's sake, using the fingers of his right hand only. The man's bicycle was lying on the asphalt, the rear wheel still revolving with a faint, rhythmical, clicking sound.

Alekhin rolled the customs officer into the ditch, got rid of the lantern and made sure there were no telltale traces in the roadway.

Then he mounted the bicycle and rode off.

Thanks to the customs officer's bicycle he reached the dinghy at one-forty A.M., twenty minutes earlier than planned.

The small craft was at the prearranged spot, a hundred yards downstream from the landing stage. The lights of Wolgast were visible on the far side of the Peene. He ferried the bicycle across with him. It had been suggested before he left Petrograd that he spend the night at a safe house and travel the rest of the way by truck, but he'd refused on principle: never trust anyone. Besides, he enjoyed cycling.

There followed a thirty-five-mile ride through sleeping villages whose watchdogs only occasionally barked as he passed.

He got to Demmin well before five A.M., located the railway station and rode on past it to an empty barn. It was an ideal place to shelter in. Having removed his oilskin jacket and his boots, he hid them under some straw with the flashlight and bicycle. Then he donned shoes and a cap, brushed the mud off his clothes and padded out his satchel with an old newspaper to make it look as if it contained a workman's packed lunch.

Two hours to wait and not a twinge of impatience. Alekhin had no nerves at all; he could have waited three days if need be.

He deliberately missed the first train, which would have gotten him to Berlin too early, and caught the second, armed with a season ticket like those of the laborers, whose clothing resembled his own. Nothing untoward occurred. Dawn was breaking by the time they reached Neustrelitz. Overlooked by a drab, grey sky and lashed by an incessant downpour that would turn to snow as soon as the temperature dropped another degree or two, the countryside was utterly devoid of interest: lakes, marshes, streams, farmsteads and isolated cottages, modest little abodes but luxurious compared to their counterparts in Russia. Then came a string of big suburban stations, one of them called Lehnitz-Biesenthal—a name he would have cause to remember.

Oranienburg, then Berlin. The major railway lines had been independent during Alekhin's days in prewar Berlin, but the German capital's municipal authorities were already planning a general link-up and the construction of a central station connected to the others by a metropolitan line. This scheme was now complete, so he entered the city by way of Friedrichstrasse Station on the bank of the Spree. A few porters were touting for business among the early-morning travelers, and a policeman with the rigid bearing of a Prussian sergeant-major was stationed at the exit distributing numbered copper tokens for the reservation of seats in taxis or horse buses, but Alekhin's satchel and workman's getup attracted barely a glance.

Although his sleepless night and physical exertions had given him an appetite, Alekhin made sure he wasn't being tailed before tucking into an ample Scandinavian breakfast at a *Frühkost-Salon* he selected because it had two exits. Then he went shopping: shirts and ties here, suits at another store, a suitcase a little farther on, shoes somewhere else, an overcoat, a hat, underclothes, socks.

He took a room at the Wittelsbacher Hof, 35 Wilhelmstrasse, in the name of Karl Mohren, actor, a false identity of his own choosing. Zinoviev and Radek had found the choice surprising, but it amused him. Perhaps it denoted that he'd missed his true vocation.

Toward eleven that morning, attired respectably but with just a hint of actorish flamboyance, he went to sign on as an extra at the studios of the only two major film production companies in Germany, Bioscope and UFA, of which the latter had been founded two years earlier (Alekhin had done his homework) by Krupp, I. G. Farben, and a consortium of banks. When asked if he'd worked before he said yes. He'd been engaged—with fifteen thousand others, admittedly—for *Plague in Florence,* directed by Joe May, Fritz Lang's screenwriter, and had played bit parts for Biograph and Messter.

"Pagu, too. I was in a scene with Max Reinhardt—you can check."

He wasn't lying. At the time he'd found it a way of financing his stay in Berlin. He'd appeared in a scene with the celebrated Austrian actor-producer, cast as a blond colossus of a hotel porter.

They took down the name he gave and his address and said they would write if they ever needed him again.

The rain had stopped by the time he left the studios, but the sky was heavily overcast.

For the last few hours—ever since his Stockholm rendezvous with Tieck, in fact—he'd been racking his brains for the stroke of inspiration that would enable him to return to Moscow with a reasonable chance of survival and, more than that, of personal advancement. He hadn't come up with anything.

Not yet.

◆　◆　◆

There were two coins lying on the chair beside the projectionist's camp bed when Candido woke up. He hadn't spotted them before.

The girl must have left them there. Really kind of her.

He left the cinema by the emergency exit, locked it behind him and slid the key under the door. Then he went and retrieved his suitcase from the station checkroom where he'd left it the day before, changed his underclothes and freshened up a little. A quick breakfast, and he was on his way.

Oskar Kuppelweiser, Andreasstrasse 39.

If he could borrow fifty marks from Kuppelweiser, that would be fine. Or even a hundred. Herr Doktor would pay him back.

Number 39 Andreasstrasse turned out to be a shop. Candido walked in and promptly stopped short, startled less by what he saw than by what he could hear: a strange, composite sound made up of countless mechanical clicks and whirs augmented by the creaking floorboards beneath his feet. The shop was so ill lit that semidarkness reigned within two or three yards of the entrance. The dust-laden air was redolent of lubricating oil and moth-eaten fur, and the shelves that lined the walls were piled high with dolls, cuddly animals and mechanical toys of every shape and size.

They were all working at once.

"Anyone there?"

No reply, just a chorus of clicks and whirs. Candido raised his voice.

"I'm looking for Herr Oskar Kuppelweiser the toy maker."

Someone finally emerged from a gap between two shelves so narrow that the only way to negotiate it was sideways, like a figure in an ancient Egyptian mural. It was a little old lady whose walk and gestures had a mechanical regularity that suggested that she, too, was an automaton.

She fixed Candido with a pair of forget-me-not-blue eyes, her lips set in a grim line, her expression that of someone confronted by a child killer.

"Herr Kuppelweiser," Candido said, "Herr Oskar Kuppelweiser. Policarpo Moravec sent me."

The old lady toddled mechanically off to the back of the shop. Candido, having debated whether or not to follow her, did so. He squeezed between serried rows of rabbits beating red and white drums, then past an army of dolls that waved their white celluloid arms in the air as if trying to capture him.

"Shouting Policarpo's name from the rooftops! Are you insane?"

The author of this rebuke was a sallow-faced man in his fifties with pale blue, deepset eyes, bushy eyebrows and a shock of bristly hair parted in the middle. His physiognomy was less than reassuring.

"I wasn't on the rooftops, I was in your shop."

"Someone apart from my mother might be lurking here, spying on me."

"I checked first," Candido said firmly, determined not to be intimidated. "Are you Oskar Kuppelweiser?"

"You want to see my papers?" Kuppelweiser demanded.

He seemed so eager for an affirmative that Candido obliged him.

"I do," he said. "I never take anyone on trust."

The sallow-faced man showed him his papers. He was Kuppelweiser sure enough.

"Now you. Prove you're who you say you are."

Candido produced his passport.

"All right," said Kuppelweiser, "but that's not all. The letter I had about you mentions a favorite book of yours."

"Der Abenteuerliche Simplicissimus Teutsch" by Hans Jakob von Grimmelshausen."

Kuppelweiser invited Candido to share a snack of apple fritters and coffee. They ate and drank, seated on packing cases and eyeing each other like two dogs of recent acquaintance.

"You don't look like a revolutionary," said Kuppelweiser, devouring fritter after fritter as if he bore each one a grudge for political reasons.

A revolutionary? Why would this pathetic creature take him for a revolutionary? This revolution business seemed to be in the air. What the hell. If he wants a revolutionary, I'll be a revolutionary.

"Camouflage," Candido replied with his mouth full.

The fritters were very good.

"Been in Berlin long?"

"A while."

They finished the fritters.

"Well," said Kuppelweiser, "it seems I've got to extend you every possible assistance. What can I do for you?"

Candido hesitated. He'd thought of borrowing a hundred marks. Was it an appropriate sum?

"You can speak freely," Kuppelweiser went on, "Mother's watching the street. What kind of bomb do you need?"

"Ah," said Candido, thoroughly taken aback, "that's the question."

"Immediate or delayed action? Designed to kill or only maim? What are you planning to do, make a lot of noise or demolish a building? How big a building—it *is* a building you want to blow up, I can see it in your eyes. What building?"

Meu Deus!

"It won't go any further?"

"What do you take me for?"

"I was thinking of the Reichstag," said Candido, who had hesitated between the Reichstag and the Brandenburg Gate.

Silence.

That shook him—me too. What on earth possessed me? The Reichstag? I must be mad!

"Remarkable," Kuppelweiser said gravely. "A stroke of genius."

"Let's not exaggerate. It's only one of several projects I have in mind."

I'm going to touch him for five hundred—a mere bagatelle to anyone willing to help me blow up half of Berlin. . . .

A few minutes later he was walking off down the street, stunned by his own success. He felt half inclined to retrace his steps, purely to convince himself that he wasn't dreaming. Had he really gone into that toy shop and accosted a madman prepared to supply him with a bomb powerful enough to blow up the German parliament building?

The wad of bank notes stuffed into his coat pocket reassured him. Kuppelweiser had advanced him a thousand marks from what he termed "secret funds."

A thousand marks!

He wondered what on earth Policarpo Moravec could have said about him in his letter to the toy maker.

A revolutionary!

But who cared? They were lunatics, both of them. Once Herr Doktor turned up and repaid the thousand marks, that would be the end of it.

He celebrated his newfound wealth by taking a taxi to the Hotel Adlon. Still no word from Herr Doktor, but he wasn't disheartened. When it came to repaying Kuppelweiser, a couple of days would be neither here nor there.

His high spirits were somewhat dampened that evening when he found
the Opal Cinema in Münzstrasse closed and could see no sign of the girl.

◆ ◆ ◆

Alekhin had wasted no time in mobilizing Karl Radek's network. He'd
already attended three meetings under three different pseudonyms.

He was neither surprised nor dismayed by the unpromising nature of
the reports submitted to him. They merely confirmed his suspicion that
it would take at least a century to bring about a revolution in Germany,
and by then the Russian Revolution would itself have ceased to exist
outside the pages of a history book.

On the evening of his second day in Berlin he returned to Wilhelmstrasse and closeted himself in his room at the Wittelsbacher Hof with a
bunch of situation reports, some of them neatly typed. *Written* reports
. . . He almost smiled at such crass amateurishness. There were hundreds
of pages, but he forced himself to skim through them before burning
them in the grate.

It took him hours to wade through this sea of platitudes, mentally
noting any names, addresses or facts that struck him as even faintly
interesting. Toward three in the morning he came across a brief, handwritten note from someone whose code name identified him as Oskar
Kuppelweiser, reputedly a skilled pyrotechnist capable of supplying any
form of explosive charge to order.

Nothing earthshaking, though the sum withdrawn from "secret funds"
was quite substantial: one thousand marks, or as much as many Berliners
earned in a year. The transaction was dated that day.

Nothing earthshaking, but what caught Alekhin's eye and rather
amused him was the code name of the person who had benefited from
Kuppelweiser's generosity: *"Jaguar."* It meant nothing to him.

Three A.M. was a bit late to go calling on Kuppelweiser. Alekhin
decided to go and see him the following night.

◆ ◆ ◆

"How did you get hold of all this money?"

"It came from secret funds," said Candido, like someone divulging a
state secret.

Samantha put down her fork, sat back against the restaurant's imitation
leather upholstery, and subjected him to an unabashed stare.

I may not impress her, but at least she finds me intriguing. My green eyes leave

*her cold (unless she's pretending), but, like everyone else in this crazy place,
whenever I talk revolution—bingo! she hangs on my every word.*

All right, if that's the way she wants it . . .

"If you want to know the truth," she said, "I don't believe for a minute
you're a Brazilian revolutionary. 'Access to secret funds' is a lot of crap.
You're pulling my leg."

The night before, when he found the cinema closed, Candido had been
tempted to take a suite at the Hotel Adlon. It wasn't until he hailed a cab
that he changed his mind and checked into the first hotel he came to, a
stone's throw from Alexanderplatz. Chance did the rest. He hadn't gone
a hundred yards that morning when he saw her emerge from Rosenthalstrasse and set off along the opposite side of the street. He ran after her,
repaid the money he owed her and invited her to lunch. She accepted,
but only just. Candido found her as disconcerting as ever. First she glared
as if she could have struck him dead for accosting her; next she looked
away and gazed into the middle distance; then she scrutinized him again;
finally she said yes. She chose the restaurant and ordered for two without
consulting him; he let her. It had never been in his nature to argue with
anyone.

"You're pulling my leg," she repeated. She picked up her fork and
tucked in again with a thoroughly satisfied air, as if she'd just found the
answer to some nagging question. Candido experienced a pang of alarm.
He was losing the game. Lunch was almost over and Samantha—if that
was her real name—would depart, never to be seen again. He had to say
something, no matter what.

"The truth is," he said, "I'm like a man walking behind his own coffin."

He was on target: she stared at him openmouthed. "Meaning what,
exactly?" she demanded.

"It's a quotation from one of my favorite writers, Franz Grillparzer."

"Never heard of him."

"He was an Austrian playwright, from 1791 to 1872." For some
reason that escaped Candido, Herr Doktor adored Grillparzer.

"You enjoy reading?"

"Immensely," said Candido.

Samantha's eyes strayed again, then returned to his face.

"Have you read Karl Marx?"

Karl who? Herr Doktor's never mentioned him, so he can't be very well known.

"Every line," he said.

"And Engels?"

"Twice."

"And Bakunin?"

Where the devil does she dig up all these names?

"Only the first hundred pages. It wasn't too easy, reading in the Mato Grosso with all those caymans around."

Silence. He'd scored some points.

Except that she gave a sudden snigger. She'd obviously decided he was lying through his teeth.

He got carried away. Her expression alternated between skepticism and interest as the words came tumbling out.

"All right," he said, "I haven't read any of them. It's because I'm a man of action."

"How would you define a man of action?"

He replied without thinking, "Someone who blows things up."

"What kind of things?"

"All kinds."

"And how are you able to blow things up? With what?"

"If I need explosives I can get them within the hour. I've got connections."

"Perfect," she said. "It just so happens I want something blown up."

"Like what?"

"Like a movie theater. The Plücks movie theater, to be precise."

Ten minutes later they were on their way to Oskar Kuppelweiser's toy shop.

"Oskar who?"

"Kuppelweiser. Please keep your voice down. He's a secret agent."

She shrugged, clearly suspicious of everything he told her. Perhaps it was better that way.

They were nearing Andreasstrasse. Candido almost brought up the subject of Herr Doktor, whom he considered describing as his tutor in revolutionary ideology, but thought better of it. Herr Doktor would turn up tonight or tomorrow or the next day. Samantha might meet him, and then the truth would out. "Revolution, Candido, is the term applied to any cyclical movement whereby persons or things, having come full circle, end up back where they started." Thus Herr Doktor was the most *un*revolutionary type imaginable.

Apart from himself.

Samantha was striding along with a depressingly resolute air. How had he got himself into this? He was worried, but not unduly so. It was inconceivable that Kuppelweiser would really supply them with a bomb, so why should he be concerned? The situation was more amusing than anything else. All at once his natural gaiety returned. He'd been studying Samantha over lunch. It wasn't easy to assess her figure under all those winter clothes, but he suspected it was good. Better than good, in fact. He'd always had an eye for such things. One glimpse of a girl's wrist or ankle and he could visualize the rest of her with a percentage of error verging on zero. It wasn't something you could learn; it was an inborn knack. All the same, it puzzled him that he should find her as attractive as he did.

They got to the toy shop. The old woman with the forget-me-not eyes and the barbed-wire mouth emerged from the shadows like a ghost, inspected Samantha from head to toe and inquired as to her identity.

"I'll vouch for her," Candido declared.

With the old woman shuffling ahead of them, they followed the circuitous route he remembered from his previous visit. It led to the workshop and Oskar Kuppelweiser.

"This time I want a bomb," Candido said.

The manufacturer of toys—and possibly of bombs as well—eyed him inscrutably before transferring his gaze to Samantha.

"A bomb for what purpose?"

"What business is that of yours?" Samantha demanded.

"We . . . I want to blow up a cinema," said Candido. "It might be better if you left this to me," he added in English to Samantha.

"If he's a genuine explosives expert and you're a genuine revolutionary he shouldn't be asking you questions," she said.

"I understand English," said Kuppelweiser.

Candido failed to hear this. "He's a genuine explosives expert all right," he told Samantha.

"I have my doubts," she retorted, likewise in English. "Anyway, it's not his place to ask questions."

"You're right," Candido replied, still in English.

"A cinema?" Kuppelweiser said in German. "Why a cinema?"

"No questions," Candido said, switching to German.

"OK, you handle this," Samantha told him in English.

Kuppelweiser stared at them.

"I'll need to know the size of the building," he said.

"Around a hundred feet by fifty," Candido hazarded.

"No, smaller," Samantha said in English, "but I doubt if this guy could blow up a shoe box."

"I can blow up anything you care to name," Kuppelweiser declared in German.

"He says he can blow up anything you care to name," Candido translated into English.

"I got that," Samantha said. "But I don't want the whole building blown up, just the projection booth."

Candido translated again. He wasn't doing too well, he felt. Something was wrong somewhere.

"The projection booth and the box office," Samantha added.

"In that case you'll need two separate charges," said Kuppelweiser. "Have you ever planted a bomb? It's you I'm talking to, not her."

"I'm a little out of practice."

"You don't have to be a genius to plant a bomb," Samantha put in. "Heaps of people do it."

"I'll manage," Candido told Kuppelweiser.

"I'll make you something simple," said Kuppelweiser. "The simpler the better for all concerned."

"When do we get them?" Samantha inquired.

Kuppelweiser pretended not to have heard. With astonishingly deft fingers, he continued to repair a doll that said "Mama" when turned upside down.

"When do I get the bombs?" Candido asked.

Silence, then: "Friday afternoon at six."

"But that's a week from now," said Candido.

"I'm aware of that," said Kuppelweiser.

He replaced the doll's head and tilted its little celluloid body.

"Mama," said the doll.

"That's it," said Kuppelweiser. He replaced the doll on a shelf and picked up another one.

Maybe he's only joking. I wouldn't be surprised—in fact I hope he is. I hate to think what might happen if he took us seriously.

It was time to put the question he'd been meaning to ask all along.

"You received a letter about me from Buenos Aires, right?"

Kuppelweiser nodded.

"Did it mention the nickname they gave me in Brazil?"

The toy maker turned. If he'd been joking before, he wasn't now. "The Jaguar," he replied.

Candido, watching Samantha's face, wasn't disappointed. This time she seemed genuinely impressed.

Samantha paused when they got to Alexanderplatz. She hadn't said a word since they left the shop. It was just after three P.M., and Candido was chilled to the bone. He would have liked to suggest going back to his hotel, taking refuge in a café, seeing a film, window-shopping in the Kaiser Arcade—anything to get out of this icy rain—but he took care to keep his mouth shut and confined himself to glancing at her out of the corner of his eye.

She's making up her mind. I've done all I can.

Her silence and immobility persisted. At last she came to a decision. "Are you keen to stay on at your present hotel?"

"Not especially."

She nodded.

"OK if we take a taxi?"

They took one. She gave an address in Rosenthalstrasse, asked the driver to wait, got out and disappeared into a small apartment house. Before long she emerged carrying two suitcases. An hour later they were sitting in a train. She still hadn't offered a word of explanation, nor had he asked for one.

"Let me carry your bags."

"I'm stronger than you are."

"You could be right," Candido admitted.

They were walking along a country road. He ended by carrying her heavy suitcases while she carried his things and a bag containing some food purchased at a grocery store outside the station. The Brandenburg countryside was a bleak and barren expanse made still more dismal by the falling snow, which was sticking better here than in town. They eventually came to an isolated cottage on the bank of a canal. Candido managed to open the back door by forcing it with a rusty spade—and just in time: darkness was closing in.

"I'll get a fire going. Am I allowed to know where we are?"

Candido had never made a fire in his life—in Brazil fire-making was a servant's job—but he performed this miracle with the aid of some old copies of a newspaper entitled *Die Rote Fahne.* Samantha explained that the cottage belonged to one Reinhold Plattnik, an anarchist currently in prison. She hadn't moved since entering the place, except to unburden herself of the things she was carrying. She'd crossed her arms—or rather, grasped them with her big hands as women do—and was gazing into the fire with her shoulders hunched and her face illuminated by the dancing flames.

"Sit down near the fire," Candido said, pulling up a chair.

It was now completely dark outside. He lit an oil lamp and secured the door. Most of the cottage was taken up by one room furnished with a bed, a table, two armchairs, a rickety closet containing some clothes and four or five plates, and a few books on a shelf. On one side of the low doorway was a tiny kitchen equipped with a wood-burning stove and a store of logs, two saucepans and a boiler, three glasses, two spoons, one fork and one large knife. On the other was a cubbyhole that Candido was unwise enough to enter without a light. The dank smell alerted him just in time. One more step and he would have fallen down an open, unprotected well sunk in the floor.

A battle with the stove ensued. He got it going at the third attempt and heated one of the six bottles of milk they'd bought. Then came another problem: how to make cocoa? Although he succeeded in breaking up the thick bar of chocolate with a spoon, the fragments refused to melt. The beverage he produced was a kind of gruel full of bits the size of walnuts, but at least it was hot. He returned to the living room, cursing his ineptitude, and thought for one moment that Samantha had deserted him.

"I was cold."

She was in bed, rendered almost invisible by the gloom and several layers of blanket.

Strange girl. What am I supposed to do, sleep in a chair?

"Would you like some hot chocolate?"

An arm emerged from the bedclothes, a hand reached out. He filled a glass. She devoured rather than drank the contents.

"The chocolate hasn't melted."

"I'm sorry," he said. "More?"

The arm reemerged. She drained another three glasses in quick succession.

"Like some more?"

A vague shake of the head. He polished off the chocolate milk, drinking it straight from the saucepan. Then, rather at a loss, he lingered beside the bed as she lay there in silence with her back to him. He was hungry. There was a big country loaf and some cold meat in the kitchen with the remaining bottles of milk, but he dared not move and couldn't think of anything to say.

"Well, what are you waiting for?"

"I, er . . . I don't understand."

"Come to bed."

"Ah . . ." Candido swallowed hard. He definitely wasn't in his usual form.

He removed his overcoat and, after a moment's reflection, his jacket. Then, loosening his tie, he slipped into bed as gingerly as if it contained a bomb (*Don't say that word!*) and stretched out on his back with his hands chastely folded on his chest. The bed was very narrow. He could feel something warm, soft and rounded against his thigh.

"Shouldn't you take your shoes off?"

"Mmm. Sorry again."

Candido got out of bed and removed his shoes. He took the opportunity to remove his tie and sweater as well, but kept his trousers and socks on. Then he resumed the same position, his thigh in contact with the same warm curve. Silence fell.

"Touch me," she said.

"Where?"

The idiotic question slipped out before he knew it.

"Anywhere you like." Calmly she added, "Anywhere appropriate."

Reaching out at random, he felt a rounded hip under his hand. He ran his fingers up and beyond it to the beginnings of a breast—how full and firm it was!—then down again. Intimidated by a woman for the first time in his life, he shifted his position slightly and pressed against her to extend the range of his hand, which scaled her thigh and descended the reverse slope.

"There?"

"Anywhere appropriate, I said. Wasn't that clear enough for you?"

"Absolutely."

"I hope you're experienced."

"At?"

"At making love."

He almost smiled. "I know what to do."

"Then do it."

"Pardon me for saying so, but it would help if you took your knickers off."

She didn't comply at once, and when she did it was with the irritable sigh of someone reluctant to be disturbed.

"Do I have to take my stockings off too?"

"Not necessarily."

"What are you doing?"

"Getting undressed."

"How much longer are you going to be?"

"It might be better if you lie on your back."

She instantly changed position.

"Like this?"

"Yes."

Should he remove his shirt and vest? No. Now, where was he? He slid his hands up under her slip, which she hadn't removed, and cupped them around her breasts. Then, baring the nipples, he venturesomely applied his tongue to them.

"Is that essential?"

"Not essential, but it feels nice."

A pause for thought.

"OK," she said at last, "go on."

"Thank you."

"No need to thank me. You're the one that's doing me a favor."

What on earth? Candido stopped short, temporarily dumbfounded, but his thoughts had already acquired a momentum of their own. He was experienced enough to know what caresses were required, what rhythm to adopt, when to bide his time.

She didn't speak again. He sensed in the gloom that she'd shut her eyes, felt her body arch and writhe, listened to her breathing, heard it quicken and, when the time came, gently mounted her.

Later, in the Great Silence, he would remember every last one of those moments. Those and the ones that were to come.

◆   ◆   ◆

The toy shop's steel shutter had already been lowered by the time Alekhin got to Andreasstrasse. He automatically circled the building, memorizing the layout and noting that it would be easy enough, by climbing a drainpipe, to break in through a window at the back.

"Show me the letter."

He hadn't taken long to form an opinion of Oskar Kuppelweiser. Despite his undoubted devotion to the cause and reputed skill with explosives, the toy maker was as hopeless a mediocrity as every other self-styled revolutionary Alekhin had encountered at his fruitless meetings yesterday and today. Going over to a supposedly secure but absurdly obvious hiding place, Kuppelweiser produced a bundle of documents from which he extracted Policarpo Moravec's letter and latest situation report.

"Are you personally acquainted with Moravec?"

"I've known him thirty years."

"Does he often send you people like this man Cavalcanti?"

"He's done so a couple of times before."

The letter was short. It asked that "every possible assistance" be extended to one Candido Cavalcanti, should he turn up while passing through Berlin, the said Cavalcanti being identifiable by a book from which he was never parted: Grimmelshausen's *Der Abenteuerliche Simplicissimus Teutsch.* Alekhin knew the seventeenth-century German author by name but had never read anything of his.

The situation report had come separately and by a more secure route than the postal system. It consisted of two closely handwritten sheets, one of them an uninteresting screed devoted to the prospects for a Brazilian revolution, of which Moravec himself appeared to have high and fervent hopes. The other sheet introduced the "Jaguar." Alekhin registered the essential points. Jaguar, real name Candido Cavalcanti de Noronha, was the only son and heir of Trajano Cavalcanti, the wealthiest man in Brazil and an extremely influential person. Father and son were at loggerheads, and rumor had it that young Candido was really the offspring of an adulterous affair between his mother and his great-uncle Amílcar, Dom Trajano's uncle. His desertion from a Mato Grosso garrison, to which his father had banished him, had fired the popular imagination. There was a possibility of using him, and his name and nickname in particular, to spearhead a revolution, either with his consent (in which case indoctrination in Russia would be desirable), or without it. He was extremely docile and malleable by nature. Although the "Jaguar" sobriquet was only derisory, one should not underestimate the impact a leader bearing that nickname might have on the masses.

That's it!

An idea had taken root in Alekhin's mind—an idea that had no connection with Brazil.

"Has anyone read this file apart from you and me?"

"I enclosed a copy of it with my report."

"The one in which you mentioned the loan of a thousand marks?"

"Yes."

They must have either filed it in the wrong place or forgotten to pass it on—he would have to check. Meantime, he was preoccupied with the embryonic idea that had just occurred to him.

"This Cavalcanti—any idea where he's staying?"

"No, but I know where he'll be next Friday: here on the premises. He's coming to pick up a couple of bombs—or so he thinks."

"Bombs?"

Kuppelweiser grinned dismissively. He'd never had the slightest intention of supplying the youngster with any bombs, he said, least of all for the purpose of demolishing a cinema. He'd submitted a second report on the subject, but Matthäus—the name by which Alekhin had introduced himself—couldn't have received it yet.

"Tell me the whole story," Alekhin said.

Kuppelweiser did so, not omitting to describe the girl who had accompanied Cavalcanti. Alekhin barely listened. Thanks to a series of split-second deductive, extrapolative and associative thought processes, his original idea had just undergone infinite expansion.

This is it—the thing I've been looking for ever since Petrograd, when I sensed they were sending me here on a suicide mission. I've got it at last.

He experienced no hint of triumph or exultation.

The machine was functioning perfectly.

"You'll do it," he told Kuppelweiser. "You'll burn these papers, every last one of them, and you'll make those bombs to the Jaguar's requirements."

The Jaguar . . .

His lips almost curled in the ghost of a smile.

◆　◆　◆

It wasn't until the end of their third day in Reinhold Plattnik's cottage at Biesenthal that Samantha clarified her position. They'd made love repeatedly, she with such mounting ardor that Candido began to wilt. He was obliged to explain that he couldn't, well, do it *ad infinitum*— no man could. And as for her questions! "Can a woman join in, so to speak?"— "Yes, of course."—"But how?"—"Well . . ."—"Like this, for instance?"—"Yes."—"And this?"—*(Meu Deus!)* "Yes."—"How about that, is that allowed?"—(No immediate response from Candido.)—"Is this the kind of thing a respectable woman does—one that isn't a prostitute, I mean?"—"There aren't any rules, it isn't a game of football."— "Tell me, Candido, are you exactly the same as other men?"—"How do you mean?"—"I mean the number of times a day you can do it. Are you above average or below?"—"Just average, I guess."—"Well, you're very gentle, I must say, even though you do know how to accelerate at the right moment."—*(Jesus, what does she think I am, a car?)* "I do my best."— "All things considered, I guess I was pretty lucky to bump into you, we're so good together. I'm starving, aren't you? No, don't move, I'll do it. I'm not much of a cook, but eggs I can manage. Sing me something, I like it when you sing. Won't you sing me that *cachaça* song again? It's my favorite. It sounds lovely in this silent place, a Brazilian song with the snow falling outside."

Candido's remaining doubts had vanished. He was definitely in love with her—the thought had broken over his head like a tropical storm. That morning, the morning of the third day, they'd walked to the grocery store to replenish their supplies because Samantha wanted to make a pudding. She'd spent all day at the stove with disastrous results. Now they were in bed in front of the fire after making love yet again. He said nothing—he didn't even feel like singing. The hush that enveloped them seemed to underline the gravity of the moment.

All at once, drawing as far away from him as the bed allowed, she broke the silence in a muffled but resolute voice. Their combined ages totaled less than forty, she began. They'd only just arrived in Germany, but she had plans. She aspired to become another Rosa Luxemburg—she'd dreamed of it for years—so falling in love was out of the question. She was grateful for his services and for being so nice to her, naturally, but a future together simply wasn't on. She preferred to be frank—she'd thought things over carefully and didn't want to keep him guessing. Their appointment with the toy maker was in three days' time. She would quite understand if he declined to come with her. Wrecking the Plücks' cinema would be only a gesture, but every anarchist had to start somewhere and she was determined to go all the way. If he wanted to leave he should do so tomorrow morning; if he stayed it would only be to help her get the bombs from Kuppelweiser. Whatever happened, she wanted him to know that theirs was destined to be a short-term relationship.

"I felt I had to tell you, Candido, you understand?"

"I understand."

"Didn't you notice anything, Samantha?"

"When?"

She was carrying one of the bombs in a shopping bag. Candido had wrapped his in a raincoat bought for him at Buenos Aires by Policarpo Moravec.

"At Kuppelweiser's place," he said. "I found his manner odd."

"I didn't."

"He spoke in a funny way—he didn't sound natural."

No reply. Kuppelweiser had explained how to detonate the bombs, which were packed in shoe boxes, and Samantha had allowed for every contingency. To avoid inflicting casualties they would go into action after midnight, when the cinema was shut and Münzstrasse deserted. Then, after grabbing a few hours' sleep at the Grand Hôtel de Russie on Georgstrasse, near Friedrichstrasse Station, they would catch the first outbound train at five-forty-two A.M..

It was seven P.M. now, so they still had five hours to kill. The best way of passing the time, Samantha had decided, would be to have dinner and then go—where else?—to a cinema.

She'd also picked the film. A German production entitled *Madame du Barry,* it dealt with the French Revolution.

◆　◆　◆

Alekhin followed the couple into Koenigstrasse. He'd had them under surveillance ever since they got to Kuppelweiser's shop, where he witnessed the handover from behind a partition. Kuppelweiser was such a poor actor, anyone but those two youngsters would have smelled a rat—for youngsters they were, that was the first surprise. Cavalcanti was a small youth, handsome and well built but quite unintimidating. He bore no resemblance to a Mexican-style revolutionary, and his open, innocent face was as good as a disguise. As for his partner, the girl . . . Alekhin, usually so immune to surprises, had been bowled over by her. She was American, he guessed, and very tall—five feet ten or more: big hands, big feet, a resolute chin, flashing eyes, an impatient manner. There was something ungainly about her movements, but at times, when she bent her head and exposed the soft curve of her neck, the big, rather gangling body acquired a graceful, sensual, voluptuous quality. It was only too easy, almost painfully so, to picture her making love.

Were they really going to plant those bombs?

Moravec's file had reached Alekhin that afternoon, on his return from some meetings in Bremen as devoid of promise and interest as those he'd attended in Berlin. János "Policarpo" Moravec was a Prague-born veteran revolutionary who had joined the Bolsheviks in 1902 and had become a member of the Iskra group at Geneva in company with Kamenev. A friend of Mikhail Markovich Grunenberg, a.k.a. Borodin, he had emigrated like the latter to America, first to Valparaiso, Indiana, then to Mexico, then farther south to Argentina and Brazil. Intelligent and trustworthy but inclined to be overexcitable, he was committed to a hypothetical revolution in Brazil, the country whose citizenship he had adopted.

As Alekhin walked on, keeping pace with the couple ahead of him, his machinelike brain gathered and stored a mass of information. This, for example: the boy was crazy about the girl and would do anything for her, even to the extent of carrying and planting bombs of which he was obviously terrified. An interesting thought . . .

Alekhin had been working on the idea born in Oskar Kuppelweiser's workshop. He now felt sure that it was the perfect antidote to what might happen if he returned to Moscow as a bird of ill omen, bringing news that the Russian Revolution could never hope for support from a similar revolution in Germany. His idea had taken on shape and substance—so much so that he would soon be ready to submit it to higher authority. Vladimir Ilyich Lenin included. Failure meant certain death, but he wouldn't be alone in trying to sell his theory. Although he would be up against Trotsky, who favored the steady spread of worldwide revolution, he might with luck enlist the support of that fellow Djugashvili, who had nicknamed himself Stalin, or Man of Steel.

It only remained to incorporate the Jaguar in his grand design. Every important message required some flamboyant, symbolic example to ram it home.

Seven-thirty. The couple were having an early dinner. Alekhin, stationed in a restaurant across the street, was having dinner too. He paid in advance in case they left in a hurry, but it proved to be an unnecessary precaution. The youngsters took their time.

A little while later they went off to a cinema. The one they meant to blow up? Aware of the risk he was running, Alekhin seated himself two rows behind them. If they slipped out, leaving the bombs under their seats, he would have to leave too, and his height and build were a liability. Someone might remember him after the explosion.

He just had time to glance at the posters outside. The first feature was *Madame du Barry* directed by Ernst Lubitsch, usually a filmmaker of great talent.

◆　◆　◆

Candido didn't enjoy the film. He was quite unmoved by the French Revolution, which Herr Doktor had never mentioned, and even more so by the misfortunes of the heroine and a certain Armand, who was ultimately beheaded by a peculiar contraption. He almost tittered at this incident, but a glance at Samantha deterred him: like most of the filmgoers around them, she was moist-eyed with emotion. Obviously, he was the odd man out.

"Hungry, Candido?"

Anything but. His throat was too tight, but he dreaded thwarting Samantha in her present edgy mood. They went into a café, where she ordered buns and hot chocolate for two. She sat staring into space but ate and drank with apparent relish.

I won't leave her. She'll have to tell me to go, but I won't even then. . . .

Eleven-thirty. The statues adorning the royal castle's lofty balustrade were barely visible in the darkness. Leaving the castle on their right and the snow-laden trees of the Lustgarten on their left, they walked back across the Spree. Münzstrasse lay seven or eight hundred yards ahead of them.

◆　◆　◆

Alekhin crossed the Spree bridge in his turn. The youngsters were still carrying their bombs, so they must either have abandoned their scheme or be heading for another objective.

The Lubitsch film had disappointed him, perhaps because he'd always thought the French Revolution overrated. Like all revolutions, it had culminated—once the initial bloodshed was over—in the advent of a dictator not unlike the lionized Bolshevik who was now ruling Russia with a frigid cynicism far surpassing that of Napoleon Bonaparte himself.

He consulted his watch: nearly midnight. He'd lived in this neighborhood once upon a time. Those were the days when he aspired to be a writer, or even a painter. He used to read *Die Aktion*—did the magazine still exist?—and rub shoulders with the likes of Kandinsky and Marc, Heinrich Campendonck and Jacoba van Heemskerck. It seemed a lifetime ago.

The couple turned into Münzstrasse. The street, which was almost deserted, contained certain cinemas specializing in erotic films. The American girl and the Brazilian youth headed for one of these. Suddenly they slowed. Sensing that they were about to look around, Alekhin dodged back into a gloomy doorway. Seconds later he risked a quick glance. They had paused outside a cinema called the Opal, which was advertising a film entitled *Das Mädchen und die Männer.*

◆ ◆ ◆

"Stop whispering, it's getting on my nerves," said Samantha.

"I'm sorry," Candido said in a strangled undertone.

They'd looked in both directions without seeing a soul. It was odd, all the same: Candido had had a vague feeling that someone was following them. Swiftly, he laid a restraining hand on Samantha's arm.

"Don't use your key!"

"Why not? I had an extra one cut. The Plücks didn't know that, and I returned the one they gave me."

"I think it would be better to break in."

She acquiesced with a shrug. Instead of unlocking the main entrance they made their way around the back. The emergency exit was also locked, but there was a transom above it. Samantha threw her weight against the door without success.

"The best plan," said Candido, "would be to sneeze."

"To *what*?"

"You sneeze and I'll break the glass at the same moment. Then we can reach down, unlock the door and get in without a key."

"What's the point, if I wake the whole neighborhood?"

"Please, Samantha."

"Atchoo!"

"Too soon, not loud enough. I'll count to three. One, two . . ."

"ATCHOO!"

A third-floor window above the Konditorei Lambschad lit up and a nightcapped head emerged. Nothing to be seen. The head was withdrawn, the light went out.

"Quiet, Candido. You're making too much noise walking on that broken glass."

"Awfully sorry."

One of Candido's worries vanished when they entered the projection booth: there was no one asleep on the camp bed. He planted the first of their two bombs under the projector.

It'll never go off. Kuppelweiser's an old fool, him and his so-called gunpowder made from saltpeter scraped off the walls of a stable! According to him, this place will be reduced to rubble just because a few cab horses peed against the walls while they slept.

"What are you waiting for?" said Samantha. "Light the fuse."

"Christ, I don't have any matches."

Samantha had brought three boxes. "Lucky I'm here," she said scornfully.

In the foyer she perched on the cashier's stool for the last time, nodded with evident satisfaction, planted her bomb and prepared to light the second fuse.

"Kuppelweiser advised us to cut off about four centimeters," Candido pointed out before he could stop himself.

She rummaged in her purse and produced some nail scissors.

"You're cutting it too short," Candido couldn't help saying.

"Damn!"

"Maybe he got it wrong. What if we blow the whole street sky-high?"

"Come on."

Through the auditorium, then out by way of the emergency exit and into the side alley that led back to Münzstrasse, where they almost bumped into a passing couple and had to beat a hasty retreat. A few moments later the street was empty. They set off at a leisurely pace.

"We must have gone at least a hundred yards," Samantha said. "That should be far enough."

"A bit farther would be better."

She shook her head. Candido had a wild urge to take her in his arms. Seconds dragged by. She started fidgeting.

"What did he say he made his bombs out of?"

"Horsepiss and borage."

"Borage? Are you sure? That's what you use for making a kind of herb tea."

"Maybe, but it also contains nitrate of something."

Just then the first bomb exploded. Candido closed his eyes.

"It worked," said Samantha. Her voice was even, calm. "I'm disappointed, though. It didn't make much of a bang, did it?"

Another detonation, not as loud as the first, but by this time lights were going on everywhere.

"I'm really disappointed," Samantha insisted. "They were downright pathetic, those bombs."

Candido opened his eyes. He took a deep breath, controlled the trembling in his legs and hustled her away.

◆ ◆ ◆

Alekhin waited another twenty minutes in case they reemerged from the Grand Hôtel de Russie, but it seemed so unlikely at this time of night that he decided to take the risk. After all their emotional stress they were probably making love. He was surprised to find himself faintly irritated by the thought of the American girl in the Brazilian's arms.

A late-night streetcar deposited him at the Holzmarkt. He walked the rest of the way to Andreasstrasse and approached the back of the toy shop by crossing a garden he'd reconnoitered on his first visit. The high stone wall was barely visible in the darkness. A neighbor's dog barked when he vaulted it and landed on some planks that snapped beneath his weight: two hundred pounds, and not an ounce of fat. He'd had the same agreeable sensation while cycling a week or so ago: an awareness that his lithe, muscular body was equal to any demand he might make on it. A second wall, and beyond it, as foreseen, the workshop. Separating the workshop from the rest of the building was a door secured by a simple bolt. It was child's play to open it without a sound. Now he was inside: shop on the left, living room and kitchen on the right, stairs in the center. He slipped his shoes off. Once on the landing he waited until the bedrooms' two occupants had sufficiently identified themselves by the noises they made in their sleep. Tiptoeing into the room on his right, he found the old woman lying on her back with her mouth open, snoring gently.

He strangled her and broke her neck for good measure, probing her throat with thumb and forefinger to locate the cervicals, then twisting sharply. The usual, characteristic little crack made itself heard. People were easy to kill at her age.

Or at any age, for that matter.

He entered the other room, shut the door behind him and silently drew the curtains. Then, going to the bed, he bent and clamped his hand over the sleeping man's mouth.

Kuppelweiser awoke with a start and began to struggle.

"Easy, comrade, it's only me, Matthäus."

Alekhin could see very little, but he felt Kuppelweiser relax and took his hand away.

"Switch the light on, Oskar."

He sat down on the edge of the bed, nauseated by the stench of body odor and grubby sheets.

"The Brazilian Jaguar and his American girlfriend planted your bombs. What's more, they went off."

"My bombs always go off," Kuppelweiser said.

Alekhin gave him a warm smile.

"I believe you. You're a reliable type, Oskar. We're going to do good work together in the months and years ahead. A pity you didn't keep quiet about my first visit, but no matter."

Kuppelweiser looked incensed. His eyes were the same forget-me-not blue as his late mother's.

"But I didn't breathe a word about you, not to anyone!"

He's telling the truth.

"I told you, it doesn't matter."

"Not to anyone," Kuppelweiser repeated indignantly. "I didn't even tell my mother who you were."

Alekhin nodded and smiled.

"I'm sure I can trust you, you and your mother—quite sure. And I'm not a man who trusts people lightly."

Kuppelweiser, much reassured, summoned up a faint smile just as the knife skewered his throat. Blood spurted from the wound, but Alekhin moved aside in time.

Incredible how much blood the human body seems to hold.

"Do I look the trusting type, Oskar? I had to kill you. You could have identified me. But there was an even more important reason. You've just become the second of Jaguar's first two victims."

He'd been thinking as he spoke. A simple murder wasn't good enough; he would have to devise some form of signature.

He slit the dead man's throat from ear to ear. The effect was better but still unremarkable.

Got it!

He slit the cheeks from the corners of the mouth to the earlobes.

"There, Oskar, that's what I call a very broad smile."

He went back to the first bedroom and performed some identical surgery on the old woman's throat and cheeks.

Perfect.

A glance at his watch. He'd been absent from his post outside the Grand Hôtel de Russie for thirty-seven minutes. There was plenty of time. He conducted a thorough search of the house, the backyard, the workshop. No less than five hiding places came to light, all empty except the one containing the money. It seemed that Kuppelweiser had carried out his instructions to the letter and burned every document on the premises. Alekhin pocketed most of the cash but left a few hundred marks scattered around. An assassin who killed for political reasons wouldn't be interested in money.

He even left the door to Andreasstrasse ajar to signify that Kuppelweiser had known his murderer. He had either let him in or given him a key.

Another glance at his watch: an hour and a quarter gone. He set off, using the same route as before. What if the couple had decamped in his absence? He disliked uncertainty, but the only way of avoiding it would have been to employ someone else to keep watch on the hotel.

He had his answer at four-forty that morning.

◆ ◆ ◆

Candido wasn't asleep. He sat up in bed and reached for the receiver as soon as the antiquated, wall-mounted telephone began to ring.

"Yes?"

He was prepared for anything, even the voice of Herr Doktor, who might finally have arrived in Berlin and managed by some telepathic means to locate him.

"Cavalcanti? Herr Candido Cavalcanti de Noronha?"

The man spoke perfect German.

"Who is this?"

"Someone who knows you planted two bombs in a Münzstrasse cinema earlier tonight, accompanied by the girl now sharing your bed. I only want to help. You've been betrayed, either by Kuppelweiser or by someone else. The police know your names . . ."

Samantha opened her big, sleepy eyes. "Who is it?" she asked softly.

". . . but they still don't know where you are. Pack your bags and leave the hotel as quickly as you can—every second counts—but stay calm, don't run. Don't tell me where you're going, I've no wish to know. If you need help, be at the Café Josy on Potsdamerplatz at eight-thirty

Monday morning. Don't forget: Monday, eight-thirty, Café Josy, Potsdamerplatz. One last thing, Cavalcanti: whatever you do, stay away from
the Kuppelweisers, the police are on their way to arrest them. Now get
going, quick!"

Samantha, who had snatched the receiver away, heard the concluding
words. She stared at the earpiece, then at Candido.

◆　◆　◆

Alekhin hung up. A few brisk strides took him to the forecourt of Friedrichstrasse Station, where he could watch both entrances of the hotel at
once. The couple emerged only three minutes later.

They headed straight for him. He ducked out of sight before shadowing them to the ticket office, where he heard them ask for two third-class
tickets to Lehnitz-Biesenthal. Having paid, the Brazilian escorted the
American girl to the third-class waiting room.

Alekhin went off to make his last phone call of the night, this time to
police headquarters on Dirksenstrasse, near Alexanderplatz, and this time
he adopted a Russian accent so thick that it rendered his German almost
unintelligible.

"It's about that attack on a cinema in Münzstrasse tonight. Anarchists
were responsible. They're launching a terrorist campaign, and they've
hired a professional killer and explosives expert nicknamed Jaguar. The
name on his passport is Cavalcanti, Candido Cavalcanti. Jaguar is armed
and dangerous—he has murdered the man who supplied the bombs,
Oskar Kuppelweiser of 39 Andreasstrasse, and his elderly mother. If
you're quick you'll find him in room three-eleven at the Grand Hôtel de
Russie, together with his accomplice, an American girl."

Alekhin hung up. The clock in the concourse said four fifty-nine. He
wondered if he should have waited a little longer before setting the police
in motion. It would be the last straw if they actually arrested the couple.

The first-class waiting room made a perfect observation post. Alekhin
took a seat, flipped through some Berlin magazines, _Lustige Blätter_ and
Der Junggeselle, idly contemplated some French Riviera posters on the
walls, ordered a cup of coffee. The waiter brought him the morning
papers as well. The _Berliner Tageblatt_ was the only one to devote four
lines to "a minor explosion, possibly accidental, at a cinema in Münzstrasse."

◆　◆　◆

Samantha was still seething. If the decision had been hers alone they would have gone straight to Kuppelweiser's shop, not back to Plattnik's cottage.

"I'm positive it's a hoax. Why should we run like rabbits just because some anonymous call wakes us up in the middle of the night?"

She even went so far as to say—joking, Candido hoped—that if the police came to arrest her she would roll herself up in a mattress and blaze away at them with her Browning. All in all, he'd had the devil's own job persuading her to leave the hotel in a hurry, board the train and return to Biesenthal.

"I don't feel like walking around this goddamned pond," she said. "I don't feel like trudging through this goddamned snow, or spending days cooped up in that goddamned shack, or keeping that goddamned appointment at the Café Josy. I don't feel like going out and I don't feel like staying in."

"Want some chocolate?"

"No! I especially don't feel like some goddamned chocolate!"

Candido had filled his pockets with the chocolate and was munching it as they circled the gloomy pond behind Reinhold Plattnik's cottage, toiling through the snow like beasts of burden. Samantha came to a halt ten yards ahead. He paused, too, and launched into the *cachaça* song, that Brazilian hymn to the pleasures of rum drinking:

"Você pensa que a cachaça é agua. A cachaça não é agua—não, a cachaça vem do alambique e a aqua vem do ribeirão . . ."

(You think that rum is water. Rum isn't water—no, rum comes from the still and water from the stream . . .)

"And I forbid you to sing!" she said.

"We revolutionaries don't take orders from anyone."

"You're no revolutionary."

"You may be right about that," he replied in his Brazilian tone of voice, nonchalant but a trifle melancholy.

"I'm going back."

He looked at her. She was wearing an old hat and overcoat belonging to Reinhold Plattnik, but the sight of her gave him that now familiar stitch in the chest.

"All right, let's."

"I don't mean back to the cottage, I mean back to Berlin, which I never should have left. I'm going to take the first train out of here."

"All right."

"Stop saying all right, I'm going back alone. It's over between us, Candido. I told you that before. You and I are through."

He'd never felt quite like this, even when struggling through the cayman-, snake- and leech-infested mud of the Mato Grosso. It was a death far worse than the real kind. Incredible how everything could change from one minute to the next.

Samantha was making for the cottage. He trailed after her.

"Please don't say anything," she said.

She'd reached the door. Standing there with her hand on the latch, she looked back at him as if he'd already ceased to exist for her.

"I'm not angry with you, Candido. I'm grateful to you for all you've done, but let me go. That's what I want now. And please don't follow me."

Candido's gesture was quite mechanical. He fished another piece of chocolate out of his pocket and started munching it. Instantly, he reprimanded himself. He was a chocolate revolutionary like George Bernard Shaw's chocolate soldier. Even if he'd thought of something suitable to say he couldn't have said it with his mouth full.

"Don't come inside," she added. "I'll pack my bags and carry them to the station myself."

She disappeared into the cottage. He stared at the pond, munching yet another piece of chocolate, and leaned against a pine tree. Dollops of snow descended on his head.

A figure of fun to the last, that's me.

"Candido?"

Her voice sounded odd. Pride made him hesitate.

"Candido, come in here a minute, would you?"

He detached himself from the tree, walked up to the door and pushed it open. Then he froze. There was someone else in the room with Samantha, a fair-haired, blue-eyed man so huge that Plattnik's cottage seemed to have shrunk by half. Even Samantha looked small beside the stranger, who was exceptionally good-looking. His face and whole bearing radiated self-assurance, as if nothing and no one in the world could stop him. Altogether, he made an overpowering impression.

"Look."

Samantha indicated some newspapers spread out on the table with their headlines exposed to view. BERLIN UNDER TERRORIST ATTACK, proclaimed the *Berliner Tageblatt.* Other dailies carried variations on the same theme. Some spoke of "black" terrorism, "black" meaning anarchist, and all cited Candido's full name, Candido Stevenson Cavalcanti de Noronha, his date and place of birth, his date of arrival in Germany, his passport number and personal description. Cavalcanti was really Jaguar, a renegade Brazilian army officer wanted in several countries, a merciless killer and explosives expert. He and his accomplice-cum-mistress, Samantha Elizabeth Franck, who belonged to a family of notorious Chicago anarchists, had already blown up a cinema, but this, it seemed, was only a rehearsal for the demolition of the Reichstag itself. They had also, with inhuman ferocity, cut the throats of one Oskar Kuppelweiser and his elderly mother, slitting their cheeks—a peculiarly horrific detail—as if to send them to their deaths with a ghastly ear-to-ear smile on their faces. Oskar Kuppelweiser had been a militant communist, and there could be no doubt—thus the general view—that this frightful atrocity was connected with the power struggle between the communists and the anarchists, of whom the latter were proving the more dangerous by far.

Jaguar and his murderous mistress were still at large. Pursuant to inquiries that the police had conducted with their usual efficiency, a flying squad had been dispatched from the Dirksenstrasse headquarters to the Grand Hôtel de Russie, but a few minutes too late. Alerted by an anonymous telephone call, the diabolical pair had just fled their bolt-hole in room 311.

"I was the anonymous caller," the stranger announced with a smile.

Candido recognized his voice.

"But for me," the man went on, "you would now have been in custody for thirty-six hours—in fact you might already have suffered the fate reserved last year for Rosa Luxemburg and Karl Liebknecht."

Alekhin had searched the cottage thoroughly while the youngsters were trudging around the gloomy pond, so his allusion to Rosa Luxemburg wasn't fortuitous. He'd taken his cue from the contents of Samantha's suitcases.

"You must leave here at once," he said. "I've got contacts even at police headquarters, and the noose is tightening fast. The German CID have established that you left Berlin by train yesterday morning, and sooner or later they'll come looking here. The fact that this house belongs to a notorious anarchist doesn't help. Every railway station is being watched."

His name was Harry Hass, he told them, and he was a personal friend of Reinhold Plattnik, his long-time political mentor. He didn't know if Miss Franck and Senhor Cavalcanti were implicated in the double murder at Andreasstrasse. . . . They weren't? He was happy to take their word for it, but he must make one thing clear: being an undercover agent himself, he was risking his life by helping them. He would keep his promise to Plattnik but could do no more. If they refused to accompany him he would be obliged to shoot them because they'd seen him and knew his real name. He had no choice.

A mail van pulled up outside. Alekhin didn't turn to look. It was Hagler, the man he'd requested from Karl Radek's network, punctual to the minute.

"Where are you taking us?"

That was the American girl.

"Somewhere where you'll be safe till the hue and cry dies down. You've three minutes to make up your minds. Please don't compel me to use this gun. My sole aim is to see you safely out of Germany. My organization will get you to Petrograd. From there you can go on to the United States or Brazil—anywhere you like. Two minutes left."

Samantha was on the point of leaving me. Well, now we're going to stay together, and that's all that matters. Besides, if this superman had wanted to abduct us he needn't have gone to so much trouble—he could have flattened me with a single punch, to say nothing of his gun or his sidekick in the postman's uniform.

All traces of their stay at the cottage were carefully eliminated. If Reinhold Plattnik came home tomorrow he wouldn't notice that anyone had been there in his absence.

Samantha was already concealed behind a heap of parcels in the back of the mail van.

"Let's go, Cavalcanti."

He paused for a last look around before climbing aboard with the Grimmelshausen in his pocket. Samantha greeted him with a nod, took his hand and squeezed it.

She's being nice for once.

The Stranger shut them in and secured the double doors. The Stranger . . . Candido felt no inclination to call him anything else. He hadn't liked the way the Stranger had looked at Samantha.

Nor the way Samantha had looked at the Stranger.

All at once he felt cold and frightened.

THE JAGUAR WILL EAT ALL
THE LARGE MAMMALS IT CAN CATCH.
IT WILL ALSO CHASE WATERFOWL THROUGH
REEDS AND IS ADEPT AT CATCHING FISH
IN THE SHALLOWS. IT DOES NOT
SEEM DETERRED BY SNAKES
OR CAYMANS.

lekhin had been at the Kremlin for all of five hours, and this was his fifth appointment in eleven days. Each of his previous appointments had entailed hours of fruitless waiting, and there was no sign that today would be any different.

Vladimir Ilyich Lenin's apartment, an unpretentious suite of five rooms, was situated at the end of the corridor facing him. Beyond the office into which he might eventually be ushered lay the chamber where the Council of People's Commissars had held their meetings in 1918, little more than two years ago. Alekhin had heard Zinoviev describe the atmosphere prevailing at that time: the hectic bustle, the comings and goings, the virtual absence of security checks. Those days were gone. Nothing could have provided clearer proof that the regime was now firmly in the saddle than this relentless surveillance and hushed atmosphere. Vladimir Ilyich's vowed dislike of noise had acquired the force of law.

Alekhin knew that his survival depended on this interview. Tieck, his fanatical little contact at Stockholm, had returned to Russia as convinced as he was himself that Germany would not succumb to revolution. Predictably enough, he'd been executed.

Alekhin conducted a brief self-examination. On the point of gambling for his very life, he could discover no hint of nervousness. He didn't even trouble to run through the arguments he proposed to submit if given the opportunity. He felt calm to the point of indifference.

He was truly the machine he'd always aspired to be.

"Next. You've exactly ten minutes."

A secretary had just beckoned to him. He gave her a nod and a smile and set off down the corridor.

The room he entered was unremarkable, twenty feet long at most and devoid of ostentation. The two windows were uncurtained, the doors had no portieres, the blinds weren't lowered. Almost dead center stood a cluttered kneehole desk: on the right, three telephones fitted with amplifiers; on the left, some files, a set of perfectly sharpened pencils, several fountain pens and a bottle of adhesive with a pierced rubber top; in the center, a lamp with a glass shade, a carbolite inkwell surmounted by two more small lamps, an ashtray and a matching lighter in the shape of an artillery shell, and a sculpture presented by the American financier Armand Hammer: a monkey thoughtfully contemplating a human skull. More files lay everywhere. On top of one batch reposed a big pair of scissors and an old railway timetable, the latter evidently used as a desk pad.

The linen-backed map of Russia that presided between the two windows could be raised or lowered by means of a crank, and the bookshelves lining the walls contained some two thousand volumes including the complete works of Tolstoy, Gogol and Dostoevski. Revolving bookstands on either side of the desk held encyclopedias and dictionaries. (Vladimir Ilyich was reputed to have a perfect command of French and English.) A second table near the door was devoted to atlases and maps, and a third table, placed end-on to the desk, was flanked by two green leather armchairs.

"Your name is Alexis Mikhailovich Alekhin and you were born at Petrograd," said Vladimir Ilyich Lenin. "Your father was a cobbler."

"A prosperous shoemaker."

The little, balding man smiled.

No point in pretending, he knew it anyway.

"Sit down, Aliochka."

Alekhin did so. Lenin shifted his own cane armchair so that the desk no longer formed a barrier between them.

"There's a very fine chess player named Alekhin."

"We're not related."

He knew that too.

"You intrigue me, Aliochka."

No comment.

"You intrigue me because men as diverse as Zinoviev, Chicherin, Kamenev and Sokolnikov, not to mention Stalin and Dzerzhinsky, have mentioned you in recent weeks and urged me to see you. You lobbied them all in turn, didn't you?"

"Yes."

"Encirclement tactics. Do you play chess?"

"I prefer to play with live pieces."

"And with me you're dropping your guard and staking everything on candor. Is this the first time you've ever done so?"

"Yes."

Silence. Lenin's dark eyes blazed, and his customary veneer of urbanity vanished.

I've never seen such a fanatic—never even dreamed that such fanaticism could exist. It's almost disconcerting.

"I suppose," said Lenin, "that you intend your candor as a tribute to my intelligence. You must surely have weighed the odds. How would you describe yourself?"

"I'm a weapon of war. My only human failing is love of country."

"You're on the brink of paranoia, you realize that?"

And you're over the edge.

"On the brink, perhaps, but I won't fall in."

Silence.

I'm very close to death at this moment.

"You're an odd fish, Aliochka, but Felix Edmundovich warned me of that. He vouches for you, which is something he's never done for anyone else. Your report on Germany."

Dead silence. Alekhin began to speak, employing a minimum of words and a maximum of ellipses, conscious that his listener was a man of exceptional intelligence—intelligence perverted by belief in a mission, true, but in that perversity lay his only hope. He described his meetings in Berlin, Bremen, Hamburg, Saxony, the Rhineland and Bavaria. He'd even traveled to Zurich, the city from which Lenin had been shipped back to Russia in a sealed train. Dates and facts, names and places came pouring out, regurgitated by his flawless memory.

He fell silent.

"Your conclusions?"

They were still the same. His German peregrinations hadn't changed them—far from it.

"There'll never be a revolution in Germany."

Lenin rose and paced the room *(mere playacting—he isn't angry),* picked up the big pair of scissors and toyed with them. The tip of the scissors struck the glass lampshade and made it ring—only faintly, but he seemed to find the sound annoying.

"I must get a cloth shade. I detest that noise."

He passed behind Alekhin's chair. Hanging on the wall facing the desk was a calendar manufactured by Gosizdat, the newly established state publishing house. Vladimir Ilyich eyed it sardonically.

"To think we Russians can produce a technological marvel like that! Amazing, no?"

He resumed his seat.

"When a lampshade makes a noise you can have it replaced. When someone brings you unwelcome news you can have him eliminated, but the lampshade continues to make a noise after being removed and unwelcome news isn't improved by the death of the person who brought it."

More playacting. I'm disappointed in him.

Lenin discarded the scissors, propped his elbows on the arms of the cane chair and fitted his fingertips together.

"You know my own attitude to revolution in Germany?"

We're getting there at last.

" 'We shall achieve final victory,' " Alekhin quoted, " 'only in company with the united workers of other countries.' Similarly: 'We cannot bring the revolution to a victorious conclusion by confining ourselves to Russia alone and without spreading it to other countries.' Or again: 'We are a weak and backward people. . . . The banner of international socialist revolution is in feeble hands. . . . The workers of the most backward country will be able to preserve it only if the workers of advanced countries come to their aid.' "

"I did indeed write those things, Aliochka. How do you explain the fact that all the other observers who have reported to me on Germany take a view that differs from yours?"

"They were either lying or mistaken."

"What of the foreigners who visit us from all over the world?"

"They're romantics—they represent no one but themselves."

"You despise them?"

"I would try to use them."

"So your pessimism isn't absolute?"

Don't go too far. Communism is a utopia such as the world has never known before, and the only thing that can impose a utopia and make it stick is a persistent, murderous reign of terror. Not even Vladimir Ilyich Lenin, who's busy regimenting this country with the aid of his personal creation, the Cheka, and who happily employs terror as a principle of government—not even he would care to hear a truth of that kind. He would concede that I'm right, in his heart of hearts, but he'd have me liquidated just the same.

"I believe in the final victory of our revolution," said Alekhin, "but I think it'll be a unique phenomenon. In my view, we should accept this unalterable uniqueness as a fact of life. We must transform ourselves into a fortress and equip ourselves to make raids into enemy territory— secretly, by means of a new, worldwide organization employing every conceivable weapon regardless of moral considerations."

Silence. He held the other man's gaze. The door opened, the secretary put her head around the door. "Another minute," Vladimir Ilyich told her, and she withdrew. He started toying with the scissors again.

He's immensely intelligent, but it disappoints me, the way he fidgets with things or paces up and down the room whenever he grows uneasy. Me, I haven't budged an inch. He's got a simple choice: either eliminate me or employ me like a man who keeps a ferocious dog obedient to no one but himself.

"An engine of war, Aliochka—wasn't that the term you used?"

"A machine with no ambition to be other than a machine."

Another silence.

"You may go," said Vladimir Ilyich Lenin.

He passed Trotsky and Kalinin in the corridor. They exchanged glances, but only Trotsky counted. Kalinin, despite his air of peasant cunning, carried no weight.

A young official checked his pass for the last time.

"Did you really speak with Vladimir Ilyich?"

"For eleven minutes."

"How did you find him?"

"He's the greatest genius of our own or any other century."

The Kremlin's towers still sported the Romanovs' double-headed eagle, which no one had thought to remove. Alekhin squared his massive shoulders and walked off with long, lithe, powerful strides. He'd thrown the dice and they were rolling.

He felt precisely nothing, unmoved even by the knowledge that the game might prove fatal. He was a perfectly functioning machine.

A thought occurred to him: the Jaguar file had been lying open on Vladimir Ilyich's desk.

Six weeks went by, and still no response or verdict had been handed down. Although Alekhin felt inclined to regard this as a favorable sign, he didn't take it for granted that the game was won. The organization whose establishment he'd recommended during his interview—the "new, worldwide organization employing every conceivable weapon regardless of moral considerations"—would not replace the Cheka; it would complement it by carrying out operations abroad with the aid of a small and carefully selected minority of the foreigners who came flocking to Soviet Russia like pilgrims to Rome or Mecca. Among other things, it would permit the elimination of rivals such as the anarchists, who could additionally be saddled with responsibility for all the liquidations that proved necessary.

It was a novel plan and a bold one, but Alekhin was gambling on its very audacity. He had no choice: it was either that or suffer the fate of a man like Tieck. He hadn't asked to head the new organization, should it ever come into being. All he wanted was to be allowed to join it, and sooner or later his cold-blooded patience and Machiavellian cunning would enable him to carve out a niche for himself. The idea that had come to him in Oskar Kuppelweiser's workshop was taking shape. Things weren't going badly, either. He'd submitted his scheme to Lenin and he was still alive.

He worked away assiduously in the weeks following his visit to the Kremlin. Stalin encouraged him and Zinoviev gave him advice, though both men were prudent enough not to back him openly. A "no" from Lenin or Dzerzhinsky would be tantamount to a death sentence. Zinoviev saw to it that he was relieved of most of his duties as deputy head of the Petrograd Cheka and authorized the various trips he made.

He took advantage of this to make arrangements for the little Brazilian and his American girlfriend. Having induced the couple to quit the cottage near Biesenthal, he hid them for a month on the Kreuzberg in Berlin under the supervision of men from Radek's network and had them taught the rudiments of Russian.

The girl proved a readier pupil than the boy, whose sullen attitude persisted after they were spirited out of Germany and escorted to Petrograd. Candido Cavalcanti kept to himself and refused to take part in any demonstrations with Petrograd's colony of budding revolutionaries from all over the world. He also declined to speak anything but his native Portuguese except with the girl, though he'd hardly seen her since their arrival in Russia, she was so taken up with her newfound revolutionary friends, especially two fellow Americans named Emma Goldman and Harvey Bloggs. Alekhin himself had devoted a little time to Samantha insofar as his own schedule permitted. He'd dined with her on two or three occasions—without the Brazilian—and had read in her eyes that she wasn't, to say the least, indifferent to his physical charms. Well, why not? He couldn't detect any risk in bedding the girl and decided to do so at the first opportunity. Meanwhile, he assigned Afonka Tchadayev to guard Cavalcanti with orders never to leave him unattended.

He'd had the youngsters brought to Moscow two days earlier. No connection, of course, with his strangely insistent desire to have the American girl close at hand and—so to speak—available to him. It was simply that the time had come to see how well the little Jaguar would cope with the jigsaw puzzle designed for his benefit.

◆ ◆ ◆

Candido, seated beside a window in their room at the Hotel Metropol, was reading Tolstoy's *War and Peace* in the original, using Samantha's Russian dictionary to help him with the more difficult words.

A pale sun was setting over Moscow. No sound of traffic drifted up from the avenue four floors below, just the muffled tramp of countless thousands of feet trudging hither and thither. It amazed Candido that such vast numbers of people could all be so glum and silent.

Samantha had gone out early that morning, ostensibly to attend a session of the so-called Third International, or Comintern. He refrained from speculating on her true whereabouts, it would only hurt him unnecessarily.

Noises came from the adjoining lobby: a door opening, a murmur of voices. Once in a while, Afonka, their bodyguard, had visitors. Silence eventually returned—silence of a peculiar quality.

You're getting ideas. Give it a minute.

He couldn't wait. He laid his book aside and, light-footed as a cat, went to look: the lobby was deserted. Had Afonka relaxed his vigilance for the first time in weeks?

Candido opened the outside door a couple of inches. Tchadayev was there all right, but talking to another man at the far end of the corridor.

"I can't leave the Brazilian," he was saying.

"I promise I won't budge from the door," replied the other man, a hotel porter in a belted Russian smock and felt boots. "I can't help it if you're wanted on the phone—this Aliochka type was most insistent. Well, make up your mind."

Candido's wolfskin coat and cap were hanging on a peg within reach. Everything went with dreamlike rapidity. It took him only a couple of seconds to sneak out, dart to the other end of the corridor and hide around the corner. He hadn't the least idea where to go from there. What was more, he'd forgotten to close the door. The voices ceased. Someone came padding up to the door and pulled it shut. A furtive glance revealed that it was the hotel porter, who had stationed himself outside and folded his arms.

Afonka Tchadayev was getting into the lift.

Just a little outing, Candido told himself. He made his way along another corridor at right angles to the first. It led to a service exit and a flight of stairs.

"A watch—a fine gold watch."

The man was gripping his arm with one clawlike hand and holding up a pocket watch with the other.

"I don't want to buy a watch," Candido told him.

They were the first Russian words he'd ever uttered, but they tripped effortlessly off his tongue. A moment's anxiety ensued. The fellow would spot his foreign accent and take him for a spy. He would be back inside in no time.

But no, the man glanced swiftly in all directions. He looked even more nervous than Candido felt, which was faintly reassuring.

"Besides," said Candido, "I don't have any money." He was actually speaking Russian! "Leave me alone."

The man sheered off. Candido discovered that he was on the point of emerging into the big square flanked by—what was the name of that fortress? Ah yes, the Kremlin. The square was alive with policemen and soldiers with red stars on their caps. He hurriedly retraced his steps.

"I've got some more like this one."

How do you say "Get lost!" in Russian?

"Forget it," was the best he could manage.

"Watches and jewelry. I live near here, I'll show you."

Some policemen were heading straight for them. Candido hurried across the street and took the first turning he came to.

"You must surely have the price of a watch, a man with a nice fur coat and boots like yours."

Candido peered over his shoulder. Was he mistaken, or were the policemen following? He took another turning.

"I've got some icons, too—very fine ones."

Why should he be scared of the police? All he'd done was leave his hotel without informing Afonka Tchadayev, but had he ever been told he was under guard and obliged to account for his movements? Never. If only this idiot would stop pestering him with his watches and icons and stuff.

Two more changes of direction brought him out into an open-air market pervaded by a strong smell of fish. The Hotel Metropol was not far away on his right. He hesitated, turned, and found himself looking into the itinerant watch-seller's eyes for the first time.

Take care! Whatever it was about those eyes, his suspicions were instantly, inexplicably aroused. He took to his heels. A whistle shrilled as he sprinted off through the stalls. He dodged the first man to bar his path, but an iron hand gripped him by the arm and a voice barked at him in German.

"Don't move!"

"Who's moving?"

Something was rammed against his forehead. Squinting up at this cold, hard object, he identified it as the muzzle of a revolver.

"Keep quiet and come with us."

"Whatever you say."

There were three of them, all powerfully built. Two held him by the arms while the third followed close behind.

"Not a sound, or we'll kill you on the spot."

"I don't want to die, I'm much too young."

"Shut up!"

"Not that I fancy dying at any age. Do you know Herr Doktor?"

"Shut up! I'm sure you were less talkative the night you cut Kuppelweiser's throat!"

His jaw dropped. For a moment he stopped short, transfixed with horror and stupefaction, but the men on either side merely lifted him a few inches off the ground and kept on walking. As soon as his feet regained contact with the pavement his legs mechanically started functioning again.

"You're crazy! I've never killed anyone."

"You're Jaguar. We all know what that means."

He was marched into a building, along a passage and down some cellar stairs. Surely they weren't going to kill him? A key turned in a lock, a door swung open. The room beyond it looked less like a cellar than a lumber room. It was piled high with furniture, pictures, books and things under dustsheets. He had no time to see more because a violent shove in the back sent him careering down a short flight of steps into the midst of this clutter. He ended up sprawling across a table laden with crockery and saucepans.

The door slammed behind him, then silence.

They've locked me in but at least I'm alive.

More crockery went crashing to the floor as he straightened up and took stock of his surroundings. All that relieved the gloom was a high, barred window, but it was enough to reveal a shadow more substantial than the rest: the motionless figure of a man whose steel-rimmed glasses caught what little light there was. He was sitting there, staring fixedly at Candido.

"I honestly don't know what I'm doing here," Candido said.

The man continued to stare at him. Candido could distinguish his features more clearly now. He seemed to be smiling.

"I don't speak much Russian—I'm a foreigner, as you can tell. Know any German? English? French? Spanish? Portuguese, maybe?" Candido indicated the door at the top of the steps. "I was walking along the street, minding my own business, when this man tried to sell me a watch. I saw the look in his eyes and ran for it, but they caught me. They marched me off with a gun to my head and threw me in here."

I'm making him laugh. Bozo the Brazilian Clown, that's me.

He headed for his silent companion, broken china crunching underfoot as he threaded his way between the furniture separating them. That was when his foot struck something soft. He looked down.

Dear God!

The corpse belonged to someone around his own age and build. Most noticeably of all, the throat was gaping open and the cheeks had been slit from ear to ear.

What about the other man?

Candido went over to him.

"*Gospodin?* Sir? Monsieur?"

One touch on the shoulder and the second corpse keeled over and toppled to the floor. This one, too, had its throat cut and its cheeks slit, hence the ghastly semblance of a smile.

The wounds were so fresh that blood was still oozing from them.

He attacked the door first. Locked from the outside, it didn't even rattle when he hammered on it with his fists, then kicked it.

The window.

It was not only barred but set into a sloping embrasure at least ten feet from the ground. Candido dragged an old sideboard over to it, climbed on top and unsuccessfully tried to break the dusty glass.

Convinced of the impossibility of escaping by either of these routes, he began wildly to look for alternatives. Leading off the lumber room was a series of cellars, all similarly vaulted and unlit. They got steadily darker the farther he went. At last, unable to see a thing, he retraced his steps and searched the lumber room for a lamp. No luck.

He overcame his repugnance sufficiently to search the bodies, which yielded identity cards, money, a pocketknife and a watch apiece. It occurred to him, looking at the time, that he must already have been there for two hours. On the second corpse, the one with glasses, he additionally found a pipe, a tobacco pouch and a lighter. The next thing was to improvise some torches. These he fashioned out of the dead men's papers, which he supplemented with pages torn from some old books—reluctantly, because the thought of mutilating any book appalled him.

There were six cellars in all. An unpleasant surprise awaited him in the last of them. There was no door: the succession of underground chambers led nowhere.

Then he caught a whiff of freshly turned soil and felt a breath of air on his cheek. He discovered the aperture a moment later. The old stone facing had been breached, and lying on the ground was the implement used for the purpose, a pickax. Instantly, an idea took shape in Candido's mind: perhaps there had been three of them, and the third had killed the other two before making good his escape.

In other words, if he took the same route he might bump into the third man—who probably wouldn't appreciate being followed and would kill him too.

Ideas like that I can do without.

He armed himself with the pickax just in case, and crawled through the hole in the wall. It proved to be the mouth of a tunnel so narrow in places that he had to squeeze through. He soon abandoned his fur coat, which not only hampered him but threatened to cause a cave-in. No question now of reaching into his pocket for the lighter: he was in pitch darkness. There were places where he had to scrape away the soil like his predecessor in this rat-hole, and one particular stretch had him panicking, unable to advance or retreat and convinced that he would be entombed for ever.

How about singing something?

The going got better. Pushing the pickax ahead of him, he managed to dig it into the floor of the tunnel. From then on he hauled himself along like a mountaineer wielding an ice ax.

He came out in another cellar. Lighting one of his makeshift torches, he glimpsed some big wooden trunks and wicker baskets, all of them covered with mildew. Dozens more trunks reposed on the concrete floor of the adjoining chamber, very capacious and stenciled with numbers in red, blue, green and black paint. A naked bulb dangled from the ceiling.

He tiptoed off in search of a switch. Three rooms farther on, having guided himself by the electric cable whenever possible, he felt one under his fingers.

He hesitated before turning the light on. What if the murderer or murderers of the two men in the first cellar were lying in wait for him?

He took the plunge.

A split-second later he let out a yell. His heart seemed to hit the roof of his mouth: looming over him not three feet away was a giant figure clad in armor and a horned helmet.

"Congratulations, you really threw a scare into me!"

The giant wasn't alone—there must have been at least a hundred of them, all around eight feet tall and mounted on circular wooden stands. Some were dressed as Tatars, others as naval officers, troubadours, Roman centurions, Swiss peasants, demon kings, aristocrats male and female.

They were dummies attired in theatrical costumes.

I must be in the bowels of the Bolshoi. I've always adored Swan Lake, *but this has put me off it for good.*

He was seated on the great throne of the king of Persia, or possibly of Boris Godunov, and he was hungry as hell. The shelves around him groaned with roast chickens, legs of lamb, haunches of venison, loaves of bread by the dozen—even a whole ox impaled on a spit from muzzle to tail—but they were all made of papier-mâché. As for the countless bottles of wine, flasks of elixir, vials of poison, goblets and drinking horns, they were all bone dry. Candido was hungry and thirsty, but at least he wasn't cold: he'd borrowed a doublet belonging to Falstaff or the Barber of Seville, whichever, and wrapped himself in Othello's cloak, a voluminous garment trimmed with fake ermine.

Why? Because he hadn't a hope of getting out. He'd banged on the only door, an iron door that couldn't be opened from the inside, but his repeated blows had failed to produce a single echo. If the Bolshoi remained closed for long he stood a good chance of becoming the Phantom of the Opera.

He was awakened by the sound of voices. Ten feet away, on the far side of a wall of dummies in stage costumes, two men were lugging a trunk along. A moment later he was slinking between rows of overladen coat hangers to the door, which was now open.

Up one flight of stairs, then another. He kept on going, unchallenged by the stage hands he passed, who eyed him curiously but said nothing.

Passages, dressing rooms, administrative offices. Through one last door, and a refreshing blast of icy night air smote him in the face. He set off briskly. Then it occurred to him: *night* air? He must have been gone for twenty-four hours! Samantha would be really anxious by now.

The approaches to the hotel were almost deserted. No sign of Afonka on the prowl, yet he too must be wondering where he'd got to.

Unless he let me escape on purpose, which isn't beyond the bounds of possibility.

He avoided the main entrance in favor of the kitchens, and there managed to skirt the few staff on duty at this hour. This getup would certainly attract some attention if he was seen.

"Where are you off to?"

He hadn't noticed the policeman lurking around the corner on the second-floor landing of the service stairs. Inspiration came to his aid.

"Cheka," he snapped.

"Excuse me, comrade," said the policeman.

The third-floor corridor was deserted. What if the door to the suite was locked? It wasn't. He tiptoed in. *No lights—she must be asleep already.* He went straight to the bathroom and admired himself in the mirror. Just his size—he couldn't wait to see Samantha's face.

He went into the bedroom and switched on the light.

The big bed was empty.

As yet he didn't feel alarmed, just mildly disappointed. He would have liked to find her there, surprise her with his getup, recount his adventures. A cold supper had been left on the table in the sitting room: tender young leeks and cold meat, herrings, anchovies, *blini* with fresh cream. He sat down and tucked in. Vodka had also been provided, but he didn't touch it. One regrettable experiment had taught him that he was allergic to hard liquor. He was on his sixth glass of iced water when he heard the outside door open.

"Samantha? I'm in here. Come and see."

He rose and spread his arms to show off his costume. Three men walked in with Afonka Tchadayev at their heels. One of them deposited a bulging canvas bag on the table and opened the neck.

"Your suit, comrade. And your coat."

He was flabbergasted. They were the clothes he'd left behind in the cellars of the Bolshoi. His crawl through the tunnel had stained them so badly with evil-smelling mud that he'd decided to abandon them.

They were now sodden with blood.

"We also recovered the knife you used to cut their throats," the man added, "—all six of them. Seems you had a busy day."

◆ ◆ ◆

Felix Edmundovich Dzerzhinsky was a pale-faced man with a fair mustache and a sparse goatee. His calm manner and quiet voice gave no indication of the heart attack that was to carry him off in six years' time.

"Tell me what you said to Vladimir Ilyich, Aliochka, word for word."

Alekhin complied. They were strolling side by side through the Lubyanskaya Gardens. The building opposite, which people had already begun to call the Lubyanka, was the headquarters of the Cheka. It had been so for two years now, ever since that organization had moved into the offices of the Rossya Insurance Company.

Moscow was bathed in watery sunlight, a timid harbinger of approaching spring, and it was on this account—or because he wanted to avoid eavesdroppers—that Dzerzhinsky had suggested a little stroll outside. He was just back from Nizhni Novgorod, now Gorki, where he had spent

two days at Lenin's country house and had gone fox hunting with him.
He nodded thoughtfully.

"You annoyed him, to say the least. I'm sure you noticed."

Alekhin merely smiled.

"It seems he wasn't altogether convinced that you knew what you were
doing and had weighed the risks with sufficient care."

"It was my only chance of persuading him," said Alekhin.

"I saw him the same evening and spent the next two days with him,
fortunately for you, but it was touch and go. Please don't trouble to thank
me."

"I feel no obligation to do so, Felix Edmundovich. Whether or not I
survive, my analysis of the situation remains correct."

Silence.

"Have you ever had designs on my job, Aliochka?"

Alekhin laughed. "No, that's the last thing I covet."

Dzerzhinsky gazed up at the leafless trees with a faintly mournful
expression on his gaunt, Slav face.

"The strange thing is," he said, "I believe you."

"If you didn't I'd be dead," Alekhin replied casually, and the pensive,
unsmiling nod that greeted his response was an exact measure of the risk
he'd run.

"Point one, revolution in Germany," Dzerzhinsky resumed. "Vladimir Ilyich rejects your theory. Whether or not he thinks it valid is immate-
rial. What matters is that everyone should continue to believe in the
possibility that the German proletariat will rise and seize power. Not only
is your opposing view rejected; you never submitted it."

"Understood."

*We might just as well end the conversation here. The essential point has been
made, and I already know what's coming.*

"Point two," Dzerzhinsky went on. "We're going to set up a new
organization distinct from the Cheka and unbeknown to it, or as good as.
Manned by different operatives recruited and trained for the purpose, it
will be reserved for external use only—like certain medicines—under the
joint command of Chicherin and myself. . . ."

Alekhin's memory slipped into gear all the more smoothly because that
name, more than any other, was the one he'd been expecting to hear:
Georgi Vasilyevich Chicherin, born 1872, aristocratic background;
started work as an archivist at the Ministry of Foreign Affairs in 1896;
espoused Marxism at the outbreak of war; allied himself with Trotsky,
becoming first his deputy and then his successor as People's Commissar
for Foreign Affairs; intelligent, cultured, erudite, fluent in six languages,

highly conscientious, excellent at carrying out orders, poor at organization.

Dzerzhinsky will be in charge. Chicherin is just a pawn.

"All your orders will come from one of us or, of course, from Vladimir Ilyich himself, and all your reports must be submitted directly to us. You'll require foreign currency. I gather you know where to get it."

"I do."

The idea had first occurred to him at one of those tedious meetings in Berlin. There existed in Germany—and not in Germany alone—a certain number of big industrialists and bankers who were already disposed to believe in the permanence of the Russian Revolution.

"For a start, we could sell them real estate. There's a demand for landed property."

"Vladimir Ilyich will shortly be announcing details of our new economic policy. The NEP envisages an end to nationalization, the encouragement of commerce and craftsmanship, free enterprise, a friendly reception for foreign capitalists."

Alekhin, who had already heard about the NEP from Bukharin, didn't believe in it for a moment. Though convinced that Dzerzhinsky was just as skeptical, he wouldn't have dreamed of saying so; the situation was becoming more surrealistic every day, but who cared? The German billionaire Hugo Stinnes, whom he had approached, would believe or pretend to believe in the NEP, as would plenty of others. Why? Because all utopias were attractive and it suited them to do so—nothing else mattered. Once Lenin's declarations had been made official and broadcast to the capitalist world at large, money would come pouring into the Soviet coffers.

"Those fools will end by giving us the rope to hang them with," Dzerzhinsky said rapturously.

That's just where I disagree with the likes of you and Lenin, Felix Edmundovich. I don't think "those fools" are destined for the gallows at all, but they'll certainly help us survive in the years ahead—us and me in particular.

The sun was still shining in the Moscow sky as they strolled back to the Lubyanka.

"Now about this Jaguar scheme of yours, Aliochka. A somewhat bizarre idea, you must admit."

"I'm constructing a myth, creating an international terrorist—one who's all the more elusive because he doesn't exist. He'll strike down those whom we wish to eliminate, whenever and wherever in the world we choose. The fact that he's merciless, unstoppable and ubiquitous will inspire fear and trepidation. Thanks to him I shall be able to turn situations to our advantage and help to install pro-Soviet governments. That was my basic idea. I needed a puppet, a hook on which to hang the name Jaguar. I chose this young Brazilian precisely because he's a harmless nonentity. If ever he were captured, who would believe him to be a mass murderer? What's more, the anarchist sympathies of his American mistress are a matter of record, so it should be easy enough to foist his assassinations on the anarchists."

"How many murders does he have to his credit?"

"He increased his score by six last night. The men whose throats were cut—"

"I know who they were, Aliochka. They'd have been shot in any case—you chose well. I was referring to the deaths in Germany."

"Eighteen. We put the boy up at the safe house on the Kreuzberg. He and his girlfriend are wanted by the German police."

"Does he realize that he was manipulated yesterday, when your man Tchadayev deliberately allowed him to escape?"

"It wouldn't matter if he did," Alekhin replied.

"What about the girl?"

Their eyes met.

Don't underrate the importance of that question. Above all, don't lie.

"I dined with her last night. I also slept with her."

"And that doesn't matter either?"

"Not at all. It'll only strengthen my hold over him. He's crazy about her."

Alekhin countered Dzerzhinsky's speculative gaze with a self-assured smile. He felt confident that, if circumstances required him to send Samantha Franck to her death, he would do so without the least compunction. As for his being jealous of Cavalcanti, that was inconceivable.

Dzerzhinsky nodded. "When do they leave Moscow?" he asked.

"Next Monday. They should be there in a month's time. My team is already in position."

"They've little chance of survival, especially if the operation succeeds. Aren't you afraid of losing your Jaguar?"

"I can always find a replacement if necessary, but I've taken certain precautions."

Silence. They were twenty yards from the doors of the Lubyanka.

"Vladimir Ilyich finds this Jaguar business quite amusing," Dzerzhinsky said suddenly. "He'd like to meet the boy. Arrange it somehow. Not just the youngsters on their own. Include them in a party."

"It's done."

◆ ◆ ◆

"I didn't know you played the guitar," said Harvey Bloggs.

"It's a balalaika, not a guitar," Candido replied. "We all play the guitar in Brazil—that and football. The rest of the time we eat beans."

Harvey Bloggs guffawed.

"We also grow coffee and drink it to help us pass the beans," Candido added.

This time everyone laughed. They were on a train, having left Moscow in a small, select group. It was an honor to be chosen, apparently. There were fifteen special invitees apart from Harvey "Call me Harv" Bloggs, with his big yellow buckteeth, his huge, back-slapping hands, his equine laugh and his love of scatological jokes. Candido was sorry he'd opened his mouth—it was the first time since the business of the Bloody Cellar, which had happened a week ago. He bowed his head and concentrated on the balalaika, which he was beginning to master.

But the impulse was too strong: he couldn't help looking at Samantha. She was sitting beside Afonka Tchadayev at the far end of the carriage, chatting with him in Russian.

Theirs was a first-class or "soft" carriage, as the Russians termed it, and they were bound for Nizhni Novgorod, where they would be the guests of someone by the name of Vladimir Ilyich Lenin. Night had come and gone, rather in the manner of the white nights at Petrograd. Visible in the daylight now streaming through the double-glazed windows were somber pine forests dappled with pale green patches by birch trees attired in their springtime finery.

The motion of the train was very slight. Harvey Bloggs, who knew everything, explained that this was because of the gauge, which was wider than on railway networks elsewhere. "That's because the Russians are concerned for the welfare of all, comrades. It isn't surprising revolution has triumphed in Russia before conquering the rest of the world. It's a country where human needs take priority over everything else." Candido's fingers had regained their touch. Just now, when everyone had woken up and the samovars and breakfast arrived, a man named Borodin had asked him to play the "Internationale." He hadn't replied.

Samantha and the Stranger . . . Samantha in the Stranger's arms . . . He didn't feel angry—in fact he reproached himself for being incapable of rage and hatred, even of genuine resentment.

It hurts, that's all.

He hadn't spoken to her since, though she'd made several attempts to break the ice. He'd slept on the sitting-room sofa, and he hadn't, of course, touched her again.

He played softly—too softly for anyone to hear above the noise of the train—and sang in his head, filled with nostalgia for the sun, for Brazil, for the music he used to make with the black servants (to Dom Trajano's great displeasure), for Samantha's soft, fragrant skin, her lips and hair. *Você pensa que Samantha . . .*

They were pulling into Nizhni Novgorod.

A motorboat ferried them across a river—the Oka, according to Harvey Bloggs—which mingled its waters with those of the Volga beneath the walls of a castle, a kind of Kremlin in miniature. Some horse-drawn *telegas* transported them along potholed streets to a hotel, where they freshened up and had lunch. Toward four o'clock a convoy of cars turned up.

They drove through the grounds of an estate—a large one, from the look of it. Candido spotted a number of soldiers discreetly mounting guard at various points. His fellow passengers were Harvey Bloggs and two Chinese. The car, which was driven by a chauffeur in a baggy blouse belted at the waist, pulled up outside a two-storied house that looked neither new nor particularly luxurious. Harvey was in a state of high excitement. "Just imagine," he kept saying, "we're about to meet the greatest genius of the twentieth century!"

Maidservants ushered the visitors into a spacious but ill-furnished drawing room. Numerous paintings adorned the walls, some of them hanging awry.

"An amazing lack of ostentation! It's a lesson to us all!" Harvey exclaimed, and the others chimed in. Candido sat down at the end of a sofa whose protruding springs dug into his buttocks. This man Lenin was president of Russia, or the equivalent, and Candido was no stranger to presidents. Brazilian presidents were almost as numerous as termites and regularly frequented Dom Trajano's dinner table. He drank his coffee and ate some pastries, thanking the maidservants with a nod. After thirty or forty minutes a short, balding man came downstairs and everyone rose, looking ecstatic. The visitors were introduced. When it was Candido's turn to shake hands, the bald man stared at him intently.

"You're Brazilian, I gather?"

"From São Paulo."

"How long has your family been in Brazil?"

"Three centuries or so. Maybe a bit longer."

"Your Russian is perfect and your accent excellent," said the bald man.

"So is yours," Candido replied.

Everyone roared with laughter. He hated himself for making people laugh whenever he opened his mouth, and above all for having been tricked into speaking Russian. He was soon forgotten, however, and no one showed any interest in him for the next half hour. Now and then he sensed that Samantha was trying to catch his eye, but he refrained from looking in her direction.

The reception came to an end. He was just emerging from the house, relieved to be going, when a man buttonholed him.

"Vladimir Ilyich has heard you're an excellent shot for your age. He'd like you to go hunting with him tomorrow."

"Tomorrow?"

"Tomorrow morning. You can't decline such a flattering invitation, naturally. A chauffeur will pick you up at four A.M., so be sure you're ready. The necessary equipment will be delivered to your hotel."

"He's about two hundred sazhens from here," said the huntsman called Porochin.

"I don't know what a sazhen is," said Candido.

He kept his head averted, and his eyes flickered a little. The Stranger was there.

"A sazhen is just over two meters," the huntsman told him. "Two hundred sazhens are about four hundred and twenty-five meters, understand?"

"No, but never mind."

"Over there," said Porochin. "To the right of the three birches. Take care, it's very muddy."

The time was four-forty A.M. and the place Zavidovo, not far from Nizhni Novgorod. Candido, guided by gestures from the men around him, had walked a mile and a half since leaving the relative warmth of the car. The thick mud into which he sometimes sank calf-deep reminded him of the Mato Grosso. At daybreak the Stranger had unexpectedly appeared beside the track and handed him a rifle. They hadn't exchanged a word as they tramped along side by side. *The long and the short of it* . . . Candido couldn't help thinking how comical they must look, like a couple of circus freaks.

Drop the idea. You could never kill anyone, not even him. . . .

Rain had soaked the track during the night, so it was easy to follow the fresh footprints. They'd finally come upon Porochin and two other men, one of whom bore a distinct resemblance to Lenin and introduced himself as Dmitry Ilyich Ulyanov. Porochin suggested splitting up into two groups, one to hunt woodcock and the other—including Candido and Vladimir Ilyich—grouse.

Candido was alone now. He doubted if one of his strides covered a meter, but he wouldn't be far off if he counted to five hundred. He'd gone hunting many times before, and for bigger game than grouse. His father had often taken him along in the old days, when he still hoped that he, Candido, would turn out to be the son he'd always wanted. Candido well remembered the gun he'd been given at the age of eight: a twin-barreled, silver-inlaid shotgun made by James Purdey & Sons of 57 South Audley Street, London. Ishmael Tavarés, foreman of the Bragança Boa Vista estate, had taught him how to use it.

Four hundred and ninety-seven . . . In theory he should by now have reached the president of the Soviet Union—or a man-trap set for him by the Stranger. He was in among the reeds of a marsh, and the water came up to the knees of his waders.

"That's my left foot you stepped on," said Lenin. "I didn't hear you coming. You made remarkably little noise."

"I beg your pardon," Candido said politely.

There were two other men there, but one of them was no hunter. He carried an army rifle and a Nagant revolver in a black leather holster belted over his padded canvas jacket.

A bodyguard, and all because of me. If I pointed my gun at Lenin that thug would riddle me with bullets before I could pull the trigger.

Lenin gestured to Candido to squat down beside him. They looked like two men relieving themselves in a field latrine.

"The grouse don't take long to appear as a rule," Lenin said.

"I'll watch out for them," Candido whispered back.

The bodyguard's eyes never left him.

"Why did they call you Jaguar?"

The question took Candido by surprise. Samantha had never asked him, yet here he was, out after grouse with his backside in the icy water of a marsh, being interrogated by the president of Russia.

He told the unvarnished truth: the story of his early days in the Mato Grosso and the garrison's visit from the *bilheteiro,* the seller of lottery tickets.

"Brazilian lottery tickets often bear pictures of familiar creatures like pigs, cockerels, horses—"

"And jaguars," Lenin said with a smile.

So they'd bullied him into buying the whole jaguar series. Weeks later he found he'd won five contos, a conto being a thousand milreis.

"Is that a great deal of money?"

Not having been in the habit of handling money in Brazil, Candido couldn't say. In any case, he'd never seen any of his five contos. His fellow soldiers had spent them all on drink.

"And they christened you Jaguar on the spot?"

"For fun," said Candido. "They were having a laugh at my expense, that's all."

So saying, he aimed and fired at a grouse that had just taken wing. The bird hit the water thirty yards away.

"They told me you were a good shot," Lenin said, "and they weren't exaggerating."

"I was lucky," said Candido.

The impression had been brief but singularly powerful, like an electric shock. Just before firing he'd turned to the president of Russia to see how his story had gone down, but the look on Lenin's face was quite unexpected. A veil had lifted from those dark eyes: they were blazing, piercing, ferocious.

He isn't after grouse. It's me he's after, and I was almost taken in. I'd forgotten something: he's the Stranger's lord and master—he rules a country far bigger and more populous than Brazil.

"You're too modest, my young friend," Lenin said, and the veil descended again.

One of the men, not the bodyguard but the other one, had gone to recover the grouse.

"That was a very fine shot," Lenin said, "but there's no point in waiting any longer. Hunting's over for the day—the grouse are busy mating. That's the last we'll see of them.

"Let's go," he said. "It's getting chilly."

Candido's teeth were chattering. As for the president of Russia, he was blue with cold. They waded back to the cars, where the other guns joined them with bulging game bags. Needless to say, the Stranger had the best tally.

"I've come back empty-handed," Lenin said with a chuckle, "but our young Brazilian comrade is a first-class shot. He can also creep up on you like a cat and tell amusing stories. Look at this nice, plump bird he bagged. The rest of us never even saw it coming."

Candido noted the look that passed between Lenin and the Stranger (by now he knew his real name was Alexis Mikhailovich Alekhin, but he couldn't bring himself to utter it). He could have sworn that an unspoken message had just been transmitted. It was as if Lenin had said, "All right, he'll do."

They left Nizhni Novgorod the next day, but without most of the original group. The only ones to go aboard apart from Samantha and Candido were the two Chinese, a bespectacled German who never spoke and Harvey Bloggs—plus Afonka Tchadayev and, of course, the Stranger. The small steamer pointed her bow at the rising sun and sailed at daybreak. It was a strange, scenically spectacular voyage. Vast plains stretched away on either side of the Volga, which was swollen with melted snow.

Installed in the best cabins on the upper deck, the party had a special dining saloon to themselves. The two meals they ate there consisted of borscht, woodland grouse, semolina mush and caviar. Down below, herded together on the decks fore and aft and even in the engine-room gangway, were scores of ordinary passengers, many of them barefoot or shod with birch bark, all of them hungry and dressed in rags but all apparently resigned to their lot.

The cabin allotted to him and Samantha contained two bunks. He avoided her all day by remaining on deck, immersed in his favorite book. When evening came he lingered in the dining saloon for as long as possible, still pretending to read, but the moment of decision came at last. He entered the cabin to find that she'd removed the horrible, unfeminine trousers, jumper and jacket she'd been sporting for the last few weeks.

"I'd like a word with you, Candido."

She was already in bed, thank God—but she was naked.

Think of something else!

"Any idea where we're going?"

"Kazan."

"And then?"

He shrugged.

"You mean you don't care?"

That was just what he did mean. "Why not ask *Him*? He should know, if anyone does." The words were on the tip of his tongue but he left them unsaid. He undressed at lightning speed, got into his bunk and turned to face the bulkhead.

"They're shuttling us around like a couple of parcels, Candido."

What am I supposed to say?

"Haven't you anything to tell me?"

"Nothing special."

"You went hunting with Vladimir Ilyich, just the two of you. What did you talk about?"

"I shot a grouse."

"What's that?"

"An edible thing with feathers on it."

An interminable silence.

"How much longer are you going to keep this up?"

Don't ask her what she means, you know it perfectly well. She's annoyed because you're sulking.

No, don't crack!

She got out of bed and switched off the little ceiling light, which he'd forgotten to turn off.

She's waiting, but don't crack now.

At last she returned to her bunk. Then she started crying, and that was the bitter end. She wept very softly, almost inaudibly. He had to strain his ears to hear her at all.

She isn't crying to get around me, she's just crying. For herself.

Candido awoke before first light. As soon as he sensed that Samantha was beginning to stir he went out on deck and stationed himself right up forward, where the pounding of the engines was least noticeable. Bluish mist was rising from the Volga. From the right bank came the crack of a whip and the hoarse shouts of a driver urging his horses on. All at once, a large wagon drawn by a team of four emerged from the mist enshrouding the towpath, and slumped on the benches that ran the length of the vehicle were a score of dejected men in chains. Short-lived as a fleeting dream, this apparition vanished into the mist as suddenly as it had come. Minutes later some peculiar-looking church spires showed up dead ahead.

"Minarets."

Candido recognized the voice. And the hand on the rail beside his own.

"Most of Kazan's inhabitants are Moslem Tatars," the Stranger went on. "We've already left Europe behind us."

He's waiting for me to ask where he's sending us and why, but I won't.

"You made a good impression on Vladimir Ilyich, Cavalcanti."

Candido said nothing.

Other buildings were taking shape around the minarets, which had seemed until then to be floating in midair. A landing stage appeared, already crowded with waiting figures.

"Kazan," said Alekhin. "It used to be a very beautiful city in the old days, before Pugachev and his rebels looted the place and left three-quarters of it in ruins. From here you'll go by rail to Perm, where you'll board the Trans-Siberian.''

If he's still expecting me to question him he can wait till hell freezes over. It would be pointless anyway—he'd only tell me what he wants me to know or believe.

Candido turned and walked off. Samantha had finished washing. She was fully dressed and doing her hair, which was still damp.

"We're going to Siberia," he said.

Harvey Bloggs parted company with them too. He took a train, but not the same one, and returned to Moscow. Their only remaining companions were the taciturn German, the two Chinese and Afonka. Some drozhki—two-horse cabs—transported them from the landing stage to the Kazan station, which was several miles from the river.

In the waiting room Harvey delivered a lecture on the Trans-Siberian. He claimed to have traveled aboard it in 1914, taking nine days to complete the journey from Manchuria to Moscow.

"There was a gymnasium, a music car, an observation car, another parlor car containing a bar and a restaurant, a car where you could take a Russian bath, a library, a second bar open around the clock for the benefit of night owls—even a chapel."

There wasn't any chapel or library these days. There wasn't much of anything except two very ornate and luxurious sleeping cars still bearing the name of the Belgian company that used to run them. Each was guarded by four soldiers with rifles and fixed bayonets, two at either end of the corridor.

To keep undesirables out, or to keep us in?

Candido wished he had a map so that he could find out where Siberia was.

"Technically," said Samantha, "if we travel far enough east we should wind up in America."

Her geography was almost as sketchy as his.

Harvey's description of the prewar; prerevolutionary Trans-Siberian express had been accurate in one respect: there were books on board. Afonka Tchadayev brought Candido a few he'd found beneath the seat in his own cramped compartment, which had formerly been occupied by the conductor. They comprised Dostoyevski's *House of the Dead* and two books each by Turgenev and Saltykov-Shedrin, all in Russian; Novalis's *Hymns to the Night* in German; in English, Poe's *Narrative of Arthur Gordon*

Pym (Candido had already read it); and in French, Jules Verne's *Michel Strogoff,* three novels by Dumas, and the eighth or East Asia volume of Élysée Reclus's *Nouvelle Géographie Universelle.*

An interesting selection. Who had made it?

Candido could guess.

He read. Six days went by, then seven. The Trans-Siberian had left the Urals behind long ago. Rain lashed the windows, but sometimes, when the train stopped and they were permitted to stretch their legs on rickety wooden platforms or simple earth embankments (some of which adjoined rows of bodies swinging from gibbets or mass graves containing hundreds of corpses barely covered with soil)—sometimes, when they managed to ignore the many faces still imprinted with terror by civil war, they detected that the cold was less intense, and that gusts of warm air were wafting faint springtime scents to their nostrils. Candido read *House of the Dead* and reread Novalis, to whom Herr Doktor had introduced him. Novalis was a fine poet, but to acknowledge that Alekhin had selected *Hymns to the Night* would be to credit him with an aesthetic sense, and that was out of the question.

Samantha, who was bored and on edge, kept trying to pick a quarrel. One of her targets was Herr Doktor.

"Take his name for a start. Taxile Grüssgott, I ask you! No one could possibly have a name like that."

"*He* does," Candido retorted calmly.

"He didn't join you in Berlin, either. He let you down."

"I'm sure it wasn't his fault if he got there too late. Anyway, he thought I was staying with his sister."

"As for the education he gave you . . . You'd never even heard of Napoleon Bonaparte."

"Herr Doktor prefers poets to generals. So do I."

"What about Alexander the Great, Attila, Julius Caesar, Hannibal, Davy Crockett?"

"Davy Crockett I've heard of," he said. "Not the others, though, I grant you."

He knew of a Julio Cesar who was the goalkeeper for Botafogo but was pretty sure it couldn't be the same man.

"You're a total ignoramus, Candido."

"Absolutely."

The light of dawn was unveiling blue mountains, seething torrents, rivers of crystalline clarity.

They were nearing Irkutsk.

Afonka Tchadayev had produced passports for all of them (in this country you needed a passport to get from one town to the next). The two Chinese, with whom no one had exchanged a word, disappeared. So did the taciturn German, who was led off by two men. They didn't say who they were, but they had policemen's eyes.

Irkutsk was nothing to write home about. Candido glimpsed a cathedral and a fortress jutting above the steep banks of the Angara, the river that separated the city from its suburbs. The city itself was an almost medieval-looking jumble of timber-framed buildings slung together any old how. Patches of stale snow still adhered to their steeply pitched, overhanging roofs, many of which were of corrugated iron painted green. There was a long, broad boulevard flanked by raised board-walks—a discolored old street sign identified it as "Bolshoi Avenue"—but even this contained no buildings of note and very few that were constructed of stone. Visible here and there, however, was the onion dome of a church with glazed tiles overlapping like snake scales, or a house built of faceted bricks in the Russian style.

Afonka told the slit-eyed driver to pull up outside one of the latter.

"Yes, this is it," he announced. "This will be your home for the time being. By the way," he added, "the driver isn't Chinese, he's a Buryat. You do come across genuine Chinese in Irkutsk, but not as many as you might think. Almost all these slit-eyed men and women are Buryats or Mongols, not Chinese."

The house was spacious and comfortable. The driver, whose name was Khoro, doubled as a manservant, and his wife did the cooking. The rooms were fully furnished. The wardrobes and chests of drawers still contained clothes and even children's toys abandoned by the former occupants, and the bookshelves were well stocked with Russian and English editions. Samantha was curious.

"Who used to live here, Afonka?"

"I don't know."

"Were the people who lived here shot to make room for us?"

"I don't know."

"How long will we be staying?"

He didn't know that either.

He chuckled and smiled, spread his hands apologetically, shuffled from foot to foot, swung his short but fearsomely muscular arms. Afonka was twenty-five, stocky and barrel-chested but light on his feet. Just when you thought he was half asleep he would come to life and move with incredible rapidity. His face was flat, especially his nose, which had no bridge worth mentioning, and his cheekbones were high and broad. He smiled all the time. "Gentle as a lamb" was Samantha's verdict on him. Yes, as long as you didn't look too closely at his eyes, which sent shivers down your spine. They were as pale as off-white snow, all except the pupils: two minute black dots that scurried around those pale grey irises like agitated ants.

They were doing that now. Even as Afonka shuffled from foot to foot and pleaded ignorance and begged Samantha's pardon, those little black insects were darting to and fro in the depths of his whitish, sightless-looking orbs.

"And what are we supposed to do here?"

"Wait," he said. "Wait, that's all."

Ten days went by, then two weeks. Spring was setting in. Khoro drove them wherever they wanted, sometimes to places of interest suggested by himself. Candido asked to see Lake Baikal, an hour and a half's drive from Irkutsk. To the northeast, the lake seemed to stretch away into infinity. According to Élysée Reclus and some books Candido had found in the library, it was a genuine inland sea nearly four hundred miles long and twenty to sixty miles wide.

Khoro spoke fluent Russian and could read and write. Five or six years earlier he'd been a foreman working on the Trans-Siberian extension that skirted the southern end of Lake Baikal, a project entailing the construction of thirty-three tunnels. Before this stretch was completed in 1916, trains had to be ferried across the lake by steamships—in winter, ice-breakers—capable of carrying twenty-five carriages apiece. At the height of winter, when the ice became too thick, the carriages were uncoupled from their locomotives and hauled across by teams of horses. As for the passengers, they covered the forty-odd miles to the eastern shore in troikas.

"There were even inns and staging posts on the ice, and the horses that drew the troikas and *telegas* wore jingling bells."

"It must have been a beautiful sight," said Samantha. "Incidentally," she added, "when we reached Irkutsk all the passengers got out. Don't the trains go any farther these days?"

"The line has been cut beyond the thirty-three tunnels. Ataman Semyonov and his bandits control large sections of track in Transbaikalia, over toward the Mongolian border. Besides, there's the Mad Baron, too."

"The Mad Baron?"

They were sitting beside the sun-drenched lake on a sandy beach fringed with pine trees.

Khoro launched into an account of the Mad Baron's career, occasionally lowering his voice and glancing around to make sure that Afonka was out of earshot. Candido paid little attention.

"Did you hear that extraordinary story, Candido?"

"Every word. He was telling us about the Mad Baron." They were getting back into the car.

"Liar," said Samantha. "You didn't listen at all—you never do—but it was fascinating. The Mad Baron sounds awfully romantic."

There was no malice in her tone. She'd been giving Candido wistful looks for some time, obviously waiting for him to make the first move.

I don't know why I keep it up. Hurt pride, that's all.

Instead of heading straight back to Irkutsk the car turned left along the south bank of the Angara.

"Are we still going to visit your family, Khoro?" Afonka asked.

"Yes," the Buryat replied, "but only if you agree."

Afonka laughed. "I agree," he said.

It would be their third trip to Khoro's family home at the southernmost tip of Lake Baikal.

The car turned off the main road and stopped. Samantha and Candido climbed the goat track side by side with Khoro in the lead and Afonka bringing up the rear. Before long they came to a narrow gorge and crossed the foaming torrent in its depths by way of some boulders black and glistening enough to be mistaken for slumbering hippos. Candido paused and looked back. The view was magnificent. Framed by blue mountains, the immensity of Lake Baikal stretched away to Chuzir, a large island barely visible in the distance. The air was filled with the scent of oozing pine resin. Afonka, too, had come to a halt. There was a cold light in his pale, watchful eyes.

"Shall we go on?" he said, smiling.

Candido set off again. Immediately after the gorge the path dropped away steeply to a valley. Some eight hundred yards to the left was a cluster of felt and birch-bark yurts, four or five in all, enclosed by wooden fences weathered by the snows of many winters. Khoro's relatives belonged to the Ekhirit clan and were reputed to be descendants of Bukha-Noyon, the Grey Bull. They didn't cultivate the soil, and the less they saw of the Russians the better it suited them. This valley was their winter home. They would soon move to the summer pastures higher up. The Ekhirits bred sheep and cattle, some of which they deigned to sell at market in Irkutsk, but they were fiercely possessive of their reindeer and horses.

Though Buddhist by religion they were also shamanists. Candido knew little about Buddhism and nothing at all about shamanism. He knew only that he would soon be regaled with curdled milk, tea full of millet grains and fatty, undercooked mutton.

A shot!

The vicious report went echoing down the rocky defile toward the valley. Candido was already in motion when another two shots rang out. He hurled himself at Samantha, knocked her over and dragged her into a cleft in the rocks.

"Are you hit?"

"No, but you knocked the wind out of me."

Always complaining, that's her.

Ahead of them, Khoro had also taken cover and was scanning the heights for a hidden marksman.

That fool Afonka is armed. Why doesn't he do something?

Afonka Tchadayev was lying sprawled on the ground with his cheek against a stone. There was a big hole in his black leather jacket. He'd had time to draw the two Nagants in his belt but not to use them. One of the revolvers was still in his hand, the other had gone flying.

"Afonka?"

Ah, the terrifying expression in those blind-looking orbs! The little black ants were scurrying around, wild with rage. Afonka raised his head and tried to smile, but two or three big gobs of blood oozed from between his lips like dark red vomit. His chin hit the ground and he lay still, with his eyes staring and the smile frozen on his face.

"You can go back to Irkutsk," Khoro said. "But without me."

"You didn't kill him," said Samantha. "We can swear to that."

The creases in the Buryat's slanting eyelids deepened. He shook his head. It wouldn't matter whether or not he'd killed Tchadayev, his family would be accused in any case. The violent death of a Cheka officer was never good news, even if the killer was only a distant cousin. It was best to make oneself scarce on such occasions.

Some horsemen had appeared. Mounted bareback on shaggy little ponies, they were armed with ancient muskets or rifles half a century old and wore sheepskin caps with the earflaps turned up to expose the fleece. They searched the surrounding area, then signaled to Candido and Samantha that the coast was clear.

They also searched Afonka's corpse, which yielded a wad of documents: passports in the names of Candido and Samantha; a card identifying Afonka as a member of the Cheka; a letter signed by someone called Felix Edmundovich Dzerzhinsky summarily instructing all concerned, no matter what their civilian or military status, to render every form of aid and assistance to Comrade Alphonse Anfimovich Tchadayev; written orders authorizing the said Tchadayev to requisition whatever he needed in the way of men and equipment; general orders addressed to named individuals along the Trans-Siberian route; and two photographs of Afonka with a fair-haired, rather plump young woman holding a very young baby in her arms *(Afonka married? He never mentioned it)*; two more photographs *(obviously of his parents)*; some train tickets; a good deal of cash, some of it in dollars and sterling; and—

Just a minute . . .

"Samantha, take a look at these."

"Ugh, they're all bloody."

"Come and look."

Four movement orders, all signed by F. E. Dzerzhinsky and made out in the names of Alphonse Anfimovich Tchadayev, Samantha Elizabeth Franck, Candido Stevenson Cavalcanti and Otto Herbert Krantz. They demanded that everything possible be done to facilitate the transportation of the said four persons to Krasnoyarsk, which journey was to be granted "absolute priority."

They stared at each other.

"The train stopped at Krasnoyarsk," she said. "That was where we saw all those horrid gallows."

"The orders are dated five days from now. Afonka must have received them after we reached Irkutsk."

"I don't want to go back to Krasnoyarsk," Samantha said firmly.

The villagers, who had finished loading their packhorses and rounding up their cattle, were moving off. Khoro had been brought a horse and was waiting impassively.

At least we'd be beyond His reach in Mongolia, but if Samantha doesn't want to go . . . What will I do? I could leave her. I could leave her for Him. Yes, that's what I'll do.

He looked over at her. Beautiful as ever. And smiling at him, or as close to smiling as she ever gets.

A buzzing, circling swarm of flies had been attracted by the blood and were trying to crawl beneath the blanket draped over Afonka's corpse. Candido went and leaned against a rock some yards away.

"Maybe he's not as crazy as all that," Samantha said suddenly.

Who's "he"? Surely she can't mean . . .

"I'm talking about the Mad Baron," she went on. "He's got such cute names, too: Roman Nikolai Fyodorovich von Ungern-Sternberg. He really is a baron, apparently. From Estonia."

Candido yelled with all his might. One of the Buryat horsemen turned to look, then another. Khoro rode back to them leading two ponies. Bridles only, no saddles, but that could be remedied later. Candido hadn't sat on a horse for ages, but he'd always enjoyed riding.

Let's give it a try. Spring's here and the sun's shining. What better time for a trip through Mongolia?

PROVIDED IT CAN FIND
SUFFICIENT FOOD AND IS
UNDISTURBED, THE JAGUAR WILL KEEP
TO A FIXED TERRITORY. IT ALWAYS MOVES
AT NIGHT. BEING AN EXCELLENT SWIMMER,
IT WILL IF NECESSARY CROSS THE
WIDEST OF RIVERS.

They had been riding up to sixteen hours a day for fourteen days, avoiding the main roads in favor of lonely tracks through the mountains. The original Buryat encampment had split up. The women, children and old men joined forces with another group and were migrating south, but more slowly. The rest, together with Samantha and Candido, had soon taken on the appearance of a band of partisans.

"Is that it, Khoro? Are you off to the wars?"

"There'll soon be more fighting in Mongolia, and we've never liked the Russians, Red or White. They take our land and put frontiers where there weren't any. Give a Russian peasant a plot of soil and he'll happily cultivate it, whereas we, with our horses and cattle . . . The death of that Cheka man only brought matters to a head."

"Who killed him?"

"It's unimportant."

"One of your people?"

"It's unimportant."

The column was descending a steep slope in single file, hemmed in by dark pinewoods. Having ridden east for the past four days, they had now been heading south-southeast for several hours. The derelict tracks of the Trans-Siberian were behind them.

"Are they really going to leave us, Candido?"

"You heard what Khoro said."

It was around eight o'clock in the morning. They reached the foot of the slope, where birches took the place of pines and the countryside opened out.

"Tired?"

Samantha shook her head. The Buryats had done their best to pad her saddle with sheepskins. She'd never been on a horse before, but she hadn't uttered a word of complaint. Looking at her drooping head, Candido felt himself melt with tenderness.

Khoro reined in while the rest of the column proceeded due south.

"It's time," he said. "We must split up here. To get to Urga, keep heading southeast—it's not difficult. Follow that valley and you'll hit a dirt road bearing tire tracks. It goes left to Ulan-Ude and right to Urga. Turn right and keep straight on. Around midday you should come to a village, but take care. Ataman Semyonov's men may be there."

His slanting eyes twinkled briefly.

"Good-bye and good luck. I shall ask the fifty-five white *tengris* to protect you and the forty-five black *tengris* to avert their gaze from you."

"Very nice of you," said Samantha.

With a parting glance at Candido, who merely nodded, the Buryat spurred his pony into a gallop. They stared after him.

"Would you like to stop here, Samantha? There's no hurry."

No, she wanted water—river water. To bathe in.

Candido was pervaded by a potent and delicious sensation: for the first time in three or four months—ever since Biesenthal, in fact—they were alone together.

◆   ◆   ◆

They came to the dirt road, whose dusty surface did indeed betray that it was regularly used by motor vehicles. At last, after a mile or so, they spotted some threads of water trickling down a small escarpment.

"Will this do?"

"No, let's go on a bit."

Farther on the rivulets combined to form a stream flowing east, which wasn't the direction Khoro had indicated.

"We're heading east," Samantha pointed out.

"I know. We're following the water, that's all."

They rode on in single file for nearly an hour. The stream became a river enclosed by banks. The water wasn't deep, but deep enough.

"Here?"

"Yes."

While Samantha dismounted with a sigh of relief, Candido sat his horse and surveyed their surroundings. He estimated that they must be eight or ten miles off the Buryat's recommended route.

Samantha removed her man's jacket and battered hat and stretched out on a carpet of moss. The little river took a bend at this point and widened slightly.

"We won't find anywhere better," she said.

Candido was staring into the trees.

"What is it?"

"Wait here, I won't be long."

Not more than a hundred yards to go. Almost imperceptible at first, the buzzing sound grew louder as he walked his horse into the wood. All he could smell was the heady scent of spring foliage. The trees had been thinned, and the woodcutters' sawhorses were still there. A new smell: sawdust.

I'm scaring myself unnecessarily—there's nothing here. . . .

Nothing but that persistent buzz, which swelled until it sounded like a multitude of maddened wasps. The far side of the wood was already in sight, a blaze of white sunlight less than two hundred yards away. He was on the point of turning back despite the inexplicable sound, which had now reached a supreme pitch of intensity, when he noticed a peculiar excrescence on a tree trunk.

The man was stark naked. His arms were above his head, and he was lashed to the trunk by his wrists and ankles. Someone had cut his throat and severed the windpipe. His cheeks, too, had been slit from the corners of the mouth to the ears, creating the semblance of a gruesome, demented smile.

The buzzing sound was explained: hundreds of fat, blue blowflies were swarming over the fresh wounds.

Another thing: there were three men hanging there, not one, and each had undergone the same treatment.

Candido rode to the far side of the wood. No sign of life for miles, though there were enough hollows and depressions in the undulating plain to have concealed a whole army. Nothing was stirring except some smoke from the remains of a fire nearby. There were scraps of charred cloth among the ashes.

Uniforms? If so, of what army?

What was going on?

"You were gone long enough."

Samantha was standing there with one hand on the wooden pommel of her saddle. She watched him ride his horse down the bank.

"See any Sioux, Davy Crockett?"

"All quiet," he said.

He managed a smile. He hadn't even vomited at the sight of those three mutilated corpses.

I'm getting used to it. A few more like that and I won't even notice them. My voice sounds quite normal—she hasn't spotted a thing.

Samantha was getting undressed.

"You ought to do the same," she said. "Wash, I mean."

The water was only knee deep. Naked now, she waded in and stretched luxuriously, rotating on the spot with her arms out and her face tilted to catch the sunlight.

"The water's not too bad. Aren't you going to get off that horse?"

Candido took another look around before he dismounted. He untied a leather camping mat and a rolled blanket from the cantle of his saddle and spread them neatly on the ground. Then, taking care to keep out of Samantha's field of vision, he undressed, waded into the river and promptly sat down.

God Almighty, it's cold!

"It feels a bit chilly at first, but it wears off."

"Oh, sure, it only hurts for the first two hours."

May as well do it properly.

He immersed himself face down, clinging to some stones to hold himself under. Herr Doktor had taught him to remain submerged for long periods without coming up for breath. "It's just a question of will-power, my boy. With practice you should be able to manage five minutes. Why come up so soon? Only three minutes forty-nine seconds that time. Try to show a little strength of character. . . ."

A stinging pain in his right buttock. He sprang to his feet, convinced that he'd been bitten by an insect.

Samantha, who was kneeling on the blanket, giggled.

"Don't bother to look," she said, "I threw a pebble at you. What were you doing down there? I could only see your backside."

I'm an idiot.

"Come on out," she went on. "You were underwater for at least two minutes, do you know that? You must have gills or something."

She fixed him with her big, blue eyes.

"Please, Candido."

All right, if you insist.

He got out and sat down on the blanket. After that things took an unexpected turn. Very gently, she proceeded to rub him down.

"You're frozen, silly. Here, let me warm you."

She opened her arms. Her naked body was warm.

"What was in there?"

"Where?"

"The wood, of course. You were as white as a sheet when you came back."

"Three men with their throats cut," he said.

"I see."

"Is that all you have to say?"

"I'm not squeamish."

She kissed him. On the hair, the forehead, the nose. The breath from her parted lips fanned his face.

"Forget about them, Candido. Think about me."

They had some food in their saddlebags: curds, hunks of semismoked mutton and a bag of dried apricots.

"We could make a fire and cook some of that awful meat."

"If we do, all the Mongols in Mongolia will spot the smoke and know where we are."

"There's no one around."

They ate sitting apart. Not very far apart, but still.

"Khoro advised us to make for Urga," Candido said with his mouth full. "As far as I can remember from the atlas, it's the Mongolian capital."

She nodded but said nothing. Candido was disappointed. He would have preferred an argument to this mutually exclusive silence. He felt a trifle sad—overcome by a fit of Brazilian melancholy.

"It's all my fault," she said. "We shouldn't have lit that fire."

He didn't know what she meant until he looked up. The mounted men, at least a score of them, were wearing Cossack *papashas* on their heads. Bearded, mustachioed and armed to the teeth, they formed an almost perfect semicircle at the top of the riverbank.

What first struck Candido was the horsemen's size. They weren't Buryats and they weren't mounted on ponies, and their stature was accentuated still further by their elevated position. One of them was even bigger than the rest. A colossus with a bushy beard and a saber-cut across his forehead, he demanded to know who they were.

He seemed wholly unconvinced by the answers he got. Candido and Samantha explained that they weren't Russians of any kind, neither White nor Red. They were simply travelers who'd lost their way, having left the Trans-Siberian at Irkutsk because they couldn't continue their journey by rail.

They were searched, Samantha first. Candido, who sprang to her defense, earned himself a preliminary blow from a carbine butt that knocked him to the ground. Next, the Cossacks examined their saddlebags with surprising results: not only did they find a revolver wrapped in oilskin at the bottom of the bag of curds, but beneath Samantha's saddle, concealed by the sheepskins placed there for her comfort, was a knife with a six-inch blade as sharp as a razor.

"So you're unarmed, eh? What's this, then? And these stains on the blade? Dried blood, wouldn't you say? Those three men—who were they? Not Reds. Anyone who kills Reds is honored here—it's almost better than a letter of recommendation from Ataman Semyonov or a passport signed by the General Baron himself. So who were they—Whites who would have unmasked you? You aren't spies, you say? Well, for one thing your Russian's a bit too good for foreigners in transit. . . ."

The flat of a saber landed smack on Candido's shoulder blade. He went sprawling, convinced that the bone was broken but heedless of what might happen to him. Samantha was all that mattered. Two of the horsemen had pounced on her and lifted her off the ground between them. When they dropped her yards away her jacket had been torn off. It was easy to predict what would happen next. The Cossacks galloped past her in pairs, yelling with delight and leaning low out of the saddle, and at every pass they removed another of her garments with the aid of their sharp, curved daggers: her jumper, her shirt, the slip she'd washed in the river that morning. Candido struggled up ten times at least, infuriating the Cossacks with his dogged, insane persistence. He could feel his skin being shredded by their plaited leather whips, which were loaded with lead, but nothing would prevent him—nothing in this world—from trying to join the girl who, standing proud and erect in the midst of those wheeling horsemen, was angrily damning them to hell.

God, what a magnificent creature she is!

And then, quite suddenly, the pandemonium ceased and the Cossacks reined in. All that could be heard in the ensuing silence was Samantha's voice. It was trembling, but only with rage. Listening to it, Candido could have sworn she wasn't frightened in the least, just angry.

And he crawled, blinded by the blood running down his face—crawled, yard by yard, in the direction of that voice. Samantha tried to lift him, cupped his head between her hands and sobbed.

Maybe she does care for me a little after all.

"Oh, Candido!" she said. "My God, what have they done to you? Can you hear me, Candido? Answer me, answer me. . . ."

"All right?"

"I'm feeling fine, honestly."

Several days they'd been riding, and Candido was finding it hard to stay in the saddle. What were these cords around his waist and thighs? For some reason that escaped him, they must have tied him to his horse.

His limbs and his back hurt like hell, but he was fine just the same.

Samantha was beside him, riding knee to knee on his left. Standing up in the armored car that was rattling along twenty yards ahead, a white-haired man in rimless glasses was scanning the horizon through binoculars.

Pamphily Merkulov, that's his name, but how the devil do I know it?

The scarred colossus was there too, bringing up the rear with his Cossacks.

Candido became aware that his head was aching as well as everything else. He touched his forehead and found that it was bandaged. Memories returned: the riverbank and the horsemen who'd appeared like magic; then a black hole; then the village where Samantha had bent over him, stroking his cheek and murmuring; then another black hole; then someone roping him to his horse to prevent him falling off; then the white-haired man introducing himself as Pamphily Merkulov, Ataman Semyonov's second-in-command.

There, I can remember nearly everything.

Pamphily Merkulov was a mixed blessing. On the asset side, he'd stopped the Cossacks from raping Samantha. Less reassuringly, he was mad as a hatter. Like Herr Doktor, he employed professorial turns of phrase. "Speaking for myself," he'd declared, "it's a matter of supreme indifference to me whether or not you're Bolshevik spies. The sole task incumbent upon me is to escort you to Chita, where Ataman Semyonov will pronounce on your case. In the interim, Tatarchuk (the scarred muscle man) will cut you into strips should you take it into your heads to be uncooperative."

Pamphily Merkulov wasn't the joking kind, either. The other day Tatarchuk had rounded up some male and female villagers who might, or might not, have been Red sympathizers. On Pamphily's orders the Cossacks adorned their bare flesh with the hammer-and-sickle emblem, some using knives, others a branding iron. They were subsequently roasted alive while Pamphily lectured them on the absurdities of communism in a tone reminiscent of Herr Doktor discoursing on Plato's *Republic*.

"All right, Candido?"

"I'm feeling fine. You asked me that two minutes ago."

"Two hours ago, you mean, and you've nearly fallen off a dozen times since then. You were dangling upside down on one occasion. I asked that bastard Pamphily to take you in his armored car, but he says you're better."

What does she mean, I nearly fell off? I've been riding since I was two and a half. I may have dozed off for a moment, but that's all. I'm fine, really I am.

"All right, Candido?"

There she goes again—it's a regular obsession. Hey, I'm lying flat on my tummy. Odd . . .

"I'm a bit cold."

"I'm not surprised. You're stark naked and it's the middle of the night. We've been here for hours—they're questioning some prisoners. Keep still. Oh, Jesus . . ."

She was working on his back. It felt as if she were tearing off the skin strip by strip. The pain was excruciating.

"Any time you want to stop it's all right with me," he said.

He thought that would cheer her up, but no, she was sobbing.

"My poor darling," she said, "I'm trying not to hurt you, but if I don't change your dressings they'll go bad."

"There's nothing to cry about."

"Please don't play the hero."

"Was that me yelling?"

"It's the prisoners. I told you, they're being interrogated."

He clenched his teeth to stop himself joining in.

That's unfair of her. I've never pretended to be a hero.

This time he knew he'd fainted.

"In response to your question," he said, surfacing once more, "I'm feeling fine, honestly I am."

She raised her head and kissed him interminably. He felt salt tears on his lips. He must have been weeping without knowing it.

"What's that you're putting on my back?"

"Just water, it's all I've got. There's a doctor at Chita—we'll be there tomorrow. Try to get some more sleep."

"Don't go away."

"No danger of that."

No danger . . . That sounds really nice, especially the way she said it. And to think I couldn't even protect her from those goddamned Cossacks.

"Samantha?"

"Yes, what is it?"

I'd like to ask her why she called me "darling" just now, but it would only embarrass her. Anyway, it doesn't mean much in English. My governess, Miss Robertson, used to say "darling" to her idiotic mutt of a dog.

"Nothing," he said. "I don't think I've got a temperature any more."

"I know, you told me: you're feeling fine."

"Thanks for looking after me."

"Don't be silly."

He was feeling so fine at dawn the next day, he tried to mount his horse unaided. In the end Tatarchuk picked him up one-handed and plunked him astride the saddle.

"Where are we going?"

"First," Pamphily Merkulov said serenely, "we're going to pay a visit to Ataman Semyonov's armored train. After that, if you're still alive, you'll be taken to Chita."

The armored train was camouflaged black and ocher. It resembled a caterpillar bristling with antennae to which leaves had adhered at random during its progress through undergrowth. Candido made out two locomotives complete with tenders, one in front and one behind. Installed on the roofs were machine guns, two per car, enclosed by a low breastwork of sandbags and cross-ties. Three of the wagons were ordinary freight cars, but the sliding doors had been replaced with ramps that could be lowered to facilitate the unloading of horses. The steel plates that encased the first and last two cars had loopholes in them.

The hundred horsemen who were escorting the train kept pace as it crawled along. There were no buildings in sight. The only sign of human activity was a gash in the forest half a mile away, where the monster had taken on wood. A strange silence reigned, broken only by the locomotives' muffled exhalations and the tramp of horses' hooves.

"The ataman will see you now," said Pamphily.

Candido had found it difficult to board the moving train, but he refused all offers of help and managed it unaided. Samantha got in first, making a nimble transition from the saddle to the footboard and entering by way of the armored door that had been opened to admit them. Part of the carriage was hidden by a curtain. The remainder had been converted into a bunkhouse. The floor was littered with palliasses, blankets, oddments of uniform and weapons of all kinds. There was a smell of wine, vomit and something fainter but more nauseating still. In the center, improvised out of two boxes of dynamite, was a makeshift table on which half-empty bottles of Caucasian and Crimean wine competed for space with the debris of a meal. The men around it were snoring openmouthed, their hands, forearms and uniform jackets caked with dried blood.

"You're too late, alas," Pamphily said. "The interrogation is over— these men are relaxing after their exertions—but there's nothing to prevent you from inspecting their place of work."

He drew the curtain aside. Samantha, who was holding Candido's hand, squeezed it convulsively. Candido didn't flinch; he'd been expecting something of the kind.

This part of the carriage had been entirely gutted: there were no partitions or seats. The loopholes in the armor plating gave little light, but oil lamps suspended from a long steel rail bolted to the roof revealed the use to which this area was put: it was a charnel house. Half-a-dozen bleeding corpses hung from the rail on butcher's hooks like sides of beef. Two soldiers, stripped to the waist, were sluicing the floor with the contented air of men engaged in honest toil. One of them grinned at Samantha. He was toothless.

"You've seen enough, I think," Pamphily said in English. "Now for your visit to the ataman. Whatever you do, remember this: you hardly speak a word of Russian."

Through the concertina and into the other armor-plated carriage. All that remained of its original interior was the corridor and one of the compartments. The other partitions had been removed to form a long room, one end of which was entirely occupied by a gigantic bed. In the latter were three naked women, one plump and blond, one Asiatic and the third a tall brunette with grey-green eyes and a scornful expression on her beautiful face, which showed signs of bruising. The rest of the furniture comprised a map table, a dining table, two sofas and three or four armchairs. Oil lamps were burning everywhere, and lounging against the wall was a man with a revolver in his belt and a horsewhip in his hand.

"Did you show them my train, Pamphily?"

"As much of it as there was to see."

Ataman Semyonov was a short, thickset man with bow legs, high cheekbones, a thick mustache and a pair of slanting eyes inherited from his Buryat mother. He was obviously drunk. He gave Candido a cursory glance, but it was Samantha who interested him more.

"What's she like with her clothes off?" he demanded, looking her up and down.

"Nothing special," said Pamphily.

"She's got big hands and feet."

"That's what I meant, Grigory."

"Go to hell," said Samantha. From her smile, it might have meant "Nice place you have here."

"Is she swearing at me, Pamphily?"

"She would never dare—nobody would. She merely pointed out that her friend is wounded."

"You murdering swine," said Samantha, still in English and still smiling. "You vile, disgusting little butcher."

The ataman smiled back at her and raised his *nagaika,* a whip such as the Cossacks had used on Candido. In addition to being loaded with lead, this one had razor-sharp fragments of steel plaited into it. The *nagaika* brushed Samantha's breasts.

Candido took a step forward, but Pamphily grabbed him by the collar.

"And these are the youngsters who killed three of my Cossacks?"

"I think not."

"Tatarchuk told me so."

"Tatarchuk is mistaken. She's American and he's Brazilian. I don't believe they're capable of killing anyone, least of all three of your Cossacks. In any case, the dead men weren't Cossacks. Whoever killed them burned their clothes. I found this in the ashes."

A coin appeared in Pamphily's hand. It was slightly bent across the middle.

"What is it?"

"A recognition sign employed by Red agents. We've already found several similar coins on the communist spies we've executed."

The ataman lurched off at last and subsided onto one of the sofas. Pamphily poured him a drink and the plump little blonde snuggled up beside him. He drained his glass and held it out for a refill, but his eyes continued to dwell on Samantha.

"Can she understand what I say?"

"Possibly, if you use simple words and speak very slowly."

"I'd like to see you swinging from a butcher's hook," Samantha remarked in an affable tone.

"What did she say?"

"She asked you—very politely—if her friend can have medical attention."

"You're sure she's American?"

"Positive," said Pamphily. "I've examined her passport and spoken English with her. She's from Chicago—she's on her way to join her father, who's with the American embassy in Peking."

"And the boy?"

"His father is an equally important man, a personal friend of Marshal Chang Tso-lin's. He and the girl mistakenly thought the Trans-Siberian would get them to Harbin. They're both relieved to have escaped from the Reds. Tatarchuk was on the point of killing them. Lucky for you I turned up when I did, or their deaths would have been laid at your door."

Semyonov roared with laughter and took another swig of vodka. Tatarchuk could be a trifle unsubtle at times, he conceded. His eyelids drooped more and more often as he poured glass after glass of liquor down his throat. Eventually they stayed shut.

Candido, unable to take any more, collapsed.

He was lying on his tummy again, but in a real bed. The first thing he noticed was the scent of woodsmoke, then a fragrant whiff of toilet water—a detail that intrigued him considerably. Where had Samantha got hold of toilet water? Their baggage was back in Irkutsk.

"Sinto-me ótimo," he murmured.

"Speak English."

That was Samantha, whispering.

"I'm feeling fine," he repeated obediently, in English this time.

A minute went by. He could feel some kind of ointment being applied to his shoulders, shoulder blades, back, buttocks, thighs. It was deliciously cool.

"He has several fractured ribs," said an unknown voice, "but that's not serious. His left shoulder was dislocated but seems to have slipped back into joint by itself—several ligaments were torn. I thought at first that his hip was fractured, but it's only badly bruised. He isn't passing blood any more, which is a good sign—his kidneys can't have taken too much punishment. His other injuries are only superficial. I doubt if he'll suffer any more blackouts. Exhaustion, that was his main trouble. Don't cover those cuts and abrasions, let them dry up. They're healing well. He may not look it, but he's very resilient."

"And very brave," said Samantha.

"To have stayed on a horse in that condition—yes, undoubtedly."

The unknown man spoke German with a strong Russian accent. His footsteps receded. A murmured exchange in Russian at the door, which opened and closed.

"Can I turn over?" Candido asked in English.

"Yes, and speak any language you like."

He got onto all fours, then gingerly sat up. Logs were blazing in the fireplace. Samantha was there, of course, but so was Pamphily Merkulov, the white-haired man who had lied to Ataman Semyonov with such aplomb.

"Are you hungry, Candido?"

"Hungry and thirsty."

He drank some milk with a peculiar taste—yak's milk, Samantha told him, a yak being a kind of mountain ox with slitty eyes—and ate some cold roast lamb accompanied by cakes of crushed millet flavored with angelica.

"I really was hungry."

"I'm not surprised. You've been asleep for thirty-six hours."

His heart leapt at the sight of Samantha wearing women's clothes for the first time in ages: a blouse with a high lace collar and puffed sleeves gathered at the wrists; a long, heavy skirt in dark blue-and-green check, and a pair of elegant lace-up boots. She'd put her hair up the way he liked, though how she managed to keep it up with so few pins he could never fathom. The corona of hair was surmounted by a charming little bun, the nape of her neck was bare except for some curly little wisps.

"Where are we?"

"Chita. At his place." She indicated Pamphily Merkulov with a jerk of the head. "More milk?"

"Please."

He drained the bowl she gave him, surveying the room as he did so. It was low-ceilinged but quite large. In front of the window stood a small desk with some bookshelves beside it.

"Who fixed you up with those clothes?"

"I did."

Pamphily got in first, but Candido continued to address Samantha as if they were alone in the room.

"Did you ask him why he lied about us to the ataman?"

"He claims that Khoro was one of his pupils when he was a schoolmaster at Irkutsk. Apparently, Khoro sent him a message asking him to help us."

"And you believe him?"

"More or less."

Still ignoring Pamphily, Candido collected his thoughts.

"Has it occurred to you that Khoro, Pamphily and even Tatarchuk may be in league together?"

"With Aliochka?"

"With Alekhin," Candido amended. "They could be doing all this to get us somewhere or other."

"Pamphily says we'll soon be leaving with Ataman Semyonov. He's going to visit the Mad Baron."

"I'm not sure I trust Pamphily. How about you?"

"We've no choice. Tatarchuk and his men are on guard outside."

"No, you've no choice," Pamphily chimed in. "Tatarchuk's there to protect you. The inhabitants of Chita are quite as prone to murder as they are to drink. I managed to placate the ataman once, but I can't guarantee to do it a second time."

"Pamphily says Tatarchuk's only there to protect us," said Samantha.

Candido thought for a moment. "Has he given you one good reason why we shouldn't set off east on our own?"

"The ataman's men are east of here facing the Red Army, and we'd have to make our way through their lines. You aren't too popular with the Reds, Candido. According to Pamphily, you're supposed to have murdered masses of people while we were at Irkutsk with Afonka Tchadayev."

"I know all about Jaguar," Pamphily interrupted. "Just between ourselves, my boy, I don't believe you've ever killed anyone, not for a moment."

Candido continued to ignore him. "Has he told you why we've got to visit the Mad Baron?"

"Because in this part of Mongolia," said Pamphily, "Ungern is the only person capable of getting you to Harbin, and from Harbin to the United States or wherever you want to go."

Candido drank some more milk. He'd just caught sight of Tatarchuk's huge figure outside the window.

"On balance," he said, "I think we should visit the Mad Baron."

Samantha nodded. "So do I," she said.

"A wise decision," said Pamphily.

Ten days later they boarded Ataman Semyonov's armored train and steamed out of Chita in the direction of Dauriya, where the Mad Baron was engaged in recruiting a private army for the conquest of Mongolia, whose emperor—or something similar—he aspired to become. He and his Asiatic cavalrymen would then smash the Reds and ride in triumph to the shores of the Baltic. He had designs, eventually, on the whole of Europe.

Ataman Semyonov's armored train had been redecorated. The carriage normally used for torture and executions was now fitted out with carpets, hangings and furniture. But for the lingering stench of death, it would have graced a royal progress. The ataman himself came aboard, accompanied by Pamphily Merkulov and the customary escort commanded by Tatarchuk. Semyonov and his officers had donned their full-dress uniforms for reasons that became clear to Candido when they reached Dauriya. The ataman was greeted there by a mounted honor guard, and drawn up in the background were serried ranks of cavalrymen whose perfect dressing and disciplined bearing were in striking contrast to the slovenly appearance of the motley band of cutthroats that had comprised the garrison of Chita.

"There you see the Asiatskaya Konnaya Divisiya," Pamphily whispered, "General Baron von Ungern-Sternberg's Asiatic Cavalry Division."

A stir ran through the rigid ranks—a kind of additional stiffening to attention. A cloud of dust took shape, and ahead of it, traveling fast, came a red automobile. It pulled up beside the train, from which no one had yet descended. The throaty purr of the car's engine and the locomotive's whalelike exhalations ceased at the same instant. A great silence fell.

"The man at the wheel is Major Zheremeyev," Pamphily murmured. "The Japanese officer is General Suzuki, attached to Baron Ungern's staff by the government in Tokyo. Suzuki is a member of the Black Dragon, an ultranationalist organization, and his purpose is to pave the way for the Japanese empire's expansion to the farthest corners of Asia, China and Mongolia included, not to mention Burma and India. The third man is the Baron himself."

Samantha craned her neck, and even Candido peered closely at the man of whom Pamphily had told them so much. Thirty-five years old and born in Estonia of Pomeranian and Hungarian stock, Roman Fyodorovich von Ungern-Sternberg was a genuine baron, even if he wasn't a bona fide general. (Formerly a lieutenant in the czarist army, he had promoted himself to that rank just as Grigory Semyonov had appointed himself ataman of the Cossacks on his own initiative.) Having graduated first from the Petrograd cadet academy and then from the Paul I School of Infantry, he had fought in the Russo-Japanese War. Of medium height, he had a clipped beard, a long, drooping mustache and the compressed lips of a man of few words. His forehead was abnormally high and broad, but it was his eyes that constituted his most striking feature. Pale grey and very deep-set, they became dreamy and inward-looking whenever they weren't transfixing those around him like twin stilettos.

The baron removed his fur cap. His shaggy hair and fearsome eyes created an impression of ferocity, of indifference to the opinions of others, of burning passion, of violence liable to erupt at any moment.

Ataman Semyonov had finally alighted from his train. Ungern, with a mixture of arrogance and disdain, kissed him on the lips, Russian fashion. They clearly detested each other, but who cared? Candido could see no good reason why their antagonism should concern him. He glanced at Pamphily, who was looking thoughtful. Pamphily . . . He really didn't know what to make of the man. Then, beyond the ranks of the Asiatic Cavalry Division, he glimpsed a small group of figures.

It was like an electric shock: two of the men watching the warlords'

reunion were all too familiar to him. He would have known them anywhere—known them from that day in Moscow when he'd been marched
off with the muzzle of a revolver jammed against his forehead and locked
up in the Bloody Cellar. Then there had been three of them; now there
were only two. There was no doubt about it, though: they were here in
the far-off depths of Mongolia.

"There was this man in rimless glasses who kept lighting cigarettes, one
after the other, without ever looking at his hands."

"Here he's known as Otto Krantz."

"Maybe. There was him and the other one. In Moscow they held me
by my arms and lifted me off the ground like a child."

"They're lookalikes, that's all."

"Lookalikes my eye," Candido said firmly.

If Chita had been unimpressive, Dauriya was even less so. It was little
more than a large village huddled around the fortress that served as
Baron Ungern's headquarters. The fortress itself was inaccessible, being
guarded by the same ferocious troops who patrolled the streets after
nightfall. All lights had to be out by ten o'clock, and anyone who left a
lamp burning or struck a match to light his pipe risked a volley of rifle
shots.

"That doesn't apply to the airfield, Candido. The airfield's very well
lit."

*Precisely: too well lit. What did she propose to do, anyway, steal one of those
Japanese biplanes and fly off with him? Was she a qualified pilot or something?*

"You can't even drive a car," he told her.

He could—up to a point. Among the scores of reasons for his father's
hostility toward him, or so he believed, was his habit of wrecking Dom
Trajano's cars. Among them had been a 1913, six-cylinder, twenty-horse-
power Chenard-Walcker imported from Gennevilliers in France
(smashed against a wall); likewise a 7.7 liter Locomobile designed by the
Stanley brothers and manufactured in Bridgeport, Connecticut, and specially designed in the style of Gordon Bennett's racing cars (nine rolls
coming out of a bend—a Brazilian record—prior to submersion in a
river); and, last but not least, Dom Trajano's pride and joy, a Rolls Royce
Silver Ghost paneled in Amazonian mahogany (flattened by a train after
Candido had, as on previous occasions, jumped clear at the last moment).

"We've got to get out of here," Samantha insisted.

Not for the first time, she ran through the arguments in favor of escape.
Mark you, she wasn't saying she shared Candido's absurd suspicion that

Pamphily had deliberately brought them to this loathsome hole with a view to assassinating someone and putting the blame on the Jaguar.

"On me, in other words."

"You're joking! Who on earth would believe you're the bloodthirsty Jaguar?"

No, she wanted to get away because she was fed up. They'd spent days hanging around here waiting for an interview with the Mad Baron, and why? In the hope that he would escort them to Urga.

"If he ever captures the place. He will, sooner or later, but when? Do we really need a whole army to get us there? Are you listening, Candido?"

"Yes."

"You don't look like it. Tell me if I'm boring you."

He didn't reply. They were taking their daily walk through the streets of Dauriya with Tatarchuk a few paces to the rear accompanied by two of his men, who were, it seemed, Khalkha Mongols. Tatarchuk and his Khalkhas—it had the makings of a song. Whatever Samantha said, he firmly believed in the existence of a deep-laid plan. Irkutsk had been only one more stage in its execution. Afonka Tchadayev's death didn't fit that theory, but everything else . . . Something was going to happen soon—today, tomorrow or a few days hence. Alekhin must be behind all these machinations, that was the only possible answer.

They were walking along the edge of the small airfield, which was guarded by a detachment of Japanese troops. Three days ago an airplane had landed there and deposited a fat Chinese, who was welcomed with great ceremony. According to Pamphily he was Marshal Chang Tso-lin, a warlord currently in control of Manchuria and part of China itself, including the capital, Peking. A confederate of the Japanese, this Chang person was in the process of concluding an alliance with Ungern against the Reds. Candido wished them joy—he couldn't have cared less.

Turning for a final look at the machines on the airfield, he intercepted a signal from Tatarchuk: time to go home.

As soon as they reached the parade ground in front of the baron's headquarters, Candido was struck by the general air of feverish expectancy. Something was in the wind, he could tell.

He was right.

Pamphily Merkulov was waiting for them at their temporary quarters. "Two pieces of news," he said. "The first is, today's the day. It has just been decided that the army is to march on Urga forthwith."

The second was, Baron Ungern would see them. He'd agreed to spare them a few minutes of his precious time.

"I described the pair of you as I did to Semyonov. Cavalcanti, your father is an intimate friend and business associate of various prominent Chinese personalities. You, Miss Franck, are the daughter of a distinguished member of the American diplomatic service based in Peking. Please back me up in those lies. They shouldn't be too difficult to sustain."

The interview was scheduled for six o'clock that evening.

The Asiatic Cavalry Division spent all afternoon drilling on the parade ground and undergoing a last-minute kit inspection. Reinforcements continued to pour in and form up under the baron's colors, yellow banners adorned with a big, black U. In addition to Manchus contributed by Chang Tso-lin, they included some diminutive Tibetans mounted on shaggy little ponies and armed with curly bows and arrows fletched with multicolored feathers. Ungern's artillery, which consisted of fourteen field guns, had already left with the vanguard; his air force—a lone German Taube with batlike wings—zoomed overhead. The cavalry moved off at last under the indifferent gaze of Dauriya's inhabitants. None of them doubted that Urga would be taken, especially as the Mad Baron was on friendly terms with the Living Buddha, the supreme religious leader resident in the Mongol capital.

The square emptied, silence fell, the town seemed almost dead. All that remained at the entrance of the redoubt was a troop of twenty or thirty Cossacks and two Hotchkiss automobiles, one red and the other white, in which Baron Ungern and his staff would travel.

Pamphily Merkulov turned up just before six, accompanied by a lieutenant named Volovichenko. Candido might have been mistaken, but the lieutenant seemed peculiarly nervous.

The four of them passed the guard post at the mouth of the tunnel leading into the fortress. It was now deserted. Major Zheremeyev had ordered the escort to mount up and move out, telling them that the baron would follow by car. Candido was last into the tunnel preceded by Samantha and, three or four paces ahead of her, Pamphily and Lieutenant Volovichenko. Feeling more and more uneasy, he glanced over his shoulder. For the first time in days, Tatarchuk and his Khalkhas weren't at his heels. They had melted away into the little town's lifeless, twilit streets.

The inner courtyard was a small, rectangular area enclosed by wooden huts. Outside one of these, two orderly-room clerks were stowing documents and maps in a steel chest. Ungern could be seen through an open door on the left, pacing up and down his office. His pale grey eyes rested briefly on the four approaching figures.

Candido had just emerged from the tunnel when everything happened at once: Pamphily suddenly slowed, allowing the others to overtake him, and lingered in the rear; Volovichenko's hand went to his service revolver; on the right, four or five men in civilian clothes drew guns from the bags they were carrying. They included the man from the Bolshoi and the man in rimless glasses—the one who moved like an automaton and was known as Otto Krantz.

"Quick!"

Candido grabbed Samantha's arm and dragged her back along the tunnel. Just as they reached the exit they met Major Zheremeyev coming the other way. Candido charged into him full tilt. The major let out a yell and the handful of guards still on duty converged. At that moment shots rang out in the courtyard. Zheremeyev released Candido and headed for it at top speed, followed by his men. The way was clear.

"Get in!" he yelled at Samantha.

"You're out of your mind!"

Samantha was calm—surprised but calm. It would have taken more than a few shots to alarm her. But she didn't resist when Candido thrust her into one of the cars, so violently that she landed on her back in a flurry of legs and skirts. He swung the crank handle, scrambled in behind the wheel and took off like a rocket.

Tatarchuk and three of his men appeared while Candido was roaring around the square in search of a side street—any side street—that would swallow them up. The Cossacks simply stood and watched. Though puzzled by their immobility, Candido put it down to surprise. At last he came to an alleyway and aimed the car at it. Dauriya, which had seemed so deserted, suddenly proved to be awash with camels, donkeys, horses and Mongols of every description. He sped through the throng, swerving this way and that. And then, by some miracle, they found themselves on a track outside town. Samantha, now sitting up, was tidying her hair.

"Wasn't it rather rude," she said, "running out on the baron like that?"

"I'm the Jaguar. I can do whatever I want."

"You're as mad as he is."

"*What* did you say, Candido?"

"It makes perfect sense. The Jaguar's killed the Mad Baron. Otto Krantz and Volovi-what's-it will claim they gunned down his assassin when they're the assassins themselves. They'll put the blame on us, and we won't be able to say anything because we'll be dead."

"I wouldn't be at all surprised," she said sarcastically, "the way you drive."

"Didn't you hear those shots?"

"I heard the ones they fired at us because you thought it was smart to make a dash for it."

"But they *weren't* firing at us! They were firing at each other in the courtyard!"

Samantha shrugged. "We got away," she said, "that's the main thing."

"I'm telling you, it's as clear as daylight. They meant to kill Ungern and they needed me there on the spot—me, Jaguar."

"Are you saying they went to all that trouble just so Jaguar could be officially blamed for Ungern's murder and executed in due course?"

Candido remembered a couple of things: the strange disappearance of Tatarchuk and his Khalkhas just before they entered the fortress, and Tatarchuk's surprising inactivity at the time of their escape.

"No," he said. "Jaguar had to take the blame, but he didn't have to die. Pamphily had our escape all worked out."

He braked hard. The Hotchkiss slewed sideways, jolted over some stones at the side of the track and came to a stop. It was almost dark by now.

"I've got a bright idea," he said. "Let's go back and ask them whether or not they meant to kill us as well as the baron."

"You're crazy."

"Maybe, but I can run fast."

Straddling the door on her side, which incorporated a spare tire in a metal container, Samantha got out and looked back in the direction of Dauriya, already nine or ten miles away. Little could be seen except when the moon emerged from behind the clouds.

"There were two of these cars," Samantha said, circling the Hotchkiss like a prospective customer. "Why did you have to steal the white one?"

"There wasn't time to get political."

She smiled and came over to him. Then, propping her elbows on his door, she bent and kissed him.

"It's true, you *can* be awfully quick when you want."

She isn't angry any more. Life's wonderful.

She got in, straddling the door again instead of opening it.

He drove off the only way he knew, with his foot down hard on the pedal.

Really wonderful.

He awoke and opened his eyes. They were both on the backseat of the Hotchkiss, he with Samantha's head on his lap.

"Are you asleep, Samantha?"

"Fast asleep."

Looking around, he was immediately struck by the strangeness of their situation. They seemed to be adrift on a sea of cloud or mist. He couldn't see the ground, just those greyish, moonlit hummocks of vapor. They might have been high in the Himalayas—in fact he wouldn't have been surprised to see an angel flapping by.

"I'm hungry," Samantha said.

He'd driven for as long as he could, not daring to switch on his headlights for fear of being spotted, seeing less and less as they ascended this godforsaken track—seeing nothing at all in the end, not even the front of the car, until he had a sudden premonition that there was a sheer drop ahead. Then he'd pulled up, far too tired to get out and check.

"I'm hungry, Candido."

He was hungry too. They'd had no dinner last night, and for a very good reason: they were supposed to be murderers, either on the run or dead. He gently removed Samantha's head from his lap, opened the door and extended one tentative foot. They might be perched on a peak with nothing but thin air all around them. Looking like an amputee with his legs buried thigh-deep in mist, he made his way gingerly to the rear of the Hotchkiss and examined the contents of the half-dozen cans strapped to the wooden trunk. Five held gas, the sixth water.

"There's tea, oatcakes, dried meat and some bottles of something," Samantha announced after rummaging in the trunk, from which she produced an officer's uniform, a spare pair of boots, three shirts, four pairs of underpants, binoculars, two books of which one was a prayer book, a rifle with ten boxes of cartridges, and some photographs in a black leather wallet.

"This car belongs to a General Risushin, Candido. Know who he is?"

"No. One of the baron's aides, I imagine."

He groped his way through the mist to a stunted tree and broke off several branches. The wood was green and damp, but a little gasoline helped it to catch.

"Sit down and leave the rest to me," she said. "That was some drive last night, and I certainly slept better than you did, with your lap for a pillow."

She can be awfully sweet sometimes.

He seated himself on the running board with an extraordinary feeling of comfort, freedom and contentment. They were all alone, the two of them, just as they had been on the riverbank a couple of weeks ago. Except that this time, all his machinations notwithstanding, they'd given Alekhin the slip.

"This car is a six-cylinder Hotchkiss 40/50 with English coachwork by Gill. My great-uncle Amílcar had one of these in Rio de Janeiro. It was a 1913 model just like this."

Samantha was far too busy to pay attention. He watched her, thinking what a pretty sight it was, a woman cooking. Having slung a mess-tin of water on a strap and suspended it between a nearby branch and the car's bumper, she was tossing in fragments broken off a slab such as the Mongols made from the tea plant's tendrils, not its leaves. Then—she'd seen Pamphily's men do this at Chita and Dauriya—she added two crumbled oatcakes and, for good measure, a little jerked mutton.

"What'll we do when we get to America, Samantha?"

No reply.

Why the devil did you ask her that? Now she's gone all grim. Very smart of you! Change the subject, birdbrain!

"I was telling you about my great-uncle's car. It wasn't absolutely identical, to be honest. His was yellow and green with blue upholstery— the Brazilian national colors. He and Dom Trajano—Papa, I mean— don't get along too well. Dom Trajano thinks he's a dangerous, irresponsible madman, a disgrace to the family. One morning a long time ago Great-uncle Amílcar went out to buy some socks. He arrived back from Paris thirty years later, laden with presents for everyone. Dom Trajano's came in a great big packing case marked FRAGILE, THIS WAY UP and lined with pink silk. Inside was a young Parisienne, stark naked except for a ribbon in her hair and a red pompom on her backside."

She's laughing, thank God. I've made her forget my idiotic question.

Perched on the running board side by side, they drank their soup and contemplated the sunrise-tinged mist. A breeze was coming up.

"Any idea where we are?" she asked.

None. He'd driven east after leaving Dauriya, he was sure. Or almost sure.

"We've done a hundred and twenty miles," he estimated.

The one certainty was, they were as alone as they could possibly be.

And then they heard it: a distant murmur that seemed to come from everywhere and nowhere at once. It couldn't have happened at a worse time. Candido was just eyeing the backseat, which was almost big enough to deputize for a double bed. The murmur grew louder and dissolved into its component parts: thudding hoofs, jingling harness, clanking sabers.

At that moment the mist parted to reveal a rocky spur jutting skyward and a precipice that yawned within yards of where the Hotchkiss was standing. *Puxa vida,* he'd pulled up just in time! Another couple of seconds and they'd have needed wings.

Two hundred feet below them, the full might of the Asiatic Cavalry Division was deployed in battle order.

◆　◆　◆

"You must have gone in a circle. Where did you learn to drive, on a racetrack?"

"I take my bearings from the sun," said Candido. "There wasn't any sun last night. Push."

"What do you think I'm doing, for God's sake?"

Any fool crazy enough to drive a two-ton Hotchkiss up to the very edge of a precipice should be able to get it down again with ease. He would simply turn around or release the handbrake and reverse, QED. Not this fool, though.

He was fated. How had he coaxed the Hotchkiss over this rock in the first place? "Your insistence on smashing every car you touch, my boy, a characteristic denoting a Freudian complex of some kind, is equaled only by your singular talent for emerging unscathed every time." He dearly wished Herr Doktor were there, if only to help them push.

"I've had enough!"

Candido's knees were sagging, and he was almost vomiting with exhaustion. He inspected the obstacle. It was a rocky outcrop shaped like a springboard, shelving on one side but straight down on the other. He'd tried building a ramp of smaller stones, but without success. There was nothing to be done.

Nothing except switch on and start up, but they'd hear it in Irkutsk. He tottered over to Samantha and flopped down on his back.

"I'm sorry," Samantha said abruptly.

"What?"

He got up, fetched the binoculars from the trunk and trained them on the Asiatic Cavalry Division.

If I can see them, they can see me, so take care. These lenses could reflect the sunlight.

"I'm sorry," she said, "—sorry about before, I mean. I wasn't planning to hurt you."

I am sore, he thought as he scanned the division's line of advance. *Ridiculous, really. It isn't as if we made plans to spend the rest of our lives together in America.*

"You were absolutely terrific at Dauriya," she went on. "I went into shock, but you thought and acted so fast."

Now she's trying to sweet-talk me. She's right, though. I must hold the Mongolian record for escaping from a mad baron's headquarters.

"What are you looking for?"

"Reconnaissance patrols."

"See anything?"

"No."

"Nothing at all?"

"Only a Mongol looking at me through binoculars."

"No need for binoculars," she said. "If you mean that guy standing up in a truck around four hundred yards away, I can see him too."

He lowered the glasses, convinced now. The Mongol wasn't alone, there were six of them. Plus Tatarchuk and Pamphily Merkulov, who was sitting beside the driver.

"This is the busiest desert I've ever seen," Samantha said.

Pamphily got out of the truck and proceeded to make some odd hand signals. Samantha could see them clearly in the binoculars. She was meant to see them. The significance of the signals was unmistakable: "Don't make a sound, wait till they've gone."

"He's telling us to stay put," Samantha said. "He won't start up either till the baron's men are out of earshot."

Candido nodded. "I guess that's it. Get in and shut your door."

He stationed himself in front of the car and prepared to crank it. Glancing sideways, he saw Tatarchuk poised to do likewise.

"This is fun," Samantha said. "I feel like standing up and waving a checkered flag. Still mad at me?"

"No."

"You're impossible, you know." A pause. "Hey, he's waving again." Samantha was standing up in the Hotchkiss with the binoculars trained on the trucks. "Looks like he's warning us not to head southeast. Which way shall we go?"

Candido thought hard. "Southeast," he said.

Why should Pamphily Merkulov, who'd led them into a trap at Ungern's headquarters, be trying to protect them now? He had only to sound his horn or fire a shot and the whole of the Asiatic Cavalry Division would descend on them in two minutes flat. Not for the first time, Pamphily's motives defied explanation. Unless . . .

"Candido!"

Tatarchuk had swung his crank handle. Candido did likewise. Nothing happened.

"Don't you have to put gas in a car?" Samantha asked brightly.

"I did."

Five turns. The Hotchkiss's engine still didn't catch.

Nor did the truck's, which was some consolation.

"You could both still be at it this time tomorrow," Samantha said. Fourteen turns.

"Can I have a try?" she asked.

"No. There's a knack to it."

The Hotchkiss beat the truck by seventeen turns to eighteen. Candido gunned the engine, reversed over the obstruction, turned, smiled proudly at Samantha and roared off.

"They're still there," she said.

She was kneeling up on the seat facing backward with the binoculars leveled. Now and then a particularly violent jolt would send her reeling sideways, either against the door or into Candido. Her figure showed up clearly beneath her blouse and skirt, which were molded to her by the warm breeze. Candido eyed her appreciatively.

"For a moment I thought they'd given up, but no such luck, they were out of sight behind some rocks. I'd say they're a couple of miles behind, maybe a little more."

"Roughly four kilometers," mused Candido.

"If you say so. We could lose them if you'd go a little faster."

He thought a while. The gap between them hadn't closed or widened for the past three hours. In other words, Pamphily and his Mongols hadn't yet stopped to refuel, but they would have to sooner or later. Like the Hotchkiss, the truck must have started out with a full tank. The question was, which of them had the longer range? If the truck did, they were sunk.

They were now crossing a wide, rolling plain that stretched away for miles on either side. It was dotted with herds of horses and yaks, flocks of sheep, and even yurts with threads of smoke rising from them. An hour ago the Hotchkiss had passed two saffron-robed, shaven-headed monks, who had scrambled up some rocks in terror at the sight of such a monster.

"Hey, Candido, they're pulling up!"

He drove another hundred yards and stopped on the brow of a low hill.

"I can't see them."

She handed him the binoculars.

"Sure you can—over there beside the rock that looks like a coffee grinder."

No coffee grinder. She snatched the glasses back with an exclamation. How could he fail to see them?

"You need your eyes tested. They're there, all seven of them. Pamphily's in the cab with Tatarchuk beside him. Two of the Khalkhas are filling up. The other three are running."

"Running?"

"Running fast. They're heading in our direction."

Candido thought it over. Their pursuers had stopped to refuel as foreseen. There were only two courses of action open to him. He could either drive on and risk running out of gas in a very short time, or . . .

He opened his door and got out, already preoccupied with another piece of mental arithmetic. Pamphily knew that they themselves would have to refuel before long, so he'd sent a detachment on foot to capture them. The question was, how long would the Khalkhas take to cover four kilometers?

"They're running pretty fast!"

Ten or fifteen minutes, probably.

"They're getting closer, Candido."

Herr Doktor had been training him for the five thousand meters in the next Olympics. *Mens sana in corpore sano* was Herr Doktor's motto.

"Purely as a matter of interest, Candido, they've started firing at us."

He walked off in search of a secluded spot.

"Where are you going?"

Where does she think, funny girl? I can hardly do it down my leg, and I've been breaking my neck for hours.

He got back behind the wheel and drove off.

"Pleased with yourself?" she said. "I could see the whites of their eyes."

Yes, pretty pleased with myself and life in general. I'm driving through Mongolia and I've just had a good pee and I'm with Samantha Elizabeth Franck of Chicago. Why shouldn't I feel pleased?

Suddenly he recalled a detail that hadn't sunk in at first.

"How many of them did you say there were?"

"Pamphily, Tatarchuk and the Khalkhas."

"No, you said there were seven of them all told. This morning there were eight."

One of the Khalkhas was missing.

"Maybe he was behind the truck."

"Why?"

"Maybe nature called him, too."

Candido shook his head. The Hotchkiss was now plowing through a mass of sheep like the Israelites crossing the Red Sea. He cursed himself for not being quicker on the uptake.

"According to Élysée Reclus we're plumb in the middle of Khalkha country, Samantha. You can bet the missing man has gone off to raise the alarm. There's a Khalkha under every stone in these parts—we'll soon have hundreds of them after us."

"So we won't get much farther, will we?"

"No, we won't get much farther."

"Pull up," Samantha said. "That's far enough."

They'd had to stop to refuel before nightfall, using up the last two cans. There was only a drop in reserve and very little water left.

"Pull up, I said."

Candido's head was drooping. He was dog-tired and he couldn't see a thing any more. This wasn't a road, it was a riverbed full of boulders the size of Tatarchuk.

"Stop, for God's sake, or we'll wind up in a ravine. You've done all you humanly could, Candido. I've never known such stamina, honestly."

She's only saying that to cheer me up. Meu Deus, *if she were even the tiniest bit in love with me it would be a pure miracle.*

"Please stop. They aren't following us any more—it's been hours since I last saw their headlights. Pull up, darling."

He pulled up. Everything ached—his neck, his arms, his back—and his palms were covered with blisters. He'd been driving over rough terrain for almost twenty hours nonstop, and the left front tire had blown long ago. Ahead of him the riverbed narrowed to form a gorge.

"How do you switch the lights off?" she asked.

He switched them off and closed his eyes.

She called me "darling."

"Come on, Candido, stretch out."

She took him in her arms. He relaxed, let himself go. Had any woman ever held him like this? Not his mother Dona Idalina, whom he'd never known, and certainly not his stepmother, Dom Trajano's second wife. As for his Scottish governess, Miss Robertson, she used to say, "Go and kiss Madam good night, Master Candido" and he would give Dona Isabel a peck and the chore would be over for another day. Samantha was kissing his cheek.

"Ubé or hu auli enl'oi anta," he murmured.

"I didn't get that."

You're even prettier in the dark, Samantha. Am I dreaming? We're at Bragança Boa Vista, not the biggest of the family's fazendas but my favorite. Look at that bougainvillea—look at those roses and jacarandas and mangoes. That? That's a jabuticabeira. *What's the fruit like? A cross between a plum and a gooseberry, sort of. Here, try one, it'll turn your lips red. You're so lovely I could weep, and you're wearing that white dress with the blue ribbons. Sweet of you, it's my favorite. I love you, Samantha. Let's go for a spin in the surrey, shall we? See, I've had the top done in white with blue stripes to match your dress. . . .*

"Candido!"

All right, we'll go swimming if you prefer. Of course there's a pool at the fazenda, a hundred and twenty feet long and all blue. There's a portrait of Dom Trajano on the bottom, but nothing's perfect. . . .

"Candido, quick, wake up!"

He opened his eyes and sat up.

"Have I been asleep long?"

"Twenty minutes or so. I heard something."

She was whispering with her lips glued to his ear. His pupils dilated like a cat's. Silhouettes took shape in the gloom: rocks. Ahead of them lay the narrow gorge, the dried-up riverbed, a tree or two, a jumble of boulders and . . .

Wait a minute!

Two men.

◆ ◆ ◆

Candido swung the crank and slid behind the wheel. He was about to put the car into first when the headlights snapped on.

One, two, four, eight, ten—there must have been thirty goddamned Khalkhas. He'd always known the Khalkhas would get them in the end. Samantha clambered over the back of the passenger seat and sat down beside him with a hairpin between her teeth. She was pinning her hair up.

"I don't know about you, Candido, but I could use a shower."

"We'll take one together."

"CAVALCANTI!"

The thunderous voice went echoing around the rocky walls of the gorge.

"We'll take one together, and I warn you," said Candido, "it'll be the sexual experience of the century."

"DO YOU HEAR ME, CAVALCANTI?"

The Khalkhas were closing in from all sides.

"We'll see about that," said Samantha, "but I'm not against it in principle." She'd finished pinning up her hair. The little topknot was back in place. "And while I think of it, we must have a talk about Bragança Boa Vista some time. And its *jabuticeiros.*"

"Jabuticabeiras."
She heard me—I was dreaming aloud and she heard me! How happy I am!

◆ ◆ ◆

"I'm bound to admit," Pamphily Merkulov observed in schoolmasterly tones, "that you're an exceedingly disconcerting young man. You look as if butter wouldn't melt in your mouth, then suddenly, quite without warning, you go off like a bomb."

"Did I spoil your little game at Dauriya?"

"What little game?"

"Ungern's assassination. Jaguar was meant to cut his throat, wasn't he? How about Otto Krantz, is he dead?"

"His name isn't Otto Krantz."

"I couldn't care less. Is he dead?"

Pamphily was eyeing him closely. Candido cursed himself for talking too much with the idiotic intention of proving that he wasn't an idiot. Pamphily would end by wondering if it wouldn't be better to kill him right away. More importantly, his verbal diarrhea was putting Samantha's life in danger.

"No, he isn't dead," Pamphily replied at length. "He's a very resourceful man."

"But Volovichenko is, isn't he?"

"Yes. The last I heard, Lieutenant Volovichenko, a Red agent, was shot by Captain Kostoied just as he was about to assassinate Baron Ungern with the aid of his two accomplices, Cavalcanti and Franck."

"So I *did* spoil your little game."

Pamphily said nothing. The Hotchkiss, in which they were still sitting, was hemmed in by Khalkhas.

If they meant to kill us they'd have done so by now.

Pamphily still said nothing. An idea was threading its way through Candido's mind.

"You've received fresh orders," he said. "Alekhin has dreamed up another mission for Jaguar. You work for him, don't you?"

Looking into Pamphily's eyes, he knew he'd guessed right. The only trouble was, he'd talked too much again—he simply couldn't stop himself.

But he had no time to marvel at his own perspicacity. Pamphily was shouting orders in Mongolian. His men grabbed hold of Samantha, lifted her bodily out of the Hotchkiss and carried her off like a sack of potatoes. God, how she fought and struggled! Candido hurled himself into the fray, but it was maddening: no matter how hard he kicked and punched, they merely laughed at him.

They didn't even retaliate, just held him at arm's length like a furious little kitten. Then he felt something hard and heavy descend on his shoulders, bruising the nape of his neck. His wrists were lashed to a beam, crucifix fashion. Samantha had been borne off out of sight by now. He yelled, but to no real purpose. A noose was placed around his neck. If they meant to hang him they were certainly taking no chances.

But no, they'd simply put him on a leash like a dog.

I smell gas. They're going to burn me alive!

Wrong again. It was the Hotchkiss they set fire to.

"Do stop struggling, Cavalcanti, it's a waste of time and energy."

Pamphily Merkulov was standing over him. From a kneeling position Candido could see nothing but his boots. Someone tugged at the leash. He tried to stand up and swing the beam at his tormentors, but they only laughed louder. Utterly exhausted, he fell headlong and gashed his cheek on a stone.

A muffled detonation in the background told him that the Hotchkiss's fuel tank had exploded. They towed him along yard by yard, hauling him to his feet whenever he collapsed. He was still conscious, but only just.

He struggled up, all by himself, and stood there. He could hardly believe it, but he'd done it unaided.

"I'm acting on instructions, Cavalcanti. His original orders were to kill you, but for some unknown reason he changed his mind. All my actions are governed by him. As for the girl, I can only say I'll do my best for her. I'm awfully sorry, believe me."

Candido tried to open his eyes, but they were caked with mud and blood. He could scarcely make out the figures of Pamphily and his huge henchman.

Tatarchuk kicked him in the worst possible place. The pain was agonizing.

"Awfully sorry, believe me," Pamphily Merkulov's voice repeated.

Another kick in the groin, and another.

He passed out at last.

Warmth on his face and hands: sunlight. It took him a while to surface completely.

Silence. They'd gone. Candido lifted one eyelid—only one, the other was gummed shut—and raised his head. He commanded himself to move, to push downward with his legs and unhook the beam from the branch. It was quite simple. There were two alternatives: he could either die of hunger and thirst while waiting for the wolves and eagles to devour him, or extricate himself and go after them.

Push!

At the third attempt, straining until his muscles almost snapped, he managed to lift the beam an inch or two.

All right, try again.

No, use your brains, it's pointless to try again right away. Better count to five thousand—that'll keep you awake—and then try again, but remember: you'll only have the strength left for one last attempt.

An eternity.

Two thousand six hundred and twenty-three . . . No, forget about the pain in your gut. . . . Two thousand six hundred and twenty-four . . . You're drifting off, better not wait any longer.

Now!

The beam came unhooked at once. He fell to the ground and lay there on his back, recuperating. Then, after slithering down a fifty-yard slope, he reached what remained of the Hotchkiss. The explosion had ripped it open like a tin can. The jagged edges were good and sharp.

Twenty minutes for the first wrist, simultaneously cursing himself for being slow and forgiving himself for being in such pain.

The other wrist took far less time.

Back on his feet again, Candido managed to ungum his right eyelid. He rummaged in the debris of the car, but the trunk was burned to a cinder and the rifle—naturally—had disappeared. He did, however, find the binoculars lying among some stones nearby. One lens was smashed, but it was better than nothing. The few drops of water remaining in the discarded can were just sufficient to moisten his lips. After some hesitation, he took the tire iron and stuck it in one of his boots.

He could walk. He was stiff all over and his stomach hurt like the devil, but he could walk.

He made his way along the dry riverbed for three or four hundred yards. It was around midday, judging by the sun, which meant that they had a start of eight or nine hours. They were mounted, too, but why be pessimistic?

He spotted it from some distance away. They'd left it in a conspicuous position, propped almost upright against one of the big, round boulders that must have been carried downstream by the river when it was in flood.

The balalaika.

And, just in front of it, his copy of *Der Abenteuerliche Simplicissimus Teutsch* with the green leather binding.

If this is their idea of a joke, they're welcome to it.

Almost weeping with joy at being reunited with the Grimmelshausen, he opened it at random at Chapter 16, which described how young Teutsch, having just escaped from the Croats, fell foul of some bandits: "By all appearances, matters were going from bad to worse with me. . . . I felt that I had been born for naught but misfortune. . . ." More pessimistic than Teutsch you couldn't get.

Their tracks were easy enough to follow. Twenty or thirty horses had passed this way, and the spring rains had softened the earth sufficiently to retain their hoofprints. Darkness prevented Candido from reading any more Grimmelshausen, but he continued to head northeast, resting at regular intervals. At the end of one of these halts he awoke with a start and realized that he'd dozed off without knowing it.

Unforgivable of me to waste all that time!

He was famished. He'd eaten nothing since the morsels Samantha had fed him while he drove, but he did quite often come upon water trapped in hollows or trickling down rocks. He picked some leaves off a bush and devoured them along with several large handfuls of grass, but he couldn't keep them down and wondered how cows contrived to do so. The tire iron started to chafe his leg, so he stuck it in his belt instead and trudged along with the balalaika on his shoulder and the Grimmelshausen in his hand.

He fell asleep a second time. When he awoke at daybreak he found himself confronted on the left, or northeast of him, by an endless succession of mountains and valleys.

And on his right, well within spitting distance, by three Khalkhas.

◆　◆　◆

They seemed quite unsurprised to see him there.

Why? Because they were expecting me, that's why. They aren't in this remote spot by chance.

"Did Pamphily Merkulov put you on my track?" he asked in Russian.

Their faces remained expressionless. They all carried *berdans,* antiquated muskets, slung over their shoulders. Two of them were tall and muscular—they looked like wrestlers—and all three wore blue quilted coats gathered at the waist by broad red belts that served to support their leather pouches and long, sharp knives. Their boots had upswept toes and bands of multicolored ornamentation at ankle level, their round hats tapered to a point. Very laboriously, Candido tried out his Mongolian on them.

"You Khalkha Mongols friends of Pamphily Merkulov's?"

No reaction. They handed him a birch-bark cup filled with thick, creamy milk, bits of jerked mutton and curd balls. He downed this mixture so eagerly that they rationed him, but they did unsling some leather bags from the saddles of their shaggy Kerulen ponies, deposit them beside him and indicate in sign language that the saddlebags were his to keep.

"Girl? Where girl?"

Either they were shamming incomprehension or they weren't Khalkhas at all, but Kalmucks—or God alone knew what else.

One of them took a pipe and a packet of tobacco from the little pocket sewn to the outside of his boot and held them out.

"Thanks, I don't smoke," he said in Russian. "Herr Doktor says it's bad for the wind. You've heard of the Olympics, I'm sure. Herr Doktor wanted me to enter for them."

He reverted to Mongolian.

"You great friends, me thank you. Mongols very mongol."

In Mongolian, *mongol* meant "brave."

No acknowledgment, not even a simple nod. Two of them got back on their ponies, the third hesitated. He retraced his steps, squatted down beside Candido and deftly drew some hoofprints in the earth with his forefinger. Then he pointed southeast and shook his head.

"I mustn't follow the hoofprints leading southeast," Candido translated.

I was right all along: they're agents sent by Pamphily Merkulov. He is trying to help me, that's the only possible explanation, or he'd have left me to starve.

This Khalkha understood Russian, even though he pretended not to. His forefinger got busy again: two parallel lines.

"Railway lines? The Trans-Siberian?"

Yes. Another drawing.

"First a truck, then they took the train."

A nod. The horseman, who had neither smiled nor uttered a word, turned on his heel and swung into the saddle as nimbly as his two companions.

They trotted off and quickly disappeared behind a hill.

◆　◆　◆

On the third day Candido came to a massive wall running from horizon to horizon. If it was a perimeter wall, he thought, the fazenda it enclosed must be immense. It might have been the work of a giant anxious to protect his lettuces.

He scaled it and walked along the crenellated top for miles without meeting a soul. There were watchtowers at regular intervals—he'd already counted four hundred of them—but all that could be seen far and wide was an uninhabited wilderness.

The endless wall—he swore it would have been visible from the moon with binoculars—ran east, which wasn't his required direction. He veered off and spent the next two days trudging up and down snow-capped mountains, but every time he turned and looked back he could still see that interminable line of masonry.

By the sixth day he reckoned he'd covered nearly two hundred miles. Thirty miles a day wasn't much—Herr Doktor would have called him a slowpoke and condemned his lack of willpower—but at least the Khalk-has' trail was clearly discernible. He could pick out the hoofprints of Samantha's small mounted escort and the tire tracks of the accompanying truck.

Heartened by this minor miracle, Candido decided to put on speed: he would run ten thousand paces, then walk ten thousand to rest himself, and so on. It wasn't too easy at first. He found it exhausting, trotting along encumbered with saddlebags of provisions, two gourds of water, the balalaika, the Grimmelshausen and the tire iron with which he intended to smash Tatarchuk's skull. In time, however, his load grew lighter. He jettisoned the saddlebags, now empty; then one of the gourds, ditto; and last of all the tire iron, whose incessant chafing had rubbed his hip raw.

In the end, to his shame, he collapsed and couldn't summon up the courage or energy to struggle to his feet again. He simply crawled on until, unable to crawl any farther, he curled up and closed his eyes and resigned himself to dying right there on that mountain path without ever seeing Samantha again. And that was when his torpor was dispelled by shouts and gunfire.

Not right away, though. It took him a little while to convince himself it wasn't a dream. He opened his eyes and crawled to the edge of the path. Drawn up below him with people in, on and underneath them were four covered wagons encircled by horsemen firing _berdans_ and slashing away with curved swords.

Silence fell at last and the horsemen rode off, laden with loot. Nothing and no one was stirring now. Candido resolved to investigate, even if he had to crawl there on his hands and knees. He must surely have strength

enough left to search those wagons and see if the horsemen had overlooked anything edible.

And drinkable. Not a drop had passed his lips for . . . he couldn't
remember how long.

He made it down the slope. Two of the wagons were burning, but the
others had been largely spared. Earthenware jars were suspended from
their sides. He unstoppered them and sniffed the contents: milk. He
drank and drank, spilling a lot of it over himself and etching dark furrows
in the pounds of reddish dust he was carrying around. He felt better
already.

"I'm fine, Samantha. Don't worry, I'm coming . . ."

The words emerged in a croak. He jumped at the sound of his own
voice and told himself not to get delirious. Laying aside the balalaika and
the book, he proceeded to search the first wagon. It was heaped with
slashed and disemboweled children. The inevitable flies and the sickly
smell of blood were everywhere, but he had to eat. Other earthenware
vessels proved to contain a kind of molasses, and there was a bag filled
with flat loaves of bread. Barely pausing to put a few feet between himself
and the dead children, he feasted voraciously.

Somewhere among these silent corpses, all of which were dressed in
the Chinese style, someone was groaning softly. Candido finally located
the source of the sound. A girl of about fifteen was lying under one
of the half-charred wagons with an ancient musket beside her and her
head and the upper part of her body resting against the beam that must
have served her as a barricade. Her hair and one side of her face were
badly burned, and protruding from her stomach was the snapped-off end
of a sword blade. Candido knelt down and bent over her, then started
back in alarm.

He'd failed to notice a big, furry mound in the shadows beneath the
wagon. It was a dog, but it bore no resemblance to the lapdogs of which
his stepmother owned a whole pack. A beast like this could have eaten
half a dozen of Dona Isabel's pooches for breakfast, and when it growled,
as it had just now, it sounded like a a train in a tunnel.

The girl opened her eyes and said something in an unfamiliar, singsong
language, presumably Chinese.

"I don't understand," Candido said softly.

"Thirsty," she replied in Russian.

He went off to get some milk. What else could he do for her? Nothing.
Besides, there was the dog. One false move and it might gobble him up.

The dog had interposed itself between them. He held the milk to her
lips with his outstretched arm brushing its nose.

"Spasibo."

"You're the only one left," he told her. "What would you like?"

"Leave me."

Her voice was very faint. She was dying, he knew. She knew it too. He should move on—he was only wasting time.

He sat down beside her.

"Who were those men?"

Bandits. Her family and another Manchu family had been fleeing from Mongolia, where they'd settled a long time ago.

"More milk?"

"Kill me," she said. "Please kill me."

He wept. *Never shed tears over your own misfortunes,* he told himself, *but there's nothing to be ashamed of in weeping for her.* He fetched his balalaika and sang to her softly in Brazilian Portuguese—sang the songs taught him by his black friend Nabuco, who'd shown him more kindness than Dom Trajano, Dona Isabel and his half sisters put together, not that that took much doing. He hoped the old man hadn't died since he'd left home.

The girl was dead—even the dog realized that. It rested its huge head on its paws and whined as if overcome with remorse at having failed to save her.

Candido pulled himself together as best he could. He told himself he hadn't even known the girl, after all, and if he were going to weep for all the world's slain innocents he would need an Amazonful of tears.

He slung the bag of loaves and two jars of milk over his shoulder on a rein borrowed from the harness of the Manchus' horses, which the bandits had cut loose and driven off.

After a few hundred yards he noticed that the dog was following him.

"Why aren't you a horse?" he called.

It was true. If the animal had been just a little bigger, he could have saddled it.

"Those," Candido told the dog, "are the tracks of the Trans-Siberian."

"Grrr," went the dog.

"You remind me of someone, you know. I could christen you Dom Trajano, but it would be disrespectful. We kept about seventy-five dogs at Bragança Boa Vista alone, and they all worshiped my father, the stupid mutts. I didn't have a single friend among them. Are you listening?"

"Grrr."

"We're going to follow the tracks, if that's what you mean. Another thing: on mature reflection I'm going to call you Grrr. All right?"

"Grrr."

"Ever read Jack London's *White Fang* or *The Call of the Wild*? No? You should."

He paused for a rest. It was all he could do not to fall asleep.

"To be honest, Grrr, I'm exhausted. Please don't look at me that way, I'm not something to eat and I haven't passed out. I've simply put my ear to this godforsaken rail to see if I can hear the Trans-Siberian coming. You don't believe me? All right, so I fell and hit my head and I can't get up. Wake me when the train comes, will you?"

He started to crawl. Three cross-ties in one go—some mileage! Another cross-tie, hauling himself along hand over hand. The sun was rising dead ahead, immediately between the rails. He was heading east, no doubt about it.

"Yes, Grrr, thanks, I spotted him too: a Khalkha scout on horseback. Yes, there he goes, galloping off. Know what I think? He was waiting for me and he's gone to tell his boss. They've always known where I was, always. All right, stop tugging at my sleeve, I can get up if I want to."

"I'd love to leave you to sleep in the middle of the track, Cavalcanti, but the Trans-Siberian won't be long now. Besides, you'll feel more comfortable in a bed."

It was the voice of Pamphily Merkulov. Quiet, gentle and more melancholy than ever.

"More tea?"

There was a Trans-Siberian timetable pinned to the wall of the log cabin behind Pamphily, who was sitting opposite him. Candido shook his head. He looked down at his bandaged feet.

"What have I got on my feet?"

"It's more a question of what you *haven't* got on them—in other words, skin. They're completely raw. We had to cut your boots off."

Pamphily answered his question in the negative before he could ask it.

"I don't know where she is, Cavalcanti, I give you my word. I haven't set eyes on her since she boarded the Trans-Siberian."

"Where was she going?"

"It was an eastbound train. Harbin, perhaps, or even farther."

"Who was with her?"

"Two men and a woman. They carried her aboard."

"Drugged?"

"I fear so." Pamphily paused. "You're a remarkably tough young man. Where did you get the horse from?"

"What horse?"

"You mean you made the whole trip on foot? I find that a little hard to believe."

"Can I go to Harbin too?"

"I certainly won't stop you. You really walked all the way?"

Candido shut his eyes. He would go to Harbin. She was there—she had to be.

"Walked and ran," he said. "You knew I'd make it, didn't you?"

"I had my doubts, knowing the country as well as I do, but he was convinced of it."

"Alekhin?"

"I see no reason not to answer your question. Yes, Alekhin."

"Did he board the train with her?"

"I don't know what he looks like. All my orders come by telegraph."

Candido described him. Pamphily shook his head.

"No, he wasn't there."

"Where is he?"

"I haven't the faintest idea. My most recent instructions came from Moscow."

"And he was sure I'd make it?"

"Sure you'd reach the railway line, yes. I posted scouts along a hundred-mile section. One of them finally spotted you and informed me."

"Why do the Mongols obey you? Are you their leader?"

"No, but I'm on friendly terms with several of their chiefs. Much of my life has been spent in this area."

"Was it you that stationed those three Khalkhas on my route with food and water?"

Pamphily's schoolmasterish face remained blank.

"I know nothing of that. You must have come across some nomads. Mongols can be very hospitable to passing strangers."

He's lying. Of course it was him, but he exceeded his orders and doesn't want it known.

"Where are we?"

"Not far from a little Manchurian town called Xiguitugi. You covered some three hundred and fifty miles in nine days without abandoning your balalaika or your book—he wants you to have them back, by the way. I'm amazed. Even he couldn't believe you'd get here so soon."

Candido felt almost proud to have surpassed Alekhin's expectations. If anger had been part of his nature, he would have been furious with himself for feeling that way.

"He was right," Pamphily went on, "you're an exceptional type, like that dog of yours. What breed is he?"

"Why not ask him yourself?" Candido retorted.

"He looks like a cross between a Tibetan mastiff and a Siberian Samoyed. You sometimes come across Samoyeds with vivid blue eyes like that."

"Has Alekhin given you any further orders concerning me?"

"I've already carried them out. My part in this affair is at an end."

They sipped their tea in silence. The railway track outside the window seemed to stretch away into infinity.

"I'm leaving for Urga," Pamphily said at last. "I hope my beloved Mongolia won't suffer too badly in the fighting. If ever you should need me, write me care of the postmaster at Urga."

Candido, wondering what could possibly induce him to return to Mongolia, said, "What about the Trans-Siberian?"

"It won't be here for another nine or ten hours at least. It isn't the Trans-Siberian either, strictly speaking, because the line's still cut. It's the Harbin train."

"May I catch it?"

"I told you, I've already carried out his orders in full. A compartment has been reserved for you."

The dog declined to come aboard. He just sat there, surveying the train with no outward sign of emotion. Even on his haunches he was the height of a man.

"Good-bye, Grrr."

Candido watched through the window as Pamphily walked up to Grrr and addressed him in the soothing tones of one accustomed to telling children the facts of life. Grrr wasn't won over immediately. He sauntered off, keeping his distance, but Candido could tell that the pair of them would come to terms in the end.

If Pamphily gets accepted by Grrr it'll mean I wasn't wrong about him. He isn't completely mad, just halfway there—like me. If it was Alekhin out there, Grrr would eat him alive.

Candido fell asleep at once; it was the best way to forget his aches and pains. Sometimes his dreams turned to nightmares, as when Alekhin chased him and Samantha along an underground passage at the head of a pack of ravenous wolves led by Afonka Tchadayev and Otto Krantz, whose teeth took the form of double-edged knives. Sometimes, though, his dreams were so sweet he could have wept with happiness. This was the best one of all:

Samantha boarded the Trans-Siberian, bent down and kissed him, took him in her arms as she had that time in the Hotchkiss, and tearfully, falteringly, told him how overjoyed she was to see him again.

But it wasn't just a dream. The train had stopped, and amplified voices were announcing in every known language that this was Harbin, in Manchuria, the end of the line.

"Can you walk, Candido?"

"I could dance," he said.

IV

THE JAGUAR'S CALL BEARS
NO RESEMBLANCE TO THE CONVENTIONAL
ROAR OF THE WILD BEAST. IT IS, IN FACT, A
SILENT CREATURE. A LOW GROWL IS THE MOST IT
EVER UTTERS, THOUGH MANY TRAVELERS CLAIM
THAT IT CAN BE LOCATED BY THE DIN MADE
BY HOWLER MONKEYS WHEN IT
COMES THEIR WAY.

Y ou were sure I'd follow you?"

"Positive."

"It wasn't easy sometimes."

She's making a fuss of me again. She can be as sweet as pie when it suits her.

"No one and nothing would stop you, I never doubted it for a moment."

That's nice of her. Really nice. If I don't change the subject I may start blubbering.

"What was she like?" he asked.

"Who?"

"The woman who got you aboard that train. The one Pamphily mentioned."

"She spoke English with an American accent—sounded like an Easterner. A stunning brunette, late twenties, nearly as tall as me. I only know her first name: Matriona. When we got here we were both questioned by the Manchurian police with some White Russians sitting in."

"What happened to the two men?"

"I never saw them again. Matriona told the police we were refugees from the Reds and produced evidence to that effect. All the same, Candido, there's no proof she's an agent of Aliochka's."

Alekhin, Samantha, not Aliochka. Please.

Candido kept this plea to himself. He got out of the bed in which he'd spent the last few days and paced up and down their suite in Harbin's Imperial Hotel.

"She paid your hotel bill in advance, Samantha, and she gave you some cash."

"Yes, five hundred dollars. I didn't have a cent. She was generous, that's all. You're being overly suspicious."

Candido's feet didn't hurt too much as long as he wore slippers.

"Can we go out?" he asked.

"No reason why not."

They decided to go for a stroll through town.

"What about our passports?"

"The police have kept them, but we'll get them back before long."

Rather unnerved by the teeming streets and powerful smells of the Chinese or Manchu quarter of the city, they retreated to Novy Gorod, which had been transformed into something of a second Petrograd by all the new buildings constructed since the completion of the Trans-Siberian and, more especially, by an influx of White Russian refugees.

"We won't get far on five hundred dollars, that's for sure," said Samantha. She'd had to buy herself some dresses and shoes, and he himself would have to acquire some clothes that fitted better than the ones Pamphily Merkulov had supplied him with.

Some days later, while strolling through a largely European crowd, Candido gave a start and gripped Samantha's hand. She had stiffened, too.

"Yes, I saw him," she said. "He looked like Otto Krantz. Maybe it was only a superficial resemblance."

"Yes," he said. "I'm sure you're right."

Candido shivered. It wasn't the man with rimless glasses and robotic movements he thought he'd glimpsed amid this throng of people enjoying the last of the summer sun.

He was sure of it: even when reflected in the window of one of the few motor cars to be seen in the city's streets, those eyes were unmistakable.

They belonged to Afonka Tchadayev.

At Immigration they were informed that their passports would be returned soon.

"Think they'll try to stop us leaving here, Candido?"

"I don't know."

"I spoke with the U.S. consul a couple of days before you got here. He says these delays are normal."

"Oh, sure."

"I don't like it when you say 'Oh, sure' in that tone of voice."

"Sorry."

"I don't like it when you say 'Sorry,' either."

They were walking along the banks of the Amur. The sunshine of the last few days had given way to a light drizzle. Long barges laden with firewood were chugging downstream.

"Well, out with it," she said.

He didn't want to talk about it, not now. To cover his embarrassment he started playing soccer with a rotting corn cob some rats had been squabbling over. Sure enough, one of his Manchurian sandals flew off and landed in the river.

"You're being really childish, you know," she said. "I haven't set eyes on Aliochka, not once since we boarded the Trans-Siberian for Irkutsk, and we haven't arranged to meet in the future. Is that good enough for you?"

He said nothing. It was an answer to the right question—maybe even the right answer to the right question, except that she hadn't said whether or not she regretted Alekhin's failure to reappear.

Finding her again, that had been his one idea while trekking through Mongolia—just finding her, even if he couldn't win her back. She'd thrown herself into the Russian's arms once, so why not a second time? Alekhin had spared his life. Why? Perhaps she'd made a deal with him: he could have his way with her in return for his, Candido's, survival.

"It's a perfectly good answer," he said, "but I can't say the question bothers me much."

"Oh no? While we're on the subject, how about getting something else straight?"

"What else?"

"Don't act dumb. I mean what we're going to do if we ever get out of this place."

"We?"

So she meant to stay with him!

Almost swooning with happiness, he pretended his foot was playing up again. He leaned against one of the big clay vessels stored on the river-bank, stood on one leg like a stork and massaged his ankle so as to be able to look down and conceal the emotion he felt.

"If we *are* going to stay together a while, Candido, here's what we'll do."

Her tone conveyed that she'd only just come to a decision. For a moment or two his doubts returned. Samantha had clearly contemplated leaving him, but that was in the past. She was staying—nothing else mattered. Who cared where they went?

"Europe," she said. "Our best plan is to head for Europe. Germany's out, of course, but why not France or Italy? My father had friends there. Anarchists can always count on their friends to . . ." She broke off. "Coming, or is your foot still hurting?"

"No, the pain's worn off."

"Those letters you wrote your father—he's bound to answer them in the end. You really think he'll send you some money?"

"He is my father, after all."

Candido had thought it safer to duplicate his missive to Dom Trajano in case one copy went astray en route. Drafting it had taken him hours. He'd told the whole story—he'd even pleaded guilty to his only crime, the bombing of the Plücks' cinema, though the bombs had been downgraded to fireworks to make them sound less lethal. Most importantly, he'd disclaimed all responsibility for the Jaguar murders. It always cleared the air to make a clean breast of things.

He felt genuinely happy. Everything was going fine now. He set off again, even forgetting to limp.

"Europe," Samantha repeated, "that's our best plan. If it's all right with you, of course."

Isn't it just! France and Italy with Samantha . . .

"All we have to do," she went on, "is get our passports back and lay hands on a bit more cash."

They smiled at each other. They were in agreement on the subject of Otto Krantz: the resemblance had been only superficial.

He said nothing about Afonka Tchadayev.

It was Samantha's idea. The doctor she'd summoned to Candido had been living in Harbin since 1917 and knew everyone worth knowing. They asked him to recommend someone who would be willing to put in a word with the immigration authorities and hasten the return of their passports. The doctor introduced them to Pavel Pavlovich Komarov, an exofficer of Kolchak's army who had fought against the Reds. Komarov was sure he could settle the matter in no time. "These Asiatics are exasperatingly slow, but rely on me, I have friends in the right places." No, they mustn't dream of thanking him. Miss Franck was an American and Senhor Cavalcanti a Brazilian. What was more, they were both reputed to be members of illustrious families. Under present circumstances the United States and Brazil seemed potential places of refuge, especially if an evil fate decreed that the accursed Reds should win the day. The news wasn't good. Kolchak was dead and Denikin had thrown in his hand and fled to France. As for Wrangel, Denikin's successor, he appeared to be in difficulties after his successful offensives in the Donets steppe, Kuban and the Donbass. The latest dispatches stated that the Red dogs were counterattacking under the command of the Jew Trotsky. Baron von Ungern-Sternberg? His first attempt to capture Urga with the Asiatic Cavalry Division had just failed, but then, he was merely a crackbrained adventurer, a madman from whom no good could be expected.

Komarov began by inviting Samantha and Candido to dine at his magnificent three-storied mansion outside town on the banks of the Sungari, a tributary of the Amur, and had them fetched from the Imperial Hotel in his own limousine, a 1915 Cadillac V-8 driven by a liveried chauffeur. Champagne flowed like water at dinner, which was a highly convivial occasion. Candido and Samantha were bombarded with questions. Most of those present had emigrated from St. Petersburg to Manchuria three or four years earlier, so it was only natural that they should want to be brought up to date by two new arrivals. Was it true that the Russian people had risen in revolt and were demanding the restoration of the monarchy? Rumor had it that the peasants were slaughtering any Reds who ventured into the countryside, that a resistance movement had taken shape and was daily gaining strength, that Holy Russia had at last turned on the Revolution, which was German and Jewish, not Russian. Was this true?

A second invitation arrived three days later, accompanied by a bouquet and an envelope containing their passports, duly rubber-stamped and bearing visas entitling them to leave Manchuria. It was raining, and the liveried chauffeur had put the black leather hood up. He wasn't alone. With him came a man of thirty or so, very elegantly attired in white tie and tails. He introduced himself as Stephan Timofeyevich Onegin, "Onegin as in Eugene—yes, I've just arrived in Harbin but I'm no stranger to the place, call me Stepa, one can feel the approach of winter, no? The winters here can be frightful. . . ." Without knowing why, Candido didn't take to Stepa Onegin.

They were dropped outside the pillared portico and joined the other guests in the library, which was dominated by a portrait of the late czar bordered with black crepe. Everyone then repaired to the sumptuously decorated dining room, where the Limoges dinner service was partnered by solid gold cutlery.

"I have a surprise for you," Komarov announced as they sat down, "but not until we've eaten."

When the time came Samantha was invited to remain. The other two women diners withdrew.

Why didn't I trust my instinct? I knew we should never have left the hotel and gotten into that goddamned Cadillac.

"To tell you the truth," Komarov began, "we maintain as many spies among the Reds as those jackals have here—we even outnumber them in that respect. You've already met Stepa. That's his real name, by the way—the others were introduced to you under pseudonyms, but no matter. What matters is that you're in the presence of the general staff

of the Secret White Army. And now a question: Have you ever heard of
a terrorist known as Jaguar?"

"It's all a put-up job, you knucklehead," said Samantha. "There's a
simple explanation."

"Jaguar," Komarov pursued, ignoring this interruption, "—Jaguar and
those who chose his sobriquet—were responsible for murdering two of
our agents in the cellar at the Bolshoi Theater. They also executed several
of our men who were hiding out in the Preznaya district. Another agent,
a doctor at the Golitsin Hospital, had his throat cut while making his way
home through the Neskuchny Sad. Finally, still in Moscow, we lost a
woman agent employed at the Bakhrushin Museum. The *modus operandi*
in every case—"

"You stupid sonofabitch," said Samantha. "Are we allowed to get a word in?"

"The *modus operandi* was identical with that already used on several
White Russian refugees in Berlin. You were in Berlin, weren't you,
Cavalcanti?"

"They both were," Stepa put in.

"More murders occurred during your sojourn at Irkutsk, and still
others in Transbaikalia, where three men died while trying to infiltrate
the communists—you may comprehend my ill humor if I tell you that one
of them was my brother. After that Jaguar moved on to Chita. No
murders took place there, admittedly, but you had bigger and better
things to view. On you went to Dauriya, where your mission was to
assassinate Baron von Ungern-Sternberg. You very nearly succeeded,
according to Pamphily Merkulov."

"Pamphily? I don't believe he told you any such thing," Samantha said
impatiently. "You're lying."

"Stepa?"

"I had it from Merkulov himself," Stepa confirmed. "He's our most
trusted agent, even though the Reds are holding his entire family hostage. He also told me of the astounding way in which Jaguar managed
to escape Ungern's men by crossing the Mongolian desert on foot. Merkulov himself was compelled to send the girl to Harbin. The lives of his
grandchildren were at stake."

*God, what a complicated puzzle! Alekhin must really have had fun devising
it.*

"This, then," Komarov wound up, "is a court-martial. Do you admit
to being Jaguar, Cavalcanti?"

"We don't admit a thing, you bastards! Not a goddamned thing!"

They were led out.

_____

"You didn't open your mouth."

An aureole of yellow candlelight relieved the gloom of the cellar in which they'd been confined to await the outcome of the self-styled court-martial's deliberations. Candido was circling it and tapping the stone walls in the vague and vain expectation of discovering a hidden exit.

"You just sat there nibbling petits fours as if you weren't interested. You don't seem interested now, for that matter. Tell me if I'm boring you, Cavalcanti."

Silence.

"Will they execute us?"

Should I tell her or not? What if I'm wrong?

"I don't think so," he said.

That'll have to do. She'll think it over and come to the obvious conclusion.

"Oh, hell," she muttered at length.

"Exactly," he said resignedly.

"Will it never end?"

She was seated on the hard-packed mud floor clasping her knees. Candido had draped his jacket around her bare shoulders.

"What if you're wrong?" she asked.

"If I'm wrong we're dead."

She nodded.

"Stop prowling up and down like that, it's getting on my nerves. Come over here, I've something to tell you."

He came and stood behind her so that his legs deputized for the back of a chair.

"I wasn't being self-sacrificing, staying with you. The real reason was, I wanted to. I guess I'll want to stay with you for quite a while. Maybe even for good."

She's telling me she loves me a little, but I mustn't get overexcited. It's this jam we're in, I expect. Maybe she simply wants me to die happy.

"Did you hear?"

"Yes."

"I wanted you to know."

"I'm awfully glad to hear it."

He squatted down and ran his hands very gently, very caressingly, over her body. That way, if they put a bullet into the base of his skull, he would retain as vivid a memory of her as possible.

She turned her face toward him and they kissed, but the thought was still there, nagging away in the recesses of his mind. He rose.

When they'd been shut up in the cellar he'd distinctly heard the click of the lock.

His ears had just caught the same sound, but more muffled.

It can't hurt to check.

He tiptoed over, hesitated for moment, then pushed. The door swung open.

They took the wrong staircase and found themselves in the kitchen, which they hadn't passed going the other way. The only person in sight was a woman wearing a babushka. Her face was invisible. She'd slumped forward onto the *gâteau* that was to follow the petits fours, with her fat backside in the air and blood oozing from her throat.

The pantry door leading to the garden was locked. On the inside, even though that was how they'd gotten in.

What if I open it?

No point. They must have gotten in that way and it was pouring outside, yet there wasn't a wet footprint to be seen. They'd thought of everything as usual.

"For God's sake let's get out of here," said Samantha.

No, we may as well look while we're at it, though I already know what we'll find elsewhere in the house.

The dining room was a slaughterhouse. Pavel Pavlovich Komarov must have been among the first to be shot, possibly with a rifle from the hallway. He was still seated at the head of the table, but he now had a bullet hole in the middle of his forehead and was leaning back with his throat cut. His cheeks, of course, were slit from ear to ear. It was almost as if he'd just heard a funny story and was roaring with laughter, both hands clutching the table for support.

The bearded gentleman who had played Russian folk songs on the piano before dinner had two bullet holes in him. His throat and cheeks, too, had been cut postmortem. Some of the others had tried to defend themselves by drawing their revolvers and sheltering behind pieces of furniture or diving under the table. There were five corpses, seven counting the cook and the butler.

"I don't see Stepa anywhere," Samantha said.

Stepa, whom Pamphily Merkulov had informed of their alleged attempt on Ungern's life? Stepa, who knew that Pamphily was under pressure from Alekhin? Stepa was a barefaced liar—was *still* a barefaced liar. *He* wasn't dead, not him.

"That leaves the two women," Candido said.

"No, please let's get out of here."

What had they done with the women? No sign of them in the drawing room or the adjoining study, though that had clearly been the killers' outward route. Candido checked the papers on the desk. They were quite capable of having forged a letter from Komarov or someone else, identifying Jaguar as a duo comprising himself and Samantha.

No sign of a letter, but they're bound to have notified the Harbin police by now.

"What on earth are you doing?"

Candido had set off along the passage leading to the hall.

"Surely you're not going upstairs?"

Oh, yes I am, even if I'm not dying to set eyes on another couple of corpses.

He climbed the stairs with Samantha at his heels, so agitated that she forgot to grouse.

"You think Stepa was one of the killers, Candido?"

She'd caught on. Stepa Onegin had pitched the Jaguar yarn to Komarov and his ridiculous "general staff" so as to get them all together in a quiet spot. All that had remained was to set the dogs on them.

"He used us as bait, Samantha."

The women were lying gagged in a bedroom with their throats cut like the rest.

"Look."

Samantha pointed to a mirror. It bore the following inscription in Russian: NO ONE, NOWHERE, IS EXEMPT FROM ANARCHIST RETRIBUTION. JAGUAR. The Cyrillic characters were written in blood.

"Anarchist?" said Samantha. *"Anarchist?"*

Candido picked up a cushion and obliterated the words. So he wasn't just the ferocious Jaguar, he was an anarchist as well. That meant no one could blame the communists. Alekhin was killing two birds with one stone: eliminating anyone he chose and implicating the anarchists.

No wonder the scheme was approved by that madman I went shooting with. Lenin must have taken me for a blithering idiot. Either that or a wild beast.

"They did leave one message behind," Samantha said. "Could there be others? Was that what you were looking for on the desk?"

Yes to the second question, no to the first. He'd been mistaken, they hadn't left anything else. They'd known he would go upstairs and wipe the mirror clean—they'd foreseen his every move. If they wanted to brand Jaguar a psychopathic killer and an anarchist, they would surely employ some method more subtle than a message in blood on a mirror.

"Let's go, Samantha."

The rain was still teeming down outside. Candido switched off the lights in the dining room and the hall and shut the front door behind them. The Cadillac was parked six feet from the portico.

"Where's the chauffeur?"

"There, look."

The chauffeur lay sprawled on the sodden ground with rain trickling down his cheeks. His throat was in pristine condition; a bullet in the back of the neck had been sufficient. Throat-cutting was restricted to specially deserving cases and members of the upper crust; the lower orders had to be content with a bullet. Jaguar, it seemed, was a snob.

Candido seized the body by the ankles and dragged it behind a privet hedge.

"What's the point of that?"

"Switch off the outside light, Samantha. Then we'll get out of here."

"Why bother?"

"If they haven't called the police, someone may be surprised to see the light on tomorrow morning."

He started up and drove off.

"You don't mean we're going back to the hotel?"

"We're in evening dress, aren't we?"

The night porter inquired if they'd had an enjoyable evening. Very enjoyable, they assured him.

The envelope was lying where it couldn't possibly be missed, plumb in the middle of the carpet in the lobby of their suite. It contained two first-class rail tickets to Vladivostok and a slip of paper advising them of their time of departure: five forty-eight A.M. Also enclosed were ten thousand dollars in cash.

So they don't want us arrested by the police after all. In other words, Jaguar's still needed.

"Pack your bag, Samantha."

They changed their clothes. Five minutes later they left the Imperial Hotel by a side door and reinstalled themselves in the Cadillac. Candido headed south and put on speed as soon as possible. No sign of a tail, but that was hardly surprising: their movements were always known in advance.

They got to Mukden just before five-thirty. Abandoning the car in one of the streets that converged on the station, they turned up three minutes before the train from Harbin pulled in. Their tickets, coupled with a five-dollar tip, secured them a first-class sleeper.

The train got under way.

"Nine bodies, do you realize?"

"Ten. You're forgetting the chauffeur. Let's talk about something else."

She stretched out on the bunk.

"What, for instance?"

He looked at her.

They wanted each other madly, desperately, after that gory farce. *Candido my friend,* he told himself later, *like every animal species, mankind reacts to death by making love. The birthrate is never higher than in wartime.*

◆ ◆ ◆

The sky at Port Arthur was clear, the bay of Bo Hai a blue to rival Samantha's eyes. They were informed that there was no ship sailing for Europe direct.

For Shanghai, yes, and at Shanghai they would sooner or later be able to get a passage to Hong Kong, and from there to Europe. Genoa, Marseilles, London, anywhere.

"What about Brazil?" Candido asked the shipping clerk.

"But we don't want to go to Brazil."

Samantha was looking tired but resolute.

"Brazil might not be such a bad idea," he said. "I'd be on home ground there, and—"

No, not unless he wanted to go there on his own. She felt sure there weren't any anarchists in Brazil.

"Two tickets for Shanghai, please," said Candido.

They were hungry. They found a hotel restaurant not too overcrowded with Japanese, sat down at a table and ordered hot chocolate. No chocolate, no milk, they were told, so they settled for tea and sticky rice cakes flavored with ginger and cinnamon. They'd barely started eating when Afonka Tchadayev sat down beside them.

"No, of course I'm not dead," Afonka said, roaring with laughter.

Samantha said she regretted the fact. Afonka laughed even louder, and the little black insects in the middle of his off-white irises frisked about in an alarming manner.

"What about Khoro the Buryat?" Candido asked. "Was he in on it too?"

"Yes, but it's not worth talking about."

Afonka wasn't alone. Seated at a nearby table but taking no discernible notice of them were Otto Krantz and a companion so huge that Candido promptly christened him Man Mountain. Otto was gazing out at the street, where Japanese officers were driving around in their funny-looking motor cars. His hands extracted a cigarette from a packet, adjusted the position of a glass on the table, moved in their usual mechanical fashion. He didn't look in their direction once. Candido could readily picture him cutting a throat with the same air of detachment.

"How many of you did it take to murder all those people at Harbin?" he asked.

Afonka gave another bellow of laughter.

"I don't know what you mean. You and Samantha did it. I hope no one reports you to the police—they chop off murderers' heads in this country. The sooner you sail for America the better."

Candido made no comment.

But Samantha will, you bet.

"We're not going to America," she snapped. "We're going to Europe. And there's no way you can stop us."

"Easy, Samantha!"

"There are policemen in Europe too—not as good as the ones in America, but good enough. Your rotten little threats don't scare us, Afonka. You want to turn us in? OK, go ahead."

Afonka rocked around on his chair, wagged his head, wiped tears of laughter from his eyes. He picked up their tickets to Shanghai, pocketed them and substituted two others. His sidelong glance at Candido was almost an appeal for help.

"Say something, Candido," Samantha urged. "Jesus Christ, don't tell me you're scared!"

"Yes," he said, "scared of being scared."

He reached for the photograph lying on the table beside the tickets. It showed Herr Doktor, shortsighted eyes magnified by thick-lensed glasses, hair long and unkempt, suit crumpled. Herr Doktor was staring at the camera, but he wasn't smiling. Two men were gripping him by the arms. He was in Red Square.

Afonka rose and walked off, swinging his massive shoulders. He made an ungainly impression, but Candido couldn't fail to notice how extraordinarily light he was on his feet. He looked as if he could pounce without warning, like a Siberian tiger. Remembering his diabolical skill with a gun, and knowing that he was Alekhin's right-hand man, how could he, Candido, help feeling scared?

"America?" Samantha protested when she saw the destination on the tickets. "I'm damned if we'll go to Yokohama and San Francisco, and no one on God's earth is going to make us!"

Candido helped himself to another gooey rice cake. He felt saddened as well as scared. It was stupid of him to have imagined that their late-night flight in the Cadillac had thrown the others off the track. They were trapped in the same old vicious circle.

"Take a seat and wait," the U.S. immigration officer told him.

Candido sat down on a bench. The room was thronged with Chinese, Japanese, Koreans, Filipinos. Some of them were squatting on the floor beside their ragged bundles. To judge by their calm, patient faces, they would wait there for centuries if need be.

Hours went by.

From Port Arthur they'd finally gotten to Yokohama on a Japanese freighter that called at every island off the Korean coast. Their last ship had been full of Americans. Inches taller than Candido, they ogled Samantha over his head and either pretended not to see him or looked him up and down with an expression that clearly demanded to know what a pretty American girl was doing in the company of a flashy little foreigner.

No one had been there to meet them at San Francisco in spite of all the letters he'd sent from Japan—none of Dom Trajano's New York representatives and no one acting on behalf of Great-uncle Amílcar. No one apart from the immigration authorities, who had stopped Candido in his tracks.

"Your Brazilian passport expires in three days' time and you don't have a U.S. entry visa. You should have applied to the Brazilian Embassy and the U.S. Consulate General in Tokyo—they might have been able to regularize your status. This way, Miss Franck—no, you can't go with him, sorry, you're an American citizen, you're welcome to wait outside. It's no use hollering, young lady. Maybe I *am* a dumb ox—maybe that goes for President Wilson, too, you're entitled to your opinion—but it won't do this gentleman any good. Please move on, you're holding up the line. . . ."

Hours and hours.

The huge room was empty but for himself and two blank-faced policemen.

It must be dark outside by now, God help me. They let Samantha through, but that was only natural—she's a U.S. citizen, after all. She may be a little sad at first, but she'll forget me in the end and marry a six-foot American. At least he'll be able to scoop her up in his arms and bear her off to bed.

"Candido Stevenson Cavalcanti?"

They're calling me. Everything's all right. I can tell from their faces! Thank God!

"You're sure you understand English?"

"You're asking me if I understand, I can certainly understand that. Sure, I understand English."

"Anyone could be forgiven for doubting it from the way you filled out these forms," said the chief immigration officer. "I mean, look at your answer to the question 'What is your race?': 'Green.' And here: 'State your point of departure.' You put: 'The Mad Baron's headquarters.' Was it meant to be a joke or something?"

"Yes," said Candido, "a joke."

He and Samantha had had great fun filling out the immigration forms. The questions they asked! For instance: "Have you ever (if a man) had homosexual relations with a man?" "Yes," he'd written, "with Vladimir Ilyich Lenin while shooting grouse." Samantha had persuaded him to cross that one out.

The immigration authorities found it equally hard to fathom how Candido Stevenson Cavalcanti, never having officially left Brazil, had traveled first to Germany and then to Manchuria without crossing any intervening frontiers.

"Mr. Cavalcanti, does the name Andrew Harmond mean anything to you?"

"No."

"That's odd. He's a prominent citizen, and he's offered to vouch for you. The governor of California and the State Department intervenes on your behalf, thanks to his attorney's efforts in the last few hours, and you say you've never heard of him?"

Cuidado!

"Well, maybe. Yes, now you come to mention it . . ."

"What's your connection with him?"

Think hard! Quick!

"Someone in my family."

I got it right.

"Who, exactly?"

"My great-uncle, Amílcar Cavalcanti de Noronha of Rio de Janeiro."

It was just possible that Great-uncle Amílcar, a man of many contacts, knew this fellow Harman or Helman or whatever. Anyway, he'd got it right again. He was going to make it.

The chief immigration officer handed him a document covered with rubber stamps.

"This is a special permit authorizing you to remain in the United States for three months, but you must contact your country's consular service as soon as possible and regularize your position. You'll need a valid passport for a start. Mr. Harmond says you're a student."

"Absolutely," said Candido.

"Sign here. It's another immigration form—Mr. Harmond's attorney completed it already. Next time, cut out the wisecracks."

"Absolutely," he repeated.

I'm going to see her again—if she's waited for me.

"And here's a letter that Mr. Harmond's attorney has asked us to hand you. You can go, Mr. Cavalcanti. In spite of the circumstances, welcome to the United States."

"Thank you very much."

"And a Merry Christmas."

Samantha, who had been waiting outside for eighteen long hours, threw herself into his arms.

"You're frozen," he said. "God, what a fog."

"They let you in, that's the main thing. Oh, Candido, I was going crazy!"

Immigration had resisted all her efforts. In despair, she'd even put through a call to her home in Chicago, but her mother had told her to go to hell. Uncle Moritz, the only relatively sane member of the family, was away on business, and the attorneys she'd called had pronounced themselves uninterested in the case or not qualified to handle it.

"Samantha . . ."

He produced the letter and showed it to her. She tried to read it but gave up.

"I can't understand a word. Is it in Portuguese?"

"Yes. Here, I'll translate it for you: 'My dear Candido, welcome to the United States. I regret my inability to greet you in person, but my state of health prevents me from traveling. I have asked my old friend Andrew J. Harmond to look after you. You can trust him implicitly. Your affectionate great-uncle, Amílcar Cavalcanti.' "

"What are those other papers?"

"One's a kind of voucher for a suite at the Fairmont Hotel, here in San Francisco. The other's a check for a hundred thousand dollars."

"A hundred thousand, are you sure? Dear old Amílcar, I adore him!"

"So do I. The only trouble is, he never wrote this letter."

"Great-uncle Amílcar doesn't have a cent, Samantha—he's flat broke. He used to have a mint of money in the old days, but he spent it all."

Amílcar was the black sheep of the Cavalcanti family, Candido explained. It had all started when he was a young man, and marriage failed to cure him because he'd sailed for Europe in 1871, immediately after the ceremony.

"Ever heard of a composer called Jacques Offenbach?"

She shook her head.

"He was a great friend of Amílcar's. The old man claims he even made him the hero of one of his operas. Don't you know the aria that begins *Je suis brésilien, pom-pom-pom-pom*'?"

"No."

"The Brazilian in question was Great-uncle Amílcar. Well, based on him anyway."

They were in their suite at the Fairmont Hotel, whose windows overlooked San Francisco Bay. They'd slept for twelve solid hours, had dinner and gone back to bed for their first lovemaking on American soil— Samantha's own, personal welcome to the United States, as she put it.

Great-uncle Amílcar had returned from Europe without a dollar to his name. He lived in a big country house, to be sure, but he didn't own a thing. In thirty years of *la vie parisienne* he'd sold his houses, his estates, his shares of industrial corporations, banks and shipping lines, even his various collections. And it was Dom Trajano—

"Your father."

"That's right, Papa. It was Papa who bought them all from him—or rather, Papa and my paternal grandfather between them. They were so keen to keep up appearances, so determined to conceal the fact that a Cavalcanti de Noronha was destitute, they let Amílcar keep his house at Botafogo. They even pay his servants. When he needs a new shirt he has to send the old one to São Paulo. If they consider it beyond repair they buy him a replacement."

"You're joking."

"I'm not, I assure you."

Candido had a strange feeling. He'd never told that story to anyone. Nobody knew it apart from Dom Trajano, his two brothers and the family's attorneys and accountants. He himself had heard it from Amílcar, who cackled with laughter when passing it on. The old man found it exquisitely amusing that Dom Trajano and the Cavalcanti family should be so hidebound by their own prejudices that they felt obliged to feed, house and keep him in style. "To be honest, Candido, I always knew they'd be reduced to it in the end, so I spent my money with an easy mind—money you'll inherit anyway, being your father's heir. I needn't even feel remorseful at having dispossessed you. Isn't it a scream, my boy?"

"All right," said Samantha, "if it wasn't your great-uncle who sent you the hundred thousand, maybe your father sent it via him."

"I doubt it. Papa has always detested Amílcar."

"If your great-uncle's anything like your description of him, I'm not surprised. My mother would detest him too."

"Probably."

"Maybe he had something left to sell?"

"He doesn't own a thing, I tell you. Except Leopolda."

Leopolda being a locomotive, not a woman. It was the last remaining locomotive in Amílcar's collection, but it wasn't worth much. It didn't even go and would never go again—not if the engineer, Ezra McAuliffe, was dead, as he doubtless was.

"Do *you* know this Andrew Harmond?"

"Never heard of him," Samantha replied. "Why don't we look him up? Then you'll know who got him to give you all that lovely money."

They were back in bed playing beggar-my-neighbor, the only card game Candido claimed to understand. Samantha beat him hands down. His thoughts were elsewhere. Why didn't she want them to go to Brazil? In Brazil he could make his peace with Dom Trajano and all would be well. No Tchadayev in the world could possibly harm them there. From Great-uncle Amílcar his thoughts turned, by a natural association of ideas, to the balmy nights of Rio, to his life at São Paulo before being dragooned into the army, and to Bragança Boa Vista, the property where he'd spent his happiest days as a child. All these recollections infused him with melancholy.

It was nearly midday when Samantha woke him. She handed him the newspapers without a word: two Russian immigrants had been murdered in San Francisco the night before. They had recently disembarked and even more recently had their throats cut from ear to ear. Jaguar had been busy again.

Welcome to the United States.

◆　◆　◆

They caught the first train out.

"We should have waited for the next one," Samantha remarked, "—the one to Los Angeles. We could have gone to Hollywood. I'd love to see William Hart in the flesh."

The train stopped at Sacramento. They carefully surveyed the faces of the people getting in, but without result.

"Candido, what say we make our way down the cars one by one, just in case we see someone we know?"

Candido dismissed this idea as pointless. Even if they discovered one of Alekhin's minions on board, what would they do, inform the police?

And tell them what? They would only incriminate themselves. Besides, if Alekhin had steered them to the United States he would be watching their every move with the aid of people whose faces they didn't know.

They combed the train in both directions and scrutinized everyone on board, railroad employees included.

"Can a Red be black?"

Not much of a joke, but it gave them a fit of the giggles.

"I'm looking for someone who speaks Russian," Candido told the conductor. "I'm a student, you see, and I need some practice for my exams."

Their search had yielded nothing, but three first-class passengers had been closeted in their compartments since the train pulled out.

"Someone told me one of them speaks Russian."

"Two-A is Mr. William Fox," said the conductor. "He's from the east. Three-A is Mr. Carl Laemmle—he's in pictures too. I know them both— they often travel L.A. to New York. I don't think either of them speaks Russian."

The third passenger was a Madame Armelle, a French lady in the fashion trade. She'd boarded the train at San Francisco and didn't want to be disturbed. She was going all the way to New York.

"What's she like?" Samantha asked. "Maybe I know her—I've got relatives in the fashion trade."

Madame Armelle was tall, almost as tall as Samantha, and around thirty. Dark-haired and very elegant.

It might be Matriona, Samantha conceded, but that she found hard to believe. It would mean that the woman who had helped her at Harbin was one of the Jaguar's Claws, as Candido had christened them. A female cutthroat? It seemed improbable.

The train had climbed the twilit foothills of the Sierra Nevada by the time they sat down to eat in the dining car. Someone at the next table pointed out the Donner Pass, where, seventy-five years earlier, several dozen snow-bound emigrants trekking west had died of exposure, the survivors engaging in cannibalism. Just before Reno two men politely asked Candido and Samantha if they might share their table. They introduced themselves as Carl Laemmle and William Fox. The conductor had passed on Candido's inquiry, but neither of them spoke Russian. William Fox admitted to being Hungarian by birth, but even his Magyar was rusty. Yes, they were personally acquainted with William Hart and Douglas Fairbanks and Mary Pickford. Before long they became engrossed in movie talk.

Samantha and Candido returned to their sleeper. Beyond Reno the landscape became an endless desert interspersed with dried-up lake beds resembling sheets of burnished silver in the moonlight.

Candido brooded in silence. Alekhin had invented Jaguar as a means of eliminating anyone he considered a threat or hindrance to the Russian Revolution. By blaming all these grisly murders on Jaguar he was mobilizing public opinion against the anarchists and encouraging a belief that the communists weren't so bad after all; in short, that they were the kind of people one could do business with. Alekhin had sent Jaguar to the United States to keep up the good work. Those two murders at San Francisco were only a modest beginning. . . .

"Stop being so moody," said Samantha. "Shut that goddamned door and come to bed."

Candido was sitting where he could watch the corridor. If the Frenchwoman decided to leave her compartment he would see her.

"There'll be throats cut wherever we go," he said. "We'll be knee-deep in gore. I'm going to be more famous than William Hart and Douglas Fairbanks combined."

"I'm not listening."

"We'll have to steer clear of Russian immigrants, Red or White, not to mention politicians, journalists, secret agents, diplomats . . ."

"I'm asleep," Samantha said.

"We'll also have to avoid cities and public places—anywhere where someone might plant a bomb."

No comment. Samantha turned her face to the wall. The curve of her hip was particularly alluring.

"No alibi, that's the only trouble with hiding someplace where there aren't any throats to be cut. No one would be able to testify that we'd been good, and that wouldn't solve a thing. On the contrary."

It was an hour since Carl Laemmle and William Fox had returned from the diner and wished them good night in passing. The corridor was dim and deserted. Candido, still watching for the slightest movement, had the Grimmelshausen open on his lap at one of his favorite passages. He knew it by heart, anyway.

"Maybe we could put an announcement in the paper: 'Beware, Jaguar is here! All those with reason to think the Cheka have it in for them are advised to make themselves scarce. You have been warned.' "

Except that that would alert the U.S. police. Everything would come out: Berlin, Moscow, Harbin, San Francisco . . . At best, he'd be jailed for a hundred and fifty years. No, their best bet was Brazil—Brazil would solve everything. Dom Trajano would have to step in, and then . . .

Candido's heart leapt at the thought of showing Samantha around Bragança Boa Vista. The beauty of it would take her breath away.

Samantha jumped up and pulled on her robe. Her manner was tense but determined, her face set in a furious scowl.

"Where are you going?" he asked.

Where did he think? She was going to knock on that Frenchwoman's door and take a look at her. Once she'd satisfied herself that Madame Armelle wasn't Matriona or Afonka in drag, she would be able to get some sleep.

He watched her make her way along the darkened corridor, and pause outside the door. "Madame Armelle?" she called softly, then prepared to knock—and stopped dead.

She was rather pale when she returned.

"There's blood coming from under the door, Candido."

◆　◆　◆

"What are you going to do?"

He'd opened his suitcase and removed a shirt.

"Mop it up, of course. What do you expect me to do?"

"Mop it up?"

Yes, unless she wanted him to call the conductor—who, on finding the body of a woman with her throat cut from ear to ear, would summon the police. The police would question them and, sooner or later, put two and two together.

She produced a slip from her own bag. They were down on their hands and knees, mopping away, when the conductor appeared.

"Our dog," Candido explained. "He lifted his leg and before we could stop him . . ."

"You should have called me," the conductor said. "After forty years with the railroad I'm used to this kind of problem. You'd be amazed, the animals I've seen folks take on trains. Strange color, though."

"That's because he's a Tibetan wolfhound," said Candido. "All Tibetan wolfhounds pee red."

Attracted by the noise, William Fox and Carl Laemmle had donned their robes and were peering out into the corridor.

"A Tibetan wolfhound?" queried Carl Laemmle.

The conductor looked puzzled. "I didn't see any dog with you."

"He's a miniature Tibetan wolfhound," Candido told him.

"We'd show him to you," Samantha added, "but he's very fierce."

"You should put him under contract," William Fox told Carl Laemmle. "It'd be one in the eye for Erich von Stroheim."

"Like me to get rid of those cloths you've been using?" the conductor
suggested. "I'll dump 'em in the trash can next stop."

"A brand-new slip and shirt?" said Samantha. "Not on your life."

"Better keep your voice down or you'll wake the French lady," said
the conductor.

They all dispersed.

Silence.

Candido said, "I don't believe it's the real thing. Blood, maybe, but
not human blood."

He'd thought it over, and that was the only possible explanation.

"You think they poured it on the floor for fun, just when I got to the
door?"

"You called her name. They must have recognized your voice."

"They could have escaped through the window."

"I just put my head out and looked. It's shut."

"So why did they stage this performance?"

"To make us get off the train."

"Well, are we getting off or aren't we?"

"I don't know."

"Couldn't we pull the emergency handle?"

"In the middle of nowhere?"

"You're always so goddamned indecisive!"

The train made its next stop, a brief one, at a little place called Winnemucca. According to the Southern Pacific guide they'd bought before
leaving San Francisco, Winnemucca had two thousand inhabitants and
was nearly in the middle of nowhere as you could get. Besides, it was
snowing.

Samantha was all set to get out.

"No," he told her, "not here."

She went back to bed. The train completed its crossing of the Sierra
Nevada. By daybreak they were skirting the dreary expanse of Great Salt
Lake. Should they get out or not?

Candido turned flippant with fatigue and nervous tension. Why worry?
The self-styled Frenchwoman hibernating in Compartment 4A was a
female vampire who'd spilled her bedtime drink.

Salt Lake City was announced. The train slowed, the sky cleared.
Dominating the city in the northeast, the huge dome of the capitol stood
outlined against a panorama of snow-capped mountains. William Fox,
who joined them for breakfast in the diner, recounted the story of his life.
He'd started his career in the Bronx as half of a duo named the Schmaltz

Brothers; now he owned his own film company. Any movie starring Tom
Mix or Pearl White was his. Important pictures currently in preproduc-
tion included one about the queen of Sheba and another about the count
of Monte Cristo. . . .

"Candido!"

The platform had just swum into view. Candido followed the direction
of Samantha's gaze. The man carrying the traveling salesman's bag was
almost unrecognizable in his fedora and fur-trimmed overcoat. The train
was still moving. Brakes squealed, a loudspeaker started squawking, passengers prepared to alight.

But it was Otto Krantz sure enough. Standing only a yard from the
diner as it glided past, he caught Candido's eye and held it. There was
no surprise in his expression, just a hint of sardonic amusement.

"So we aren't getting out?"

"No," Candido said firmly.

The train was under way again. Otto Krantz hadn't boarded it. He
lingered on the platform for a while, absolutely motionless except when
putting a cigarette to his lips at precisely regular intervals. Then, just
before the whistle blew, he turned on his heel and made for the exit like
one of the late Oskar Kuppelweiser's clockwork toys.

"Well, where _do_ we get out?"

"New York. I think we should go all the way."

Candido studied the telegram he'd just been handed by the conductor.
It was addressed to "Candido Stevenson Cavalcanti, on board the San
Francisco–New York express."

LOOK FORWARD CELEBRATE YOUR ARRIVAL NEW YORK WITH
PARTY TO END ALL PARTIES STOP A REMINDER OF AMÍLCAR AND
GOOD OLD DAYS STOP YOU WILL RECOGNIZE ME BY THE FLOW-
ERS STOP SIGNED THE SCARLET PEONY.

"What's all that about?" Samantha demanded.

He hadn't the least idea, but the style was very reminiscent of Great-
uncle Amílcar. All at once he felt his spirits revive.

"Candido, there's no one left in 4A. She must have gotten off while
we were watching Otto Krantz."

He picked up the balalaika for the first time since leaving Japan. Suddenly inspired, he composed two new songs in quick succession.

"So we aren't getting out because of that telegram?"

"We aren't getting out because I think they want us to do just that."

He'd said the first thing that came into his head. The truth was, he could think of as many reasons for getting off as for staying, and all of them absolutely imperative. The telegram had nothing to do with it. He was almost sure it had been sent by someone acting on Great-uncle Amílcar's behalf.

"How much money do we have left?"

"One hundred and three thousand, six hundred and forty-three dollars."

Samantha had insisted on drawing out the entire sum in cash, and it was she who kept their accounts with loving care.

"According to the advertisements in the last paper I saw," Candido said, "we've got enough to buy seventeen four-bedroom houses, or eighty-two Studebakers, or nine hundred and eighteen refrigerators, or nineteen hundred and ninety-two wireless sets. What's the betting we can get through every last cent in a month?"

She came and lay down beside him, almost on top of him. The balalaika had a narrow escape.

"You're on!"

He hadn't boarded the train, the Man Mountain in lumberjack's attire, but he knew exactly where they were. He'd walked up to their window, flattened his massive hand against it and smiled.

But he had only smiled with his lips. His eyes were as cold as ice.

A twenty-piece orchestra was playing Offenbach's *La Vie Parisienne* when they pulled into New York. Extras dressed as Greeks from *La Belle Hélène* hurriedly unrolled a red carpet for them to step on.

"The resemblance is quite incredible, *mon chéri*! You're Amílcar as he was half a century ago. The same build, the same green eyes, the same happy, innocent, devil-may-care expression. You had only to bat an eyelash and he was into your bed before you knew it. Ah, what memories!"

There were flowers everywhere—a profusion of scarlet peonies. The old lady heading the reception committee was tall and erect. Her figure was still worth a glance, her manner vivacious, her smile dazzling. She radiated high-voltage *joie de vivre* in spite of her seventy years. Grabbing Candido, she kissed him full on the lips, drew back, contemplated him for a moment and kissed him again.

"I'm the Scarlet Peony," she said. "You speak French, I hope? I would

have given you a real reception if I'd had more time, but Amílcar's letter
only reached me the day you landed at San Francisco. You'd gone by the
time Cavanaugh—that's my husband—discovered that your ship had
berthed and mobilized his West Coast attorneys. Your resemblance to
Amílcar isn't only physical, _Dieu merci_—he always stayed at the best hotels
too. I told Cavanaugh you'd be at the Fairmont, and you were. Did you
get my telegram when the train stopped at Salt Lake City? Who's that
beanpole with you? _Bonté divine,_ what an armful! Amílcar liked them tall
too—I mean, look at me! How is the old _coquin_? He must be nearly
eighty, no? It was he that christened me the Scarlet Peony, can you guess
why? He used to say it was a physiological marvel. I'd show you if I were
twenty years younger, but I'm not. Besides, Cavanaugh wouldn't like
it—he still gets jealous."

Still playing, the orchestra preceded them across the concourse. The
thought that had struck Candido just before their arrival reasserted itself.
He looked around him.

"Call me Aurélie. Does the beanpole understand French? Not from
the look of her. She has a superb derriere, that girl—Amílcar would have
adored her. She's crazy about you, I suppose?"

Candido managed to get in a word at long last. "Yes and no," he said.

"If she isn't dying of love for you she must be mad. That's another
thing you get from Amílcar. You couldn't help wanting to mother him,
he was so touchingly innocent—innocent but an absolute demon between
the sheets. You could have heard me yelling on the other side of Paris!"

He had to be somewhere around, Candido told himself. Why not?
They were only in New York at his instigation.

But he couldn't see a thing in this crowd where everyone topped him
by a head. Aurélie Cavanaugh towed him briskly along, still chattering.
Under other circumstances he would have been delighted to make the
old lady's acquaintance. "Oh yes," he lied, "my great-uncle never stops
talking about you." How could he be expected to remember all the
women Amílcar had mentioned during his reminiscences of long ago?
Equally, how many of the women and girls he'd had at Rio and São Paulo
would remember him as fondly half a century from now? Would Samantha, for that matter?

The Scarlet Peony—_Meu Deus,_ what a nickname!—had ordered a
whole convoy of limousines. The chauffeurs were already doffing their
caps when he turned to look at Samantha. The sight of her was like a
dagger-thrust. She'd raised one tremulous hand and was patting her hair,
which needed no attention; she was also, as though under some irresistible compulsion, glancing at something or someone on her left.

It had to be him. Immensely tall and very good-looking, Alekhin was standing beside a pillar, nonchalantly tapping his palm with a rolled-up newspaper. He made a formidably potent, self-assured impression. Candido caught only the briefest glimpse of him before a movement in the crowd hid him from view.

It wasn't Candido at whom Alekhin had been gazing so intently, but Samantha.

I'm a secondary object of interest. He's going to take her away from me yet again. . . .

Life in the ensuing weeks was fast and furious. Hilarious, too.

Aurélie refused to let them stay at a hotel. She lent them an entire floor of her mansion on Fifty-ninth Street, which overlooked Central Park, and threw various parties-to-end-all-parties, not only in New York, but at her estate on the Long Island Sound and on her Arizona ranch.

They went to see Andrew J. Harmond right after they returned from one of these trips. Harmond was out the first time they called at his office on East Thirty-fourth Street. Candido left his name and address, and two weeks later a message reached him fixing an appointment at Harmond's home.

Harmond turned out to be a smallish man in his mid-thirties. The faintly oriental eyes in his olive-skinned face were those of a person more shrewd than intellectual. His duplex occupied the two top floors of an apartment house on Fifty-fifth Street. Throughout the interview another man, possibly a valet or secretary, hovered in the background like a guardian angel. For protection against Jaguar?

"I'm anxious to know," Candido began, "why you sent me a hundred thousand dollars in San Francisco."

"And paid for our suite at the Fairmont," Samantha added.

Harmond contemplated them thoughtfully.

"I know nothing about a hotel bill."

"But you did shell out the hundred thousand?"

"Yes."

"Why?"

"As a favor to a business associate."

"Called Alexis Mikhailovich Alekhin?"

"The name means nothing to me."

No reaction: he seemed to be telling the truth. Candido surveyed the walls of the big double drawing room. There were only six pictures in sight, but they weren't just any old pictures.

"Mr. Harmond," said Candido, "you're an international businessman. More specifically, you do a lot of business with Russia."

Harmond smiled.

"It's not illegal."

"You supply the Soviet authorities with grain and machinery, and when they're short of cash they pay you in works of art."

"On occasion, yes."

"Are you acquainted with Vladimir Ilyich Lenin?"

"Intimately," Harmond smiled again.

Candido switched to Russian. "Do you speak Russian with Comrade Vladimir Ilyich while taking tea together and deciding on Jaguar's next victim?"

"I didn't get that, but if you're asking whether I speak Russian, the answer's no. President Lenin has an excellent command of English."

"I've met him too. We went grouse shooting together near Nizhni Novgorod."

"An exceptional man," said Harmond. "A true friend."

"Was it he that asked you to give me the hundred thousand?"

Harmond's laugh conveyed that Lenin would never concern himself with such a trifle.

"Do you know a painter by the name of Monet, Mr. Cavalcanti?"

"Claude Monet," Candido said swiftly, "born in Paris in 1840. It was his painting 'Impression, Sunrise' that prompted a hostile critic to coin the term 'Impressionism' in 1872."

Herr Doktor had no time for Monet's "daubs," as he called them, but Candido admired them greatly. He couldn't resist glancing at Samantha. All right, so he might not know who Napoleon was, but he was well up on artists. He could bet she'd never even heard of Monet.

"Monet is one of my favorite painters," said Harmond. "Several of his canvases were included in a transaction I completed some time ago—they were part payment for some consignments I'd delivered. The hundred thousand dollars came with them. I was informed that the money was owed to a man named Cavalcanti, a Brazilian residing in Rio."

"Amílcar Cavalcanti de Noronha."

"Yes, that was the name."

"He's my great-uncle. Do you know him?"

"I don't have that honor. To be on the safe side, I made inquiries about the Cavalcanti family. The results were thoroughly reassuring. Do you think it probable that your great-uncle sold some paintings by Monet, Degas, Renoir and Bazille before the war?"

"Highly probable."

"My informants came to the same conclusion, so I paid over the hundred thousand dollars on the strength of a letter from Senhor Cavalcanti asking me to remit the money to you instead of him in settlement of all outstanding debts. I have, of course, preserved that letter, together with the receipt you signed at San Francisco and the deed of sale, dated 1905, whereby Senhor Cavalcanti sold a batch of canvases to the Hermitage Museum in St. Petersburg for a sum that was not paid in full at the time, doubtless because of the disruption caused by the first Russian revolution of 1905."

The doorbell rang, but the valet-secretary didn't move a muscle. Someone else answered the door. Voices could be heard.

"Please excuse me," Harmond said. "I was expecting some friends."

It all fitted. Great-uncle Amílcar, who was friendly with Monet, Sisley and sundry other painters, might as well have bought some paintings from them and subsequently sold them to a Russian museum. Even if the whole story was a fake, it was a well-devised one. If Candido Cavalcanti, the Jaguar, were arrested tomorrow, Andrew J. Harmond could not only affirm his own innocence but prove it.

Except for one point.

"If you hadn't vouched for me," he said, "the immigration authorities would never have let me into the country."

Harmond raised his eyebrows.

"Vouched for you?" he said. "I did no such thing."

It seemed that Great-uncle Amílcar's letter had given the date and place of Candido's arrival in the States and requested that the money be paid at that time. Harmond had complied with this request—or rather, he'd instructed his West Coast attorney to do so.

"I wasn't here then. When did you land? Christmas Day? I was abroad—thousands of miles away. I left New York around December tenth and didn't return until the end of January. The authorities said I'd vouched for you? They were mistaken, I assure you."

Andrew J. Harmond smiled with an air of total sincerity and faint amusement. Several people walked in, one of whom Candido recognized, having seen him at a Cavanaugh reception, as the governor of New York State.

"Let's go," Samantha said.

◆　◆　◆

"Going out?"

Samantha met his eye in the bathroom mirror.

"I'm having lunch with Uncle Moritz. You can come if you like."

"No, thanks."

Fat, red-faced Uncle Moritz was in the construction business like Harry Cavanaugh and worth at least fifty million dollars. Candido found him tedious rather than odious. Uncle Moritz tended to act as if he didn't exist. He'd once asked him how much Dom Trajano was worth. Candido, who hadn't the least idea, named a figure at random. Five hundred million dollars, he said. Uncle Moritz hadn't believed him, but he felt pretty sure he'd got it right to the nearest hundred million.

"I'm off," Samantha said. "Sure you won't come?"

"Positive. I'm going to read a bit. Give Uncle Moritz my best."

He went to a window and waited. Uncle Moritz's offices were in lower Manhattan. Samantha emerged, crossed East Fifty-ninth Street, skirted the railings of Central Park, and turned left onto Fifth Avenue. Uptown, in other words.

It doesn't mean a thing. Her old fool of an uncle must have arranged to meet her at a restaurant. Aren't you ashamed? Yes, but it makes no difference.

He spent the next half hour trying vainly to read one of the books he'd bought since their arrival in New York.

She's with him, I tell you. She's in his arms.

He tossed the Henry James aside and went downstairs.

It was a glorious day in late spring. He made his way along Fifth Avenue, occasionally turning right to investigate the streets facing the park. There weren't many restaurants, but he paused a couple of times and squinted through the windows. No sign of Samantha and Uncle Moritz.

You're being ridiculous.

Yes, I know.

He walked as far as Harlem. Attracted by the sound of music to a café where some black musicians were playing the blues, he ordered a sandwich and a glass of milk. He'd already sighted Otto Krantz on three separate occasions.

Krantz was now standing twenty or thirty yards away on the sidewalk across the street, chain-smoking and pretending to read a newspaper. Absolutely motionless except when consuming cigarette after cigarette with metronomic regularity, he displayed spine-chilling reserves of patience.

Candido's original intention was to keep the man hanging around for hours on end, nothing more. It was a petty form of revenge: unlike Krantz, he was sitting comfortably, eating and drinking and listening to the kind of music he liked.

We'll see who cracks first. Besides, if Samantha gets back to the Cavanaughs and finds me gone, she may wind up worrying about me. So much the better.

And then a wild idea took shape in his mind.

Otto Krantz had now been cooling his heels on Harlem's 125th Street for six hours. By nightfall Candido had consumed four sandwiches and eight glasses of milk. A black musician of his own age—he came from New Orleans and introduced himself as Louis Armstrong—had been playing the trumpet and cornet superbly. When Candido picked out the melody line of "Samantha's Song" on a guitar he joined in with a broad smile but observed that they differed in their approach to rhythm.

Candido, who had already relieved himself once in the backyard, paid it another visit. His idea had matured. It was not the most original plan but it would do. The yard was bounded by a brick wall. He got over it and into the yard next door by climbing on an old icebox, made his way through a laundry and came out on 125th Street a hundred yards from Otto Krantz, who still hadn't moved. Time went by. Having failed to see him reappear, Krantz hurried into the café. Candido secreted himself under the steps of a brownstone. He could only see the feet of the passersby, but that was enough. Krantz was identifiable less by his shoes and trousers than by his mechanical, almost zombielike gait. Candido counted to twenty, then rose and followed him.

No cab, no bus, no subway. Otto Krantz proceeded on foot in the same robotic manner. Stopping only once to buy some cigarettes, he reached Central Park and turned down Madison Avenue. He had now passed Saint Patrick's Cathedral, never having varied his pace since leaving Harlem.

Maybe he knows you're tailing him. Maybe that's why he hasn't taken a bus or the subway—so you won't lose him.

Along Forty-second Street, then Thirty-fifth. He was still heading south. It was seven-thirty. Samantha would be back by now and growing anxious.

Krantz turned left and kept going. Two hundred yards farther on he disappeared into a small hotel.

Candido waited.

Ten seconds later his heart gave a jump: the Man Mountain had just passed him, two yards away, wearing a black leather cap and a bulky red-and-black-checked lumber jacket. He, too, disappeared into the hotel.

Candido continued to wait.

Half an hour went by, and this time he spotted Stepa Onegin entering the hotel. Stepa was his usual slim, elegant self—far too elegant for such a seedy establishment.

Krantz will tell him that he lost me—or, if they always meant to lure me here, that their plan has worked and I'm right where they want me.

Stepa emerged and hailed a cab on Third Avenue. Another cab cruised by a moment later.

"Follow that cab, please."

On to East Eighty-sixth Street, a neighborhood so abounding in delicatessens and restaurants with German names that it might have been in Berlin. Stepa showed no interest in any of these. He climbed the steps of a narrow-fronted house with only one window on each of its three stories.

Candido surveyed the house, which was painted pale green. Each window had a little corbeled balcony adorned with red geraniums.

That's where he's staying. I know he's there—I can sense it.

"Six slices of Westphalian ham, please," Candido asked in German.

He'd gone into the nearest delicatessen, which was about to close its doors.

"I'd like a knife too. A big one. We've just moved in, my mother and I. She's made a roast and I've nothing to carve it with."

The proprietor eyed him and hesitated. His knives and cleavers were of finest imported Solingen steel, he stressed, and he wouldn't part with them for anything in the world. He wouldn't sell Candido a knife, but he would lend him one against a deposit of fifty dollars, duly receipted.

Candido emerged, never having taken his eyes off the pale green house. The lower windows were lit, and he caught an occasional glimpse of two tall figures—but then, Stepa Onegin was almost as tall as Alekhin.

So what are you going to do now, ring the bell and butcher everyone inside until you get to Him? You'll never kill anyone—you're not up to it.

There remained the roof. He abandoned the doorway he'd been lurking in. The street was now deserted and the delicatessen had shut like all the rest. The streetlights left little pools of shadow. He spotted a narrow alleyway, hardly more than a passage, made his way along it and scaled a wooden fence that only just supported his hundred and thirty pounds. He perched on the top, then clambered lizardlike up the back of a house with the aid of some trelliswork, until he reached a second-floor window. Having scrambled through this into the room beyond, which was clearly a nursery, he made his way out on to the landing. Someone was playing a phonograph on the floor below. On his left, a little staircase led to the attic.

He emerged onto the roof less than a minute later. The pale green house was only two doors away. Suddenly he heard a noise—from the street this time: the sound of a car idling. He crawled forward on his belly, braking himself against the pitch of the roof with his palms, until the street came into view. The driver of the cab waiting below had one arm dangling out of the window.

And there in the glow from a streetlight stood a man and a woman.

Oh God, I knew it.

Alekhin put out his huge hand and touched Samantha's arm. She didn't shake it off, just turned after a moment or two and got into the cab. He shut the door.

The cab drove off in the direction of Fifth Avenue.

Alekhin watched it go, then went inside.

Not up to killing anyone? Who says so?

The skylight in the roof of the pale green house opened at last. Candido slipped through and closed it behind him. The layout was the same as that of the first house. A murmur of voices drifted up from the ground floor. The words were unintelligible, but the language was Russian.

The voices increased in volume as Candido made his way down to the first floor, but he still couldn't pick out individual words. The upper floors had been empty. The second floor, though almost unfurnished, was illuminated. The room overlooking the street contained nothing but a rickety old table with a telephone on it. There was a mattress on the floor of one of the two back rooms. The bed in the other had no bedclothes, just a blanket and a pillow, but there were two tan leather suitcases beside it and a toilet case and a wallet on a small chest of drawers near the bathroom door.

Either He's just arrived, or He's leaving.

The wallet was open. It contained a first-class boat ticket to Stockholm bearing tomorrow's date, a thick wad of hundred-dollar bills, a driver's license, and a German passport. The photographs on the latter two documents were of Alekhin, the name was given as Peter Joachim Schugger, born in Lübeck, July 22, 1890, profession: publisher. The passport stamps indicated that Herr Schugger was a frequent traveler.

He has only to crook his finger and she comes running.

Candido put everything back, retrieved his butcher's knife, and went out on the landing. The men below were still talking. He felt tempted to creep downstairs and eavesdrop on them, but that might have meant taking on two opponents instead of one, both of them bigger and more experienced than himself.

No, better to enlist the element of surprise. He stationed himself where he couldn't be seen from the stairs, gripping the knife so hard his hand trembled. He was almost overcome by a sudden urge to vomit. The awareness of his physical inferiority made him doubt if he would be able to strike when the time came. Tears welled up in his eyes.

Twenty minutes or more. Then a door opened and the voices became intelligible at last. ". . . and that'll be that," Stepa said, completing a sentence whose opening words Candido didn't catch. "Exactly," said Alekhin. "Have a good trip" and "Thanks" were the concluding words. The front door closed. Silence.

Have they both gone?

Another surge of panic. The silence was unbroken, but he could sense that someone was there. Alekhin—it had to be. Seconds crept by, fraught with menace, before an almost inaudible creak made itself heard. He was climbing the stairs!

Candido gripped the knife even harder, blinking away the tears that blurred his vision. A moment later Alekhin materialized at the top of the stairs. He was already turning, making for the bedroom.

Candido just had time to see the big man pivot like lightning before he struck, his pent-up breath emerging in a strangled cry. The long blade darted toward Alekhin's belly and almost simultaneously stopped dead. Candido felt an agonizing pain take possession of his wrist and arm as they were crushed and twisted. The knife began to move of its own accord, against his will. The tip of the blade changed direction and headed inexorably for his own chest, penetrating his shirt, pricking the skin.

Then it came to a stop.

"Cavalcanti?"

Alekhin's tone was vaguely surprised, tinged with amusement and contempt. He hadn't even bothered to parry the blow with both hands.

"I'd drop it if I were you."

The knife dug a little deeper into Candido's chest. He opened his fingers and it fell to the floor. An instant later he was seized by the throat, lifted off his feet and flung through the door of the front room. He landed on the telephone table, smashing it. Alekhin bent down, picked him up one-handed like an old shoe and, still smiling disdainfully, sent him hurtling through the door again. He fell in a heap at the top of the stairs.

"How long have you been here, Cavalcanti? Were you here when I stripped her naked—when I took her? No, I'm sure you weren't—you wouldn't have been able to restrain yourself. Don't tell me you're crying, little man? You're not even worth killing."

Candido started to crawl away, blinded by tears, but the huge hand fastened itself on his neck again. Powerless as a puppet in the face of such terrifying physical strength, he was dragged downstairs with his arms and legs bouncing every which way.

"You don't exist, Cavalcanti. You're nothing. I'm not even annoyed with you—I'm a stranger to that emotion."

Candido traversed the hallway in the same manner, legs trailing, half strangled by the fearful pressure on his neck. At last Alekhin set him on his feet.

"I was peacefully minding my own business when I was attacked by a pathetic little runt whose identity and motives were a mystery to me. I could have called the police, but I didn't. I simply ejected him, complete with knife."

The door opened. Candido found himself standing on the steps outside the pale green house. Alekhin patted him on the head and smiled.

"Go play somewhere else."

The knife went clattering down the steps, the door closed.

◆　◆　◆

He got back to the Cavanaughs' around three A.M.

"My God, where have you been?"

Samantha had hurried out on to the landing in her dressing gown. He climbed the last few stairs and walked straight past her, brushing aside her outstretched hand.

"Candido?"

He shut himself in the bathroom, removed his jacket, tie and shirt, and deposited the knife in the washbasin. Only the tip bore traces of blood— his blood. He examined the wound in his chest. It was only superficial, half an inch deep at most, and had bled very little.

"Won't you tell me what happened, Candido? I've been worried sick."

The tears returned. He fought them off by splashing water in his face. Samantha had grown impatient and was banging on the door. He toweled his face dry, put his shirt on again and hid the knife behind the column supporting the basin. Finally, having taken several deep breaths, he emerged.

"You might at least tell me where you've been."

Candido restrained a momentary urge to slap her. He went to the wardrobe and took out his suitcases.

"What are you doing?"

"I'm off."

"Off where?"

"Brazil. I'm going home."

"Without me?"

A suitable retort eluded him.

"Candido, please . . ."

He'd sworn to say nothing while roaming the streets, but the words just slipped out.

"I shadowed them. First Otto Krantz, then Stepa Onegin."

He sounded cool and detached—that, at least, was a minor feat of self-control. So were his toings and froings across the room as he proceeded to pack his bags.

"Oh," she said at last. Then, after another pause: "Did you see Aliochka?"

"Yes, I saw him."

"You had a fight?"

"An epic fight," he said. "I broke every bone in his body. It was a walkover."

"I don't like it when you get sarcastic. Anyway, I can explain."

"Oh, sure."

He was in the bathroom now, getting his toilet things together.

"Listen, Candido. They've killed a lot of people here in the States— we'd have known it if we'd read the papers. They've pinned the murders on Jaguar and his girlfriend, but they haven't given the authorities our names the way they did in Germany. Not yet. The police haven't established a connection between these murders and the ones in Berlin and Bremen, but it won't be long before they do."

He strapped up the first bag. It occurred to him that he would need a little money, so he took some from the drawer in which they'd casually deposited their hundred thousand-plus dollars when they moved in with the Cavanaughs. There was plenty of it left in spite of all their efforts. Aurélie took umbrage whenever they tried to pay for anything.

"I agreed to have lunch with Aliochka yesterday, but only because I wanted to beg him to leave us alone. You weren't here when I got back, and no one knew where you'd gone. Hours went by. I began to think he'd done something terrible to you. Not knowing where to find him, I went back to the restaurant. Then I spotted Afonka tailing me. You know Afonka: he said he'd no idea where you were and left it at that, just rocked with laughter. Finally he gave me that address on East Eighty-sixth Street. I made it just after nine. Stepa Onegin was there too. Aliochka refused to answer any of my questions, so I came home. That's all there is to tell."

"Oh, sure."

"Jesus, how it irritates me when you say that! Are you really leaving for Brazil? You don't even know when there's a boat."

Indeed he did. He'd paid a visit to the docks in the hours since Alekhin had dismissed him with a pat on the head. There was a boat sailing for New Orleans in six hours' time. From there another boat would take him to Rio via Recife and Bahia. He'd already bought himself a ticket and reserved a cabin.

Say nothing.

He strapped up the other case.

"I'm coming with you, Candido."

Pretend you didn't hear that.

Samantha sat down on the floor with her back against the door and her long arms wrapped around her legs.

"Brazil's all right with me. We ought to have gone there in the first place. It's all settled, I'm coming with you."

No, never. Out of the question.

He sat down on the bed, close to tears again.

It was four-thirty A.M. when they slunk out of the Cavanaughs' front door. Candido wrote Aurélie a farewell letter on the edge of a table in an all-night café, and Samantha added a few words plus some crosses that she said meant kisses.

Otto Krantz had parked right outside. He wasn't alone, either. The Man Mountain was in the passenger seat.

"Think they'll try to stop us?"

"I don't know."

They killed time till daybreak over an extended breakfast. Candido went off to drop the letter in a mailbox across the street, came back, finished his hot chocolate and paid the check. Samantha picked up two suitcases and a grip while he took charge of the rest. They emerged from the café, walked past the two men in the car, who showed no sign of recognition, and hailed a cab.

Samantha kept peering out of the rear window. "There's another car following us," she reported. "I think it's Matriona."

Their cab dropped them at the docks. Otto Krantz pulled up a few yards away. He and the Man Mountain got out and leaned against the car like a couple of sightseers come to watch a ship leave port. The second car pulled up too, but the woman at the wheel stayed put. Candido couldn't see her face clearly through the windscreen, which was ablaze with reflected sunlight.

"They won't try anything here," Samantha said. "Too many people around."

Candido bought another ticket. The first-class cabin reserved in his name was big enough for two.

"Look, Candido."

Stepa Onegin had turned up too.

They entrusted their baggage to a sailor and went aboard. A loud-speaker announced that the ship would be sailing in half an hour's time. Candido accompanied the sailor to the cabin, tipped him twenty dollars and joined Samantha on deck. She was leaning over the rail.

"Afonka's there too," she said.

They were all there, all five of the Jaguar's Claws: Afonka Tchadayev, Stepa Onegin, the Man Mountain, Otto Krantz and, almost on a level with them, a woman wearing a mauve suit and a hat to match. Matriona, beyond a doubt.

"I'm sure it's her. They're letting us go, Candido."

Candido was exhausted. There were too many questions whirling around in his brain. Samantha could well have been lying, but he'd given in as usual, like the weak-kneed fool he was. Thanks to him—thanks to his initial stupidity in agreeing to plant a bomb in a Berlin cinema—Herr Doktor had been shanghaied by the Reds. He might even be dead.

Why hadn't Alekhin killed *him*? What else did he have up his sleeve?

The ship was slowly pulling away from the quayside.

Does she seriously think—

"By the way," said Samantha, "I'm going to have a baby, and if you ask me who the father is I'll jump overboard right now."

Does she seriously think the Claws will leave it at that? Well, if Afonka and Company mean to follow us to Brazil, let them come and be damned. Brazil isn't Mongolia—it isn't even the United States. As soon as I settle my little difference of opinion with Papa they'll have the whole of the Cavalcanti clan to contend with. The Cavalcantis will soon see them off. . . .

Samantha's announcement sank in at last.

Meu Deus!

THE JAGUAR AVOIDS MAN
WHEN IT MEETS HIM AND SELDOM
RETALIATES EVEN WHEN WOUNDED. IT BECOMES
A MAN-EATER ONLY IN VERY EXCEPTIONAL
CIRCUMSTANCES.

andido finally got to see Dom Trajano seven weeks after their arrival in São Paulo. Even prior to that time, nothing indicated that the return of the prodigal son had aroused any particular enthusiasm. No one was there to welcome them when they alighted from the Rio train. No one, that is, except two attorneys, of whom one was Senhor Lascalles, a member of the deputation that had been sent—light-years ago, it seemed—to notify Candido of his summary expulsion and assignment to garrison duty in the Mato Grosso.

"Point number one," Lascalles began. "We have managed to regularize your position vis-à-vis the army. You are no longer considered a deserter and will not be prosecuted. We successfully pleaded—well, a certain mental derangement on your part. Point number two: Dom Trajano does not wish you to set foot in any of his personal residences. He has, however, made his property at São Roque available to you. You may live there and will receive an allowance."

"May I see my father?"

"He's away at present. We shall advise him of your request, which he will doubtless answer as he thinks fit. Another thing: the less you're seen in São Paulo the better for all concerned. That is all we have to say, Dom Candido."

In spite of Lascalles's unfriendly demeanor, Candido and Samantha not only stayed on in São Paulo but made themselves conspicuous. Although the cabinet minister who had hounded Candido was no longer in office and thus in no real position to harm him, and although Candido's colonel in the Mato Grosso was now a general stationed at Manaus on the Amazon, São Paulo's high society joined forces against the new arrivals. The clubs of which Candido had been a member—the Jockey, Automobile and Commercial—barred their doors to him. His stepmother and half sisters were even more standoffish than before, if that was possible, and his old friends shunned him. It seemed that certain rumors were circulating about his doings in Europe—nothing definite, but . . .

All in all, the only person who stood up for him was Ciccio Vaz Vasconselos, but Ciccio was—how could one put it? He'd always had a tendency to kiss and cuddle Candido in the old days, when they used to play croquet together as boys, and now—well, his girlish manner was all too obvious. To have Ciccio fall in love with him at this stage would be the last straw.

The day finally came when Lascalles turned up at the hotel where he and Samantha were staying.

"Your father's back. He'll see you, but not until you comply with his original instructions."

So they left for São Roque, some ten miles southwest of São Paulo. It was, by Cavalcanti standards, a small property, employing only two hundred field hands and eight domestic servants, but Samantha, with a grudging smile, conceded that the house was comfortable enough. At long last, conveyed by Lascalles, the summons came: Dom Trajano would grant his son an audience.

The interview took place in Dom Trajano's majestic office atop a building in the heart of São Paulo's business district, the seat of financial and political power that aroused so much envy, if not hatred, in the rest of the country. Samantha was refused admittance.

Dom Trajano received Candido while standing behind his desk, as if to emphasize their physical disparity. He was a tall, broad-shouldered man with dark hair greying at the temples, an imperious beak of a nose and a hard mouth. He had married Candido's mother at the age of twenty-three and remarried, with a speed that raised a few eyebrows, less than twelve months after she died giving birth. He was now approaching forty-five.

"Don't sit down, it's pointless. I can only spare you a minute."

Not a word or gesture of affection.

"I'm quite uninterested in your excuses. I shall decide what to do with you in due course, provided you behave yourself. As to what exactly happened in Germany, where that imbecile of a tutor sent you, I'm not a man to be satisfied with rumors. I've initiated certain inquiries. When they bear fruit, we shall see."

"But Papa—"

"I don't wish to set eyes on that woman you've seen fit to bring with you. She doesn't exist. Get rid of her."

"Her name is Samantha, and she's—"

"She doesn't exist. I propose to do my duty by you. One more piece of foolishness, however trivial, and I'll stop your allowance and leave you to your own devices. Ask Lascalles if you need anything—he'll pass it on. That's all. Now go."

Candido stared at his father, who was by now absorbed in whatever papers and files were on his desk. When, after a few seconds, Dom Trajano did not return his gaze, Candido followed his father's wishes.

They were attending a ball at a neighboring fazenda. Samantha's figure had ripened considerably.

"Married? What ever gave you that idea?" she said to a group of matrons who were avidly gossiping beneath the jacarandas. "Candido and I merely live together. Besides, he's got several other women, all pregnant to their fingertips. He may not be big, but he's active."

"Let's dance," said Candido.

"His progress through America was positively Homeric," Samantha went on. "Women were cutting their throats for love of him."

"Let's dance."

He hauled her off like a small tug valiantly towing an ocean liner.

"Those silly cows," she said loudly. "Are they all aunts of yours?"

"Only thirty of them. Come on."

People stood aside as they headed for the dance floor.

"You can't dance with me, Candido Cavalcanti, your arms aren't long enough—not unless you hold me from behind."

"Hungry?"

"No."

"Thirsty?"

"No."

Samantha was speaking Brazilian Portuguese, but with an excruciating accent.

"Jesus Christ," Samantha said in an undertone, "let's get out of here."

Only Ciccio escorted them to their car, which had been purchased with the dollars they'd brought from the States. It was a Chandler Cleveland Six with overhead valves and an engine capacity of 3.5 liters.

"Everything will come right in the end," Ciccio assured them. "My father has promised to have a word with Dom Trajano, but not straight away. It'll be easier in a few weeks' time—six months at most. Just make sure you don't cut any throats in the meantime."

"Good thinking," said Candido. He cranked the engine into life.

"Have you read those books I lent you?"

They were by someone called Marcel Proust, Ciccio's favorite author.

"Not yet."

Candido took refuge behind the wheel to avoid being kissed and drove off. The fazenda was only ten or twelve miles from São Roque.

"Tired, Samantha?"

She had her eyes shut and her face turned to catch the breeze blowing through the open window.

"I don't want to go back to São Roque," she said suddenly.

She was sick of the heat, the mosquitoes, the people, their dreary existence at São Roque, her bulging belly.

"We could go to Great-uncle Amílcar's place in Rio," he suggested, "but not till the baby's born."

"Let's go now, right away. Please, Candido."

It was eleven at night. Three hundred miles, and what a road! He wouldn't be able to drive at his usual speed with Samantha in her present condition. It would take them at least twelve hours.

"What if the baby arrives on the way? I mean, all those bumps."

She smiled and said it better wait if it didn't want to be born in a ditch.

They returned to São Roque and packed their bags, Candido taking the Grimmelshausen and the balalaika just in case. Eglantina, the mulatto maidservant who slept in the kitchen, woke up and insisted on coming too.

They set off at daybreak. Halfway to Rio they stopped at a small town called Guaratingeta and lunched at an open-air restaurant with a view of the distant Serra de Mantiqueira in the background. The Paraíba, its ocher waters swollen by the last rains of the Brazilian winter, flowed past within a hundred yards of them. Just beyond it stood a train wreathed in smoke, and stretching away for as far as the eye could see were coffee plantations in which the work of clearing and pricking out had just begun.

"Is it much farther to Rio?"

"We're nearly halfway there."

"It'll wait till then," Samantha said, indicating her belly and helping herself to some more charcoal-broiled meat.

Candido felt a great surge of happiness. This was his native land, and she was adapting to it better than he'd dared to hope. Going to the car, he fetched his balalaika and began to play. Eglantina accompanied him with the aid of two forks and a saucepan, and it wasn't long before twelve or fifteen voices were raised in "Samantha's Song."

Candido had already improvised two new verses when rage and disappointment quenched the flow of inspiration. Well, he told himself, it was bound to happen sooner or later—what else had he expected? He played the last few chords and put the balalaika down.

Then, finally, he turned his head.

_____

"Do you like Brazil, Afonka?"

"Immensely. It's a beautiful country, and so big. A little too hot for my taste, that's all."

Afonka chuckled. He was wearing a white suit and a panama hat.

"What do you call yourself here?"

"Afonka Tchadayev, what else? It's my name." He turned to Samantha. "How are you, Sam?"

"Don't call her Sam," said Candido.

"How are you, *Samantha*?"

"You're looking well, Afonka. Where are Otto Krantz and Matriona and Stepa Onegin and that other great hulk?"

"I don't know what you mean." Afonka chuckled some more. "Those names mean nothing to me."

"Have you been tailing us ever since we left São Paulo?"

"Tailing you? Why should I do that? We met by chance, that's all." Afonka's eyes came to rest on Samantha's swollen belly.

"When is it due?"

"When it suits me," said Samantha. "Nobody gives me orders."

"Nobody would even dream of trying, Samantha."

"You're a long way from home, Afonka, and Candido isn't. Why not get lost? Go back to Russia and tell him you couldn't find us."

Afonka didn't reply. With a meditative smile, he surveyed the dozen-odd blacks and mestizos seated at tables in the arbor of the open-air restaurant. Candido grew impatient.

"Shall we go, Samantha?"

They got back into the Chandler. Afonka remained seated but politely raised his red-ribboned panama.

"A very handsome car you have there," he said in mellifluous Brazilian Portuguese. "Know something, Sam?" He gave another chuckle. "I think it's going to be a girl."

It was, and she was born the night of their arrival at Great-uncle Amílcar's house in Rio de Janeiro. She had blue eyes, but Candido was informed that this meant nothing. All babies had blue eyes at her age.

Why do I never know things like that?

"Come, Voltaire. Sit down and drink a glass of champagne with me."

"I'm not too fond of champagne, Uncle."

"That's because you haven't drunk enough. I had to get through two dozen cases before I developed a taste for it."

Great-uncle Amílcar was even shorter than Candido. His toothless mouth was framed by a white mustache and goatee, and his tremulous hands clutched the gold and ivory knob of a cane in perpetual motion, rotating swiftly and jerkily as if he were trying to drill a hole in the checkered white and indigo floor tiles. His *sobrado,* a mansion perched on the heights above Botafogo beach and set in three acres of tropical garden, was enclosed by countless iron railings in the shape of wasp-waisted Parisian cocottes with little gilded stars adorning their nipples. Sunk into the big central patio was a pool in which Candido had many times swum as a boy. Almost on a level with the garden and separated from it by a few shallow steps were four drawing rooms, two dining rooms, a study, an adjoining library, a long-disused ballroom, a billiard room, a gunroom and the kitchens. The covered gallery encircling the patio was adorned with faded photographs of *la vie parisienne.* Candido knew the story of each by heart. For instance, the name of the lady wearing nothing but a magnificent diamond necklace was Leopolda. The gentleman beside her was a certain Duc de Morny and the man in pince-nez Jacques Offenbach. As for the series of soft, rounded, opalescent hillocks, these were one of Great-uncle Amílcar's most cherished souvenirs: the buttocks of all his favorite mistresses captured on film by Félix Tournachon, alias Nadar. This heartrending farewell gift was a memento of Amílcar's personal Waterloo, the day when every Brazilian bank stopped his checks and refused to advance him another cent.

"Did I ever tell you that story, Voltaire?"

"I believe so, Uncle."

Not more than a hundred and eighty-three times.

"And the one about Emperor Napoleon III and the vicar of Saint-Germain-l'Auxerrois?"

"I think I've heard that one too."

"Something has slipped my mind, Grand-nephew. Didn't I see you with a very pretty girl just now?"

"That was yesterday, Uncle."

"What have you done with her?"

"She's asleep in the Blue Room."

"Good, excellent," said Great-uncle Amílcar, drilling the floor with his cane. Servants were coming and going as if they owned the place. Some were smoking cigars on Chinese couches encrusted with mother-of-pearl, some were lounging in *conversadeiras,* armchairs for two, and others were playing cards. They were herdsmen imported in rotation from other Cavalcantian fazendas and attired in ill-fitting livery. Their function wasn't to wait on Great-uncle Amílcar, simply to create that impression so that no one in Rio could say that a Cavalcanti de Noronha lacked for household staff.

"It has to be admitted," said Great-uncle Amílcar, "that your father doesn't like you very much."

"He has his off days."

I feel like crying, I don't know why. Papa's lack of affection for me is no news to me and hasn't been for ages.

"As for his second wife, she's a fool as well as a bitch. She must be, to have married your father. The same goes for her daughters, your half sisters."

"I'm fond of them all the same."

"You've always been too softhearted, my boy."

I really will start crying if the old man goes on like this. I don't know what's the matter with me.

"I'm leaving you this house and everything in it."

"Thank you, Uncle."

The _sobrado_ wasn't Amílcar's to leave. It belonged to Dom Trajano, but Candido certainly wasn't going to hurt the old man by reminding him of the fact. Even that stuff he was drinking, which he mistook for champagne, was horrible local fizz supplied for a few milreis a bottle by Ferrat, the wine merchant in Rua do Ouvidor.

"You're my sole heir, Grand-nephew. I'm leaving you this _sobrado_ and everything I own: my plantation at Campinas and my fazenda at Bragança Boa Vista, my shipping company, my banking shares, my real estate here in Rio, and, of course, my summer residence at Petrópolis. Have you ever been to my summer residence, Voltaire? It's very beautiful—flowers everywhere. His Imperial Majesty and the famous aviator Alberto Santos-Dumont have houses almost next door. They're nice, quiet neighbors, both of them—you'll have nothing to complain of."

Candido didn't know about Santos-Dumont, but the emperor, whose name he seemed to recall was Pedro II, must have been dead for at least thirty years. Anyway, Great-uncle Amílcar was in no position to bequeath his summer residence at Petrópolis either. It belonged to Dom Trajano like everything else.

"Thank you, Uncle. You're too generous."

The old man sniggered toothlessly.

"I've always made a point of annoying your father. Besides, my boy, I'm very attached to you. Leopolda and you have been dearer to me than anyone else in the world. I'm leaving you everything. Don't worry about Leopolda, by the way. I did the necessary a long time ago."

You can say that again. You gave her enough diamonds to finance the construction of a small palace.

"All I ask, Voltaire, is that you should take care of Domitila. She's getting on a bit now, but you should have seen her seventy-five years ago. She had the cutest little backside in all Brazil."

Amílcar smiled at the old black crone squatting not far away. No one could remember a time when she had not been in the service of Dom Amílcar Cavalcanti de Noronha of Bragança Boa Vista. Born a slave and not emancipated until 1887, Domitila had even accompanied her master to Paris. If she had ever possessed a cute little backside, considerable powers of imagination were required to picture it, because she was now as wrinkled as a fig. Of the dozen official domestics at the *sobrado* at Botafogo, Domitila was the only one to devote herself wholeheartedly to Amílcar, who would long ago have died without her care—of starvation, if nothing else.

"I trust you have some mistresses, Voltaire?"

"No problem there, Uncle."

"Good, good. No one ever invented anything finer than women, my boy—they're miraculous creatures. Even the ugliest of them can be beautiful if you know how to use your eyes. Do you have a particular favorite at the moment?"

"Yes, Uncle."

"Go to my safe—you know the combination: Leopolda 1863–9. The nine stands for the nine times I made love to her in a single night. But I digress: take as much money as you want and buy your lady friend some diamonds in Rue des Ourives. Place Vendôme has a wider selection, but she must have the best. Nothing can ever be too beautiful for a beautiful woman, so never regret your generosity."

"I'll go at once, Uncle."

The safe was empty apart from some cobwebs and several hundred frilly garters.

"What's her name, boy?"

"Samantha."

"A pretty name. Where did you say she was?"

"Asleep in the Blue Room."

"Far be it from me to criticize your family," said Samantha, "but the way they've treated Great-uncle Amílcar gives me a rash."

"At least they didn't stick him in an old folks' home."

"Those servants are impossible. The other day I found a couple of them amusing themselves by getting him drunk, the dirty swine." She paused. "Look at me, Candido. Is anything wrong?"

"The old man's absolutely broke."

"So? We knew that already."

Better change the subject.

"I've found a godfather for the baby: Clovis, one of Domitila's great-grandsons. He's a trolley-car conductor."

"A black?"

"Why, does it bother you?"

She didn't care any more than she cared about the christening, to which she'd given her perfunctory consent. They had, on the other hand, devoted hours of discussion, even at São Roque, to the choice of a name. Candido had favoured Caterina or Kathleen or Catherine for a girl because no female member of his family had ever been called that. Samantha disagreed, so they'd finally settled on Candida, the casting vote being that of Eglantina, the baby's prospective godmother.

"You just changed the subject, Candido. Are you sure everything's all right?"

"Certain."

"You've seen Afonka again, haven't you?"

"No."

I have, but I'm not saying.

"One of the others, then. Otto Krantz or Stepa."

"No, none of them. I'm a little sad about the old man, that's all."

"Uncle?"

Amílcar's eyes opened at the third mention of his name.

"Is that you, Candido?"

"Yes."

"You should come more often. I haven't seen you for ages."

"I'm staying here, Uncle."

"Did you bring Herr Doktor?"

Candido had already told him of Herr Doktor's whereabouts, more than once. The old man's eyelids drooped again. He was dying.

"He's abroad. Listen, Uncle, I want to ask you something—something important."

"I've got a lot of time for that fellow Grüssgott, you know. He stinks like a goat, but I like him."

"I wanted to ask you about my mother. Do you remember her?"

"A pretty little slip of a girl, your mother. She never comes to see me either."

"She died giving birth to me."

"Forgive me, my boy. I remember now."

"I've just been told something about her by João Pessoa."

"Never heard of him."

"Your attorney, Uncle—I saw him this afternoon about your will. Of course you know him. Think hard."

"Yes, you're right. Mind if I shut my eyes? I'm sleepy."

"Did you . . ."

How on earth can I put it?

"Did you ever sleep with my mother, Uncle?"

"She often visited me in the old days. Lovely green eyes, really lovely. Do you have green eyes, Candido?"

"Yes, but you didn't answer my question."

"I've forgotten what it was."

"I don't believe you, Uncle. According to Senhor Pessoa, Dom Trajano thinks I'm your son, not his."

"I shall be a thorn in Trajano's side till the day I die."

"Please answer my question."

"What were we talking about?"

"About you and my mother," Candido said patiently. He felt simultaneously saddened and embarrassed. "Don't pretend you've forgotten."

"Is Trajano with you now?"

"He's in São Paulo. There's no one else here."

"I've had a lot of women, you know. Thousands of them."

"And my mother?"

"Idalina, that was her name. I knew her before Trajano—I begged her not to marry that rogue. I never touched her, my boy. You should be ashamed, asking me a question like that."

"So I'm not your son?"

"Never had a legitimate child," Amílcar muttered drowsily.

"That's no answer."

The old man chuckled to himself.

"The answer is no."

"Did you know that Dom Trajano thinks I *am* your son?"

"Typical of him. He really must be a fool to believe that Idalina would have been unfaithful to him."

"How long have you known?"

Another faint chuckle.

"It's true you look more like me than Trajano."

"You knew it and you never said anything to him?"

"The more like me you looked, the more it enraged him. I'm awfully sleepy, my boy. Come back later—oh, and by the way, go and see my attorney. I've bequeathed you my entire estate. Are you pleased?"

"Yes, Uncle, very pleased."

Great-uncle Amílcar died a week later. Candido's telegram to Lascalles remained unanswered and the news elicited an equal lack of response from everyone else in São Paulo, so the funeral was a very modest affair. The only persons present were Candido, Samantha, Senhor Pessoa, three or four ancient gentlemen who had known Amílcar in the old days, and Domitila, the nonagenarian former slave. None of the so-called servants troubled to show up. They celebrated instead.

"Let's get out of here, Candido. Let's take the car and go, anywhere you like. I can't stand these drunken oafs. They'll be dancing on the old man's grave next."

There was no question of returning to the little fazenda at São Roque. Samantha found it deplorable that Candido should simply resign himself to surviving until Dom Trajano issued a second summons and deigned to pardon him. If he wanted to go to São Paulo and try again, he could go alone.

"He won't even have read those two ten-page letters you sent him, you told me so yourself. What more do you want, another dose of humiliation?"

Candido had said nothing to her of Dom Trajano's doubts about his paternity, he was too ashamed, but they did account for Trajano's permanent hostility toward him. Great-uncle Amílcar had noticed it himself: their mutual resemblance had become more and more pronounced as Candido grew up. Every passing year had transformed him little by little into a younger version of Amílcar, whom Trajano had always detested. Why? Because any Cavalcanti who squandered his patrimony heedless of scandal—any Cavalcanti whose sole preoccupations were wine, women and song—was beyond the pale.

Great-uncle Amílcar had been selfish to say the least. It must have amused him greatly to let Dom Trajano think he'd been cuckolded, but the old man had never stopped to think that Candido would suffer the consequences. Candido didn't feel resentful even so. Samantha was right: he could never be bothered to be angry with anyone. What was the point to anger? It never changed anything, except for the worse.

They got into the Chandler with Eglantina and their baby daughter. Hitherto prevented by her pregnancy from exploring Brazil, Samantha was eager to make up for lost time. She wanted to visit Bahia, Recife, Belém, even Amazonia. Candido voted against Amazonia. His former colonel was stationed there now, and he was a man to be avoided. As for Bahia and the rest, they were a long way off. Samantha didn't realize how big Brazil was—as big as the United States or even bigger.

They drove to Petrópolis, where they rented a villa near Santos-Dumont's handsome house and the late emperor's summer palace. Two excursions apart, one to Bahia and the other to Ouro Prêto, they remained there for nearly three months. Candido wrote to inform Lascalles of his new address, advise him that Dom Trajano was now a grandfather, and emphasize that they were staying in the healthful highlands for the new baby's benefit, not in deliberate defiance of his father's wishes.

He received no reply to this letter, which he had refrained from showing to Samantha, but interpreted Dom Trajano's silence as a favorable sign. Things would work out in the end. Dom Trajano must have completed his inquiries into the German affair, and the results couldn't have been too disastrous or he would have reacted by now. A letter from Ciccio Vaz Vasconselos at the end of March seemed to confirm this. The chances of a meeting with his father were better than even, Ciccio wrote. Having kept his nose clean, Candido could return whenever he chose.

It was mid-afternoon when the Chandler pulled up outside the gates of the *sobrado* where Amílcar had died. They were shut, and the garden looked neglected. The whole place was deserted.

◆   ◆   ◆

João Pessoa was nearly eighty and wore old-fashioned pince-nez secured to the lapel of his jacket by a black ribbon. If Candido was small, the attorney was positively lilliputian. His offices on Rua do Hospício, a few yards from the French embassy, resembled a cave in which decrepit old ghosts circulated with ceremonious deliberation.

"Your father's attorney, Dom Eduardo Lascalles, turned up with two colleagues a few days after you left for Petrópolis, armed with instructions from Dom Trajano. They put the *sobrado* up for sale and sent those so-called servants back to their fazendas."

"What about Domitila?"

"They made her an *ex gratia* payment of one conto in full settlement of all claims on your great-uncle's estate. Her present whereabouts are unknown to me. I'm delighted to see you, Dom Candido. Certain matters have been causing me some distress."

One conto was around two hundred dollars, Candido calculated. Two hundred dollars for seventy-five years of unflagging devotion. . . . What reckless generosity!

"Certain matters?"

"I handled all the late Dom Amílcar's affairs. In particular, I supervised his disposals of property during the last half century. I have always felt, however, that many of those transactions were made under duress."

"He was robbed, first by my grandfather and then by my father. I know it and he knew it too, but that was his business."

Candido was indifferent to such problems. Then a thought struck him.

"Could you trace the sale of some paintings to a St. Petersburg museum, somewhere around 1900 to 1905? They were by French artists of the Impressionist school. I asked Dom Amílcar about them, but he couldn't remember."

Pessoa stroked his chin. "I should have to look through a vast number of documents, and you, being the sole legatee, would have to sign a form of authority."

Candido wondered if he wasn't crediting a minor detail with too much importance. On the other hand, if he could prove to Dom Trajano that Harmond or someone at the Russian end had been lying, it would help to buttress his own version of the Jaguar story.

He signed a power of attorney authorizing Pessoa to act on his behalf. What did it matter? The little old lawyer would either fail to find anything—Dom Trajano's attorneys would run rings around him anyway—or he'd die before he was through. Still, if there was the smallest chance of substantiating his theory of a Red plot, why not give it a try?

But that wasn't all, Pessoa went on. There were a certain number of items that Dom Trajano's attorneys had omitted to remove or sell when clearing the *sobrado*. They included the collection of garters—no less than eleven hundred and twenty-seven of them.

Yes, one for each of Amílcar's official mistresses. No wonder the old man ruined himself.

"Your great-uncle," said Pessoa, "was full of surprises. He could be extremely shrewd despite his easygoing disposition—perhaps he knew himself too well. Many years ago he entrusted me with what remained of his possessions, and I've stored them in my strong room ever since. There are a number of canvases, two or three of them by an artist named Van Grog or something similar. Several statuettes, too. Does the name Rodin mean anything to you, Dom Candido? No, nor to me, but I must warn you: the ladies and gentlemen are stark naked and captured in rather improper poses. I certainly wouldn't want my great-grandchildren to see them."

Little Pessoa almost blushed. Dom Trajano's attorneys had also spurned his late client's collection of photographs, including those of the twelve—how should he put it?—female posteriors, to which Amílcar had been much attached. Finally, there was the Leopolda.

Candido thought at once of Amílcar's great love, the lady with breasts like watermelons and a backside worthy of a brewer's dray horse.

No, no, said the diminutive attorney, he was referring to *the* Leopolda.

The locomotive.

"She now belongs to you, Dom Candido, that's legally beyond dispute. By the way, may I ask you where you're staying? I own three houses in Rio, one of them on the Avenida Atlantica, immediately overlooking Copacabana beach. If you'd care to . . ."

Candido declined the attorney's offer with thanks. He didn't intend to remain in Rio. Tomorrow he would go in search of Clovis the trolley-car conductor, Candida's godfather-to-be, and through him he would find Domitila. As soon as he'd made the old woman a more generous settlement they would head for São Paulo.

Clovis lived in Maracanã, on the other side of the city. Just before ten the next morning Candido left his little clapboard hotel on deserted Ipanema beach and boarded a _bonde,_ one of the multiple trolley cars run by a Canadian corporation. All that shielded passengers from the sun and rain were oilskin awnings and curtains. The cars were jam-packed as usual, and clambering on to a running board was quite a feat.

Cuidado!

It was the figure's sheer size that had caught Candido's eye. One momentary glimpse was enough to identify it as the Man Mountain.

I'm going after him. This is my country, after all. I'd only have to spin some kind of yarn and twenty or thirty of these people around me would help me hunt him down.

Stalled by a milling crowd getting on and off at the next stop, he reached the spot too late. The Man Mountain was already disappearing into a maze of alleyways. To follow him would be to risk an ambush.

Candido leapt aboard a Maracanã streetcar at the last possible moment and looked back. There was nothing to see.

"I'm looking for Clovis do Nascimento, the trolley-car conductor."

A black man pointed to a dirt lane. Sixth house on the left. He knocked.

"I'm looking for—"

"You're Dom Candido Cavalcanti." The black girl was very pretty. She smiled. "Clovis told me about you. You'll find him in his garage—it's that big corrugated-iron building over there."

What the girl had called a garage turned out to be a warehouse filled with big metal drums. A smell of crushed fruit suggested that it was a back-street factory supplying water ices to itinerant vendors.

He heard a noise behind him, but too late. The blow caught him on the base of the neck. He collapsed without losing consciousness, only to pass out completely when someone clamped a cloth soaked in ether over his nose and mouth.

He was inside one of the drums.

I hope they haven't turned me into a water ice.

Very funny. Almost as funny as dying at the hands of these scum.

He got to his feet, swaying a little, and nearly passed out again. The drum had a lid.

The lid weighed a ton and refused to budge. Until, at last, on the eighth or ninth attempt, it abruptly gave. Objects cascaded to the floor with a clatter as it flew off. Hoisting himself on to the edge of the drum, he saw that the lid had been weighted down with stones and bits of scrap metal. The intention hadn't been to kill him or incarcerate him permanently. No, he knew what the intention had been. He slid to the ground.

It was pitch black outside.

Nighttime? But it was ten in the morning when I left Ipanema!

The only lights to be seen were wood fires and oil lamps. He made his way back up the rutted lane to Clovis's house. No one home. Neighbors emerged from their plank and cardboard shacks, roused by his repeated knocking. Clovis? They hadn't seen him all day.

"I see. Thanks."

Candido set off at a run. He'd covered two miles before he sighted a horse-drawn cab.

"Ipanema, please, and hurry. Any idea of the time?"

Four-thirty A.M. That explained the dearth of cabs.

I'm scared. I knew this had to happen some time.

Ipanema at last.

"Drop me here, would you?"

He was three hundred yards short of the hotel. The beach on his left was dotted with pinpoints of light by candles stuck in the sand beside propitiatory offerings to Umbanda, the spirit of white magic. Somewhere in the darkness voices were solemnly chanting, hands clapping, African drums thudding. Candido gave the cabbie a hundred-milreis note. He hugged the shadows as he approached. It was a wise precaution: the first two police lookouts he spotted were lurking behind a van. Others, barely visible, were lying in wait around the hotel.

If I'd told the cabbie to drop me outside they'd have jumped me.

He ducked down behind a flowering shrub just as a hand tugged at his sleeve. A little black boy had materialized beside him.

"Dom Candido?"

Thirty seconds later they were stealing off side by side. The boy, whose name was Paulo Cesar, announced that Samantha and the baby had left the hotel earlier that night accompanied by Eglantina, his aunt. He'd been keeping watch for hours, but not alone. Eglantina had mobilized every last one of her nephews and nieces, and they, reinforced by a number of their friends, had been stationed so as to intercept Candido before the police could arrest him.

"_What_ am I supposed to have blown up?"

For a start, the _sobrado_ at Botafogo, Dom Amílcar's former residence. There wasn't much left of the house, which had been dynamited just after nightfall. The headquarters of the Banco Cavalcanti e Irmãos on Rua do Benedictino had gone up an hour later, except that this time the dynamiter had been less heavy-handed. Only the interior had been wrecked.

"You should have warned me," Samantha said brightly. "If I'd known you were going to blow up half of Rio, Candy and I would have come too. It's time the little darling learned the rudiments of her father's trade."

Paulo Cesar had taken Candido to Clovis do Nascimento, the general commanding this army of lookouts, and Clovis had driven him by truck to a luxurious property to the south, on the lower slopes of the Corcovado. Samantha was already there with Candida, Eglantina and a handful of men and women, all black.

They brought each other up to date. In Samantha's case, no less a person than Afonka Tchadayev had presented himself at the hotel, smiling more broadly than ever.

"He was beside himself with glee. He said you'd just gotten your own back at Dom Trajano and his lawyers by blowing up the house at Botafogo, and that the family bank was going to suffer the same fate. The police had been tipped off and were after you. Someone was about to inform them of our new address, so I'd be wise to leave at once."

"And you lost your temper."

"How did you guess? To hear you, anyone would think I had a foul temper. Anyway, Clovis and Domitila confirmed what the sonofabitch had said and agreed it would be better to hide out here."

" 'Here' being what, exactly?"

A house belonging to some people called da Silva Campos or something. They were away in Europe and wouldn't be back for some time. The cook was one of Eglantina's innumerable elder sisters.

"Are you sure you didn't blow up those buildings, Candido?"

Meu Deus, *I honestly believe it would give her a kick to hear me say I'm the Mad Bomber.*

"You thought I'd sent Afonka to warn you?"

That convinced her. She gave a rueful smile.

"Pity. What I liked best was the thought of you blowing up Dom Trajano's bank. At least *that* would have been worthy of a genuine anarchist. *That's* what we should have done in Berlin, blow up a bank. Bombing a little movie theater was a pretty pathetic gesture, when you come down to it." She paused, half hopeful again. "You would tell me if you'd done it, wouldn't you, Candido?"

He shut his eyes.

"The police are on your track," said João Pessoa.

The little old lawyer seemed as unperturbed by this fact as he was at having been dug out of bed by Clovis in the middle of the night. Nothing appeared to faze him, not even Candido's account of his misadventures, which covered everything: Policarpo Moravec and Oskar Kuppelweiser, Biesenthal and the bombing of the Plücks' cinema, Russia, Mongolia and the exploits of the Jaguar's Claws.

"You wish me to go and tell your father the whole story?"

Silence. Pessoa pondered a while. He'd listened to Candido's recital without turning a hair, but he now felt bound to point out that things looked black. It was common knowledge that Dom Trajano didn't get on with his son—indeed, it was rumored that he'd just disinherited him. "I told you that yesterday, Dom Candido, but I don't think you were paying attention." Furthermore, rumors were circulating about certain incidents that had occurred in Europe while Candido was over there. He was even being linked with a terrorist campaign in the United States, where two anarchists, Sacco and Vanzetti, had recently been convicted of murder.

"Look at the facts. You were very fond of your great-uncle. He died, you discovered evidence that he'd been cheated, you returned to Rio and vanished under peculiar circumstances. During your absence, someone perpetrated criminal acts directly prejudicial to the interests of Dom Trajano Cavalcanti, his brothers and cousins, all of whom were responsible for the late Dom Amílcar's unhappy lot."

A delicate situation, Pessoa concluded, tapping his pince-nez. Would he agree to act as Candido's intermediary? Yes, he would. Eighty come next September, he had known Dom Amílcar for sixty years or more.

"Eyes apart, Dom Candido, you bear a striking resemblance to him.

He once suggested my joining him in Paris. To my everlasting regret, I declined the invitation. Yes, I'll go to São Paulo and do my best for you."

They arranged that Clovis should act as their go-between. Then the little lawyer departed, looking as frail and tiny as if one sneeze would blow him away like thistledown.

News of Pessoa's success reached them nine days later: Dom Trajano had consented to a meeting. They were to present themselves at Bragança Boa Vista the following Wednesday.

They set off in trucks with a party of a dozen led by Clovis and his brother-in-law Hastimphilo. All were trolley-car conductors except Hastimphilo, who was an accountant, and Zé Julio, a mechanic.

When they were less than three hours from the fazenda, Candido, Clovis and Hastimphilo exchanged their truck for some horses and headed east across the hills.

◆   ◆   ◆

Lights were burning on both floors. Candido had visited the house scores of times, and of all the Cavalcantis' Brazilian properties this was his favorite. It was in the *senzala,* the plantation's onetime slave quarters, that he'd lost his virginity to a girl of sixteen. To him, who had only just turned thirteen, she had seemed incredibly old.

"We've been spotted," Clovis said.

A man had just opened the front door. It was Bandeira, the butler.

"Good evening, Dom Candido."

"Good evening, Bandeira."

Candido had never been able to stand the man, and the feeling was mutual. Bandeira's father, grandfather and great grandfather had all been in the family's service. They used to hunt down runaway slaves and were quick to use the whip, if not the noose. Candido wondered why Dom Trajano had always surrounded himself with such men. He might equally have put the question another way. Why was it that he, a pure-blooded Cavalcanti, should differ so much from previous generations of Cavalcantis (four centuries of them, according to the family archives), all of whom must have resembled Dom Trajano in employing men like the Bandeiras as aids to the attainment of wealth? What had wrought this change, Herr Doktor's tuition or some congenital flaw in himself?

Visitors to Bragança Boa Vista in the old days had approached the house by way of an avenue of palm trees three miles long, which ended in a pair of ornate wrought-iron gates. Great-uncle Amílcar, who was extravagant but not ostentatious, had preferred his friends to enter the property through the gardens on the right, which sloped down in a series of terraces to the river below, a minor tributary of the Mogi-Guaçu. It was here that Amílcar had constructed a swimming pool and an amusingly intricate network of arbors, pergolas and summerhouses half smothered in bougainvillea, roses and passionflowers. It was here, too, Candido recalled, that Amílcar had told him of his Parisian escapades and Herr Doktor had made him read Horace and Virgil in the original, seasoning them with an occasional pinch of Pierre de Brantôme. His eyes grew moist at the recollection.

"The gentlemen are in the green drawing room," Bandeira announced.

He opened the polished oak door wider and started to step aside, then slumped to the floor with his throat cut. Blood spurted over Candido's chest. The Man Mountain, who appeared out of nowhere, pinned his arms to his sides and bundled him inside. He found himself confronted by Matriona and Afonka Tchadayev, who was smiling as usual.

"What a state you're in, Candido. You really needn't have gone to those lengths."

Stepa Onegin emerged from the green drawing room looking thoughtful, as if he'd just attended a board meeting and was still debating the agenda. His eyes came to rest on Bandeira. In spite of the gaping wound in his throat, the butler's limbs continued to twitch and his fingers clawed convulsively at the black marble floor.

"Slit his cheeks too," Stepa said in Russian. "Everyone knows that Jaguar detested him."

Matriona bent down and performed the twin incisions. Stepa turned to Candido.

"What news apart from this latest atrocity? You almost managed to butcher your cousin Firmino Luiz de Barros at Bahia, had you heard? You were angry because he refused to shelter you from the authorities. You really must control that temper of yours."

The Man Mountain was compressing Candido's tracheal artery one-handed.

I'm sure he doesn't mean to kill me, but that's what he's doing.

"On the left shoulder." Stepa's voice seemed to come from very far away. "Someone threw a punch at his head and missed. A little more blood would be good. Not too much, though."

The blow on his left shoulder was so painful he nearly passed out.

"And again. Mark his face this time."

Another agonizing blow. This time he did pass out.

◆ ◆ ◆

Candido regained consciousness to find himself lying on top of a corpse. He detached himself from the dead man, whose throat and cheeks had been slit. It was Eduardo Lascalles, and he was in the green drawing room at Bragança Boa Vista. Getting to his feet, he discovered two more bodies nearby. His heart gave a jump. *Meu Deus,* that man lying face down looked like Dom Trajano! He turned the body over. No, it was someone else.

He steeled himself to examine the other man, who proved to be Dias Gonçalves, yet another of Dom Trajano's attorneys—men of whom Great-uncle Amílcar had once remarked that even a pig would refuse to share its trough with them.

It's Harbin all over again. I must get out of here before I'm spotted.

A knock at the door restored him to complete lucidity. Someone outside was deferentially calling in Portuguese. The handle was turned, but without result. They'd locked him in.

He straddled the windowsill, landed in a flower bed ten feet below, and made off, zigzagging between arbors and summerhouses, leaping from terrace to terrace. Frenzied cries rent the air behind him, figures ran in all directions, shots rang out, bullets kicked up the gravel only a few feet away.

On he went, scrambling over trelliswork thick with greenery, trampling passionflowers underfoot, lacerating himself on climbing roses, sprinting across an old *terreiro* on which coffee beans had once been spread to dry, veering off at a tangent, hauling himself over a stone wall with the aid of a big pepper tree. At last, after racing across an orange grove, he came out in the palm-fringed avenue, so long and straight that it stretched away into the night like a tunnel.

Clovis and Hastimphilo must have galloped off at the sound of gunfire. I don't blame them—I'd have done the same myself. Either that, or they've been caught and executed. Another few deaths to my credit. I'm more lethal than yellow fever.

Then he heard a low whistle. Hastimphilo and Clovis emerged from the darkness leading his horse.

Five or six miles at a gallop until the horses' legs were trembling and their necks lathered with foam. They slowed to a walk.

"No one would think it to look at you," Clovis said, "but you run like a hare."

"Lucky the fazenda belongs to your family," said Hastimphilo. "If it didn't, they might have used some heavy artillery on you."

No sound of pursuit. The night was still. Had they seen any sign of the Jaguar's Claws?

None.

They kicked their horses into a trot and were soon beyond the boundaries of Bragança Boa Vista. The odds against his seeing the place again were pretty long.

"If you ask me," Samantha said, "your father's a complete swine."

"Let's change the subject."

"All right, as long as you don't intend to bury us in the jungle for the rest of our lives."

Samantha, Candido, Eglantina and the baby were in the back of the leading truck driven by Hastimphilo. While heading back to Rio some hours earlier they'd been ambushed by a detachment of soldiers and forced to turn about. They were now heading due west. There were bullet holes in the tarpaulin cover, and the other truck, whose tires had been shredded by rifle fire, was bouncing along on its rims.

"I'm not leaving Brazil," Candido said. "This is my home, the only place in the world where I've even half a chance of laying Jaguar's ghost. I'm only sorry Clovis and Hastimphilo got mixed up in this. They and their friends are faithful souls, but they'll have to go home to their families sooner or later."

"I'd be surprised," said Samantha.

"Why?"

"Because they're wanted by the Rio police for trying to organize a trolley-car strike. Vivaldo Maria, Zé Julio, Teotônio—they all resisted arrest when the police came to get them. They think they may even have killed a couple."

"How do you know all this?"

"Vivaldo Maria told me while you were gone."

The trucks were limping into a village.

"What's more, they're happy to accept you as their leader," Samantha added. "It's worth a lot to them, having a Cavalcanti in command."

The village had a church. Wearily, Candido climbed a ramshackle ladder to the top of the tower with Clovis at his heels. His binoculars soon picked out a column of soldiers two hours' march away.

"What do you have in mind, Clovis, a revolution?"

"*Puxa vida,* no! All we want is better wages."

"This strike at Rio—who organized it, you or Hastimphilo?"

The first detachment of troops was visible at twelve o'clock. More dust indicated that another was approaching from three o'clock.

"Me and Hastimphilo," Clovis replied.

"But mainly Hastimphilo?"

"Mainly him, yes."

A third column of soldiers showed up at eight o'clock. Obviously, they were being encircled. Remarkable that Brazilian troops should have leapt into action with such uncharacteristic alacrity, unless . . . Unless someone had alerted the authorities *before* the massacre in the green drawing room at Bragança Boa Vista.

That's it! The Jaguar's Claws are busy transforming me into a revolutionary leader, an outlaw in my own country. They've made sure I can't count on any help from my father.

"Tell me, Clovis, do you know a man called Policarpo Moravec?"

"No."

"Might Hastimphilo know him?"

"He's an accountant. He reads a lot and knows a lot of people."

A fourth column was advancing due west at six o'clock.

"Are they all round us, Candido?"

"I'm afraid so."

He could give himself up without a fight, without attempting to escape, but for two minor problems. In the first place he might be shot out of hand (perhaps that was part of the Claws' plan, to make a martyr of him). Secondly, the soldiers would gun down everyone else in the party. The arguments in favor of his remaining alive and at liberty were also twofold. On the one hand, he wouldn't be able to convince Dom Trajano of his innocence if he were dead or in prison; on the other, he'd just had another wild idea.

Clovis cleared his throat.

"Can't you think of any way out of this fix, Candido?"

"Yes," he said.

He left at once, barely pausing to exchange a word with Samantha, and sped off into the gathering gloom. Although uncertain of his route for the first three or four miles, he got his bearings as soon as he came to one of the dirt roads inside the plantation. He ran as Herr Doktor had taught him. "Don't strike out or pick your knees up too much, keep your arms supple and relaxed, let them hang limp occasionally so the bend of the elbow doesn't obstruct your circulation. I'm not sure if you're a natural five-thousand-meter man, Candido. Your physique may be better suited to the ten thousand, or even the marathon. . . ."

The thatched cottage, which came into view an hour later, looked as if it had been transplanted to Brazil from the depths of the English countryside. The long, low shed adjoining it was dimly visible in the glow from the lamp above the door.

Candido subsided on to the bench below the white casement window. Bragança Boa Vista, less than two miles away, was ablaze with light.

He didn't have long to wait.

"I heard you, whoever you are. If you're still there ten seconds from now, I'll pepper your hide."

"In Hebrew," Candido said, "Ezra means 'help.' You told me so yourself."

There was a pause. Then the door opened to reveal an old man in a nightshirt and a tasseled nightcap knitted in a mixture of green, blue and red wool. He was holding a double-barreled shotgun.

"Is Herr Doktor with you, laddie?"

"He was filming in Russia the last I heard."

"A daft question deserves a daft answer," said Ezra McAuliffe. "If Herr Doktor were with you, you wouldn't be galloping around in the dark with the police and the army on your tail. Did you really kill those men?"

"That's an even dafter question," Candido retorted.

McAuliffe sat down beside him. He planted the butt of his gun on the ground, his palm on the muzzle and his chin on the back of his hand. The other hand he used to brush aside the tassel of his Clan McAuliffe nightcap, but it was a futile gesture. The tartan tassel swung to and fro like a pendulum before centering itself between his grizzled eyebrows and coming to rest on the bridge of his nose.

"I'm seventy-three years old but fit as a fiddle. I'm not ready to die yet, laddie. This isn't a social call, so what do you want?"

"The Leopolda."

"What for?"

"A little outing. Great-uncle Amílcar's dead, had you heard?"

"Aye, I had."

"I'm his sole beneficiary."

"Much good that'll do you."

"A twisted legal mind," Candido said cautiously, "might infer that the Leopolda now belongs to me."

"What of it?"

"Is she in working order?"

"You want a clip on the lug, laddie?"

They preserved a moment's silence as if in tribute to Great-uncle Amílcar and the good old days. More lights went on in the big house beyond the trees. To judge by the activity reigning there at this time of night, the authorities had requisitioned it as a base of operations for their manhunt.

"I had a soft spot for your great-uncle," McAuliffe said. "He was crazy as a loon."

"I know."

"I took his death hard, I won't pretend I didn't. I'm just recovering from a monumental hangover. If you'd come here two days ago you'd have found me stiff as a board. Why didn't you hide here last night?"

"It never occurred to me."

"Amílcar loved you, that's all I need to know."

"That _did_ occur to me. That's why I'm here."

The old Scot grunted.

"Why would you be wanting the Leopolda?"

Candido explained. "I don't have it all worked out yet, but it's all I could think of."

McAuliffe's tassel swung to and fro as he flicked it with a wrinkled, grime-ingrained forefinger.

"It could end in a big bang, laddie, you realize that?"

"You may be right."

"Well, it'd be a fine way to go, for her and me both. Let's move. At her age she takes a while to get steam up. We won't even mention _my_ age."

They were now doing sixty or seventy miles an hour.

"Think the bridge'll hold?" Candido asked.

"It better, even if it wasn't built by a Scot."

McAuliffe hadn't lit the Leopolda's "eyes," as he called them, so very little could be seen. People, some of them armed with rifles, had rushed outdoors on two or three occasions, roused from their slumbers by the locomotive's thunderous approach, but the countryside became more and more sparsely populated as they bowled along the track that linked the plantation to the outside world.

"Not far to go now," Candido remarked, doing his best to sound casual.

"Well?"

"I remember what you said a couple of years back. You called it a pathetic little bridge—you said the Leopolda would smash it like an eggbox."

"I still say so."

Candido slid the cab window open and stuck his head out, braving a shower of soot and cinders. The pathetic little bridge was only a quarter of a mile away.

We're going to land at the bottom of the gorge with a crash they'll hear in Manchuria.

"You can still jump, laddie."

The Leopolda was panting ever harder, ever faster, like a woman in the throes of childbirth. She covered the final two hundred yards flat out. It was as if she'd lifted her five-ton skirts and broken into a gallop.

The bridge groaned, sagged, creaked. And collapsed.

But they were across. The tender had made it by inches.

The Leopolda gave a monstrous screech as McAuliffe jammed her brakes full on. At last, emitting furious jets of whitish steam, she came to a stop.

From out of this milky vapor, like a collection of severed heads, protruded the beaming faces of Clovis, Hastimphilo, Zé Julio and the others. On the embankment beyond them, with baby Candida in her arms, sat Samantha.

◆ ◆ ◆

It was a quarter of an hour after the bridge episode. The Leopolda was purring peacefully to herself in the dawn light. Everything was at rest: her four and a half thousand horsepower, her four pairs of seven-foot wheels, her two-hundred-and-twenty-five-ton body, her iron skirts—and, of course, the massive tender McAuliffe fondly referred to as her "swinging hips."

"Let me explain," said Candido. "Ezra McAuliffe first came to Brazil as a prisoner of war. He drove an armored train for the Paraguayan army in 1869. . . ."

At that time Paraguay was ruled by a dictator named Francisco López. To defend his country against the Brazilians, Uruguayans and Argentinians, who found him a troublesome neighbor, López commissioned the first armored train in the history of South America and entrusted it to an English driver, whose assistant McAuliffe was. López lost the war and McAuliffe wound up in a prison camp. Great-uncle Amílcar's lawyers secured his release and employed him to maintain their client's collection of sixty-three locomotives, of which the Leopolda became flagship some years later. Great-uncle Amílcar had squandered his last remaining assets on it.

They were now heading due south toward Mogi-Guaçu and Mogi-Mirim. Coupled to the Leopolda and her tender were a couple of armor-plated boxcars, a flatcar armed with a 75-millimeter field gun and three machine guns, a luxurious Pullman car that Amílcar had christened the

Love Nest, and, last of all, a second flatcar supporting a turret-mounted 105-millimeter howitzer.

"A howitzer?" exclaimed Samantha.

"Yes, and it works—I should know, I've fired it twenty times or more. We amused ourselves one day by putting a shell into Tasso Tavora's cistern. The only casualties were a dozen cows, but twenty thousand gallons of water came pouring into old Tasso's kitchen. Before he and his wife could put their knives and forks down they were a hundred yards away, clinging to the branches of a mango tree. Fortunately, Great-uncle Amílcar owned their house."

"You're pulling my leg, Candido."

"Word of honor—ask Ezra, he'll tell you. In the old days the Leopolda had her own track and a whole series of stations with names like Fontaine-bleau, Biarritz, Cannes, Monte Carlo and so on. Then it occurred to the plantation manager that she could haul wagonloads of coffee to São Paulo. She made two round trips a year until Dom Trajano decided that using such a monster was uneconomical and put her into retirement— Ezra too."

Samantha was entranced.

"Could I fire the howitzer, do you think?"

"Why not? The only problem with it is to make sure no one's in the line of fire and err on the generous side."

They left the Love Nest, made their way through the boxcar that housed the off-duty trolley-car conductors, negotiated the catwalk running along the right-hand side of the tender and ducked through a heart-shaped, armor-plated door into the monster's cab. Hastimphilo and Zé Julio were already there with McAuliffe.

"Well, laddie, decided where you want to go?"

"Who does he think he's talking to?" Samantha demanded.

"I don't have any precise idea," Candido told McAuliffe. "Anywhere except São Paulo, Rio, Belo Horizonte and another couple of hundred big towns, and—"

"*Laddie?*" exclaimed Samantha.

"—and I'd also like to steer clear of any properties owned by members of my family, down to and including tenth cousins once removed. I'll make you out a list."

"Listen, you whiskey-swilling toad," Samantha told McAuliffe, "call Candido 'laddie' once more and I'll split your skull with this shovel!"

"A woman in the Leopolda's cab is an offense against nature," McAuliffe declared. "Females belong in the Love Nest. Mind you, she's not a bad-looking lass."

"Females?" Samantha protested.

"Ladylike, too." McAuliffe continued to ignore her. "What we need, Candido, is a map of the Brazilian railway network."

"Mogi-Guaçu?" Candido suggested.

"Mogi-Mirim's the better bet, being a junction. Could you ask her to put that shovel down?"

"Samantha, please! Can't you see we're busy!"

"We'll also need some spare rails," McAuliffe added, "in case some idiot steals our track. There's a whole stock of them at Mogi-Mirim."

"Mogi-Mirim it is, then," said Candido. "From there we'll branch off to Pouso Alegre and Itajubá. Then I'll think again."

"Yes, sir," said McAuliffe. "I like my orders nice and clear." He grinned at Samantha. "Like to try driving a locomotive, lassie?"

The end of Bragança Boa Vista's private railway network came in sight ten minutes later. The Leopolda stopped where it joined the São Paulo state line.

"There are two possible dangers when you're traveling by rail," McAuliffe observed. "One is another train coming in the opposite direction. The other is points. Those trolley-car conductors, Candido, are they coming with us?"

"Seems so."

"In that case, everyone out."

With a surprising degree of patience, the old Scot spent the next few minutes lecturing his passengers on points and how to operate them. Candido listened a while, then stepped back for a better look at the Leopolda. The locomotive had acquired several refinements since the last time he'd seen her. McAuliffe had reinforced the huge, fan-shaped cow-catcher with a steel ram. Studded with conical teeth a foot long and running the full width of the locomotive, this formidable contraption made the Leopolda look like some terrifying mythical beast.

Samantha rejoined him on board.

"Where are we taking this monster?" she asked.

Candido honestly didn't know. It had seemed a good idea at the time. The trucks were *in extremis,* so he'd had to find some other means of transportation.

Music!

It had just blared forth, preternaturally loud, filling the air for miles around.

"I'd forgotten the loudspeaker system," he said. "That's Great-uncle

Amílcar's favorite song from Offenbach's _La Vie Parisienne._ Some mad inventor sold him this newfangled phonograph. It's worked by electricity."

"Je suis brésilien, j'arrive de Rio de Janeiro," boomed a disembodied voice. The Leopolda's huge wheels, which were partly concealed by her armorplated skirt, began to turn.

They were on their way again.

Mogi-Mirim boasted a small marshaling yard, a few warehouses, some ancient rolling stock, a dozen ragged idlers squatting on their heels and a mustachioed, potbellied stationmaster.

Although the stationmaster heard perfectly well the first time, he made Candido repeat his question.

"You want _what?_"

"Some rails and cross-ties. We'll pay for them, naturally."

It took them about an hour to load up. They stacked as many rails and cross-ties as possible inside the cars, plus the equipment needed to assemble them, then lashed still more rails to the roofs. Candido insisted on a signed receipt for the thousand dollars he paid the stationmaster, whose office turned out to contain a mass of timetables, network diagrams and maps.

"We're in luck, laddie," said McAuliffe. "Anyone would think this place was the headquarters of the Brazilian railway network. There's enough information here to get us to Canada."

Candido didn't put it down to luck. He was more inclined to believe that this superabundance of documentation had been put there solely for his benefit. In other words, THEY _wanted_ him to go charging around in his armored train.

I'm doing exactly what they expect. Again. As always! But what choice do I have?

"What fun!" Samantha kept repeating, and the former trolley-car conductors fell over themselves in their eagerness to help load the train with food and weapons. Candido's command had been reinforced by half a dozen unknown faces, and all had exchanged conspiratorial glances with Hastimphilo on arrival. "They've decided to join us," the big man explained with a look of supreme innocence. Lindolpho, a telegraphist by trade, had taken over the stationmaster's office and fired off messages in all directions.

The Leopolda steamed out of Mogi-Mirim hauling an extra wagon—one of the flatcars that had been rotting in a siding there. It was laden with dismantled points, steel girders and thirty-foot beams.

"We'll need that stuff for replacing sabotaged points or rebuilding a bridge if someone's been mean enough to blow it," McAuliffe explained.

Sabotaged points, blown bridges . . . We're going to war with a vengeance, and I'm the only one who failed to realize it.

Offenbach's music rang out like a trumpet sounding the charge. Candido, who'd been pacing up and down the track, was jubilantly hailed by Samantha, Clovis, Zé Julio and the rest.

"All aboard!" they chorused. "Come on, you're holding us up!"

As Herr Doktor had said, citing some historical figure whose name he'd forgotten: "I'm their leader; I must follow them."

He jumped aboard the moving train.

◆ ◆ ◆

Hours later the Leopolda nonchalantly demolished a barricade constructed of cross-ties and tree trunks. The cowcatcher scooped up the debris, the ram pulverized it and seven hundred and fifty tons of train ploughed through it like so much sawdust.

"What if they build a bigger one?" Samantha asked.

McAuliffe sneered. "What if they do?"

"They may send a suicide train crashing into us."

"Well?"

McAuliffe was quite categorical. No ordinary train could stand up to the Leopolda—she would go through it "like a spoon through porridge"—and ordinary trains were all the Brazilian authorities possessed. It would take them six months to construct an armored train, and even then the Leopolda would remain invincible.

"How fast are we going now, Jock?"

"Ezra to you, lassie. Around sixty."

Without a train to haul, and without her skirts, corsets and other furbelows, the Leopolda was capable of a hundred miles an hour. Even with her present load and equipment, she could exceed seventy-five.

"I've souped her up a bit. The old girl can get quite skittish."

"What if they cut the track?"

"We've got the wherewithal to repair it."

"We could run full tilt into a trainload of passengers any minute. Even if your beloved Leopolda got through we'd kill hundreds of people."

It wouldn't happen, McAuliffe assured her. Did she think he was senile or something? The first person Lindolpho had contacted by telegraph was the chief traffic controller at São Paulo, an old friend of his. Lindolpho had notified him of the Leopolda's imminent departure and disguised their prospective route by demanding that the track be cleared in the direction of São Paulo, Itajubá and even Guaxupé in the north.

"I informed the press as well," Hastimphilo put in. "If there's an accident, the government will be blamed."

Samantha was running out of arguments. "They could still take the train by boarding it," she said.

McAuliffe scoffed at this.

"Try sneaking under the Leopolda's skirts and see how far you get!"

At Itajubá several dozen policemen and soldiers had set up a second barricade consisting of an old cattle car filled with bricks and earth and tipped on its side. The Leopolda sliced through this makeshift rampart as if it were made of sand. She propelled the cattle car along the track for two hundred yards before it broke in two. But for a sound like peas rattling on a drum, no one inside the armored train would have known that the enemy had opened fire.

"Pitiful," was McAuliffe's only comment.

They made a brief stop at Maria de Fé to take on some rum, then headed along the summit of the Poço Frio range to Soledade de Minas, an important junction.

"You choose, laddie."

Candido had been poring over the map for several minutes.

"Show me," said Samantha. She traced the various lines with her forefinger. "Seems we can go in any one of four different directions."

"Including back where we came from."

"I'd like to see a bit of Brazil, Candido. Besides, think of our daughter. She hasn't been anywhere yet."

"What say we turn south to São Lourenço and join the Rio–São Paulo line?"

They looked at each other.

She's caught on—she always does. She's starting to get the hang of me, I've got to admit.

"I know what that means," she said. "You haven't given up, have you?"

Candido hesitated. "Well, er . . . no."

"What the devil are you talking about?" McAuliffe demanded.

"Dom Candido Cavalcanti," Samantha announced, "is toying with an idiotic idea. Before sampling every railroad track in South America, he plans to go and say hello to his daddy."

"I want to get to São Paulo," Candido told McAuliffe, "—the center of São Paulo, preferably. At worst, we can simply steam in and out again."

Silence. Then the pompom on the old Scot's tam-o'-shanter gave a little bob.

"You're on," he said.

The Leopolda had now been stationary in the heart of São Paulo for nine hours. She was standing a few hundred yards from the mouth of the Estação da Luz, the city's central station. Her 105 was pointing south at the Sé district, while the 75's designated targets were the station and the municipal market. The mortars and machine guns were aimed in all directions, not least at the soldiers drawn up on the far side of no-man's-land, which varied in width between a hundred and fifty and two hundred yards depending on the terrain.

The Leopolda wasn't by any means a prisoner. She could set off again whenever Candido gave the order. If the army attempted to cut the track they would be warned in good time. According to Hastimphilo, the vast crowd peering at them through the soldiers' ranks included hundreds or even thousands of sympathizers who would promptly inform them of any such interference. "My boy," Candido could recall Herr Doktor saying, "there's nothing and no one a mob won't applaud like a field of grain bending before the wind, but no field of grain has ever been known to smash the combine harvester sent to cut it."

It was six days since the Leopolda had ended her hibernation at Bragança Boa Vista and sallied forth, and her route had been lined with cheering hordes of impoverished peasants ever since Barra Mansa. She became a mobile recruiting office besieged by hundreds of volunteers, many of whom hailed from Volta Redonda and some from as far afield as the iron mines at Minas Gerais. Of these Hastimphilo recruited twenty or thirty. Two more freight cars had been added to the train and hurriedly armor-plated. In the Pullman car, Great-uncle Amílcar's former love nest on wheels, a wooden partition now separated Candido and Samantha's bedroom from the conference room where councils of war were held.

"Ciccio's back," Samantha announced.

Two ordinary locomotives had unsuccessfully tried to bar their path when they steamed into São Paulo early that morning. Badly damaged, the tank locomotives skidded backward in a shower of sparks before toppling over sideways and leaving the track clear. The Leopolda stopped precisely where Candido wanted, well within range of the big building on the Praça Patriarca that housed the headquarters of the Banco Cavalcanti & Irmãos and Dom Trajano's office. Army machine guns peppered the train for the first few minutes, but to no effect. After a heated argument, Candido persuaded Hastimphilo to retaliate in a purely symbolic fashion, and a provisional cease-fire was arranged. An officer who came to parley with Candido and referred to him as "the leader of the revolutionaries" took formal note of the following declaration: "I'm neither a leader nor a revolutionary. It's all a big misunderstanding, you *cretino,* so stop talking out of the back of your head!" Two hours later Ciccio had turned up, still bleary-eyed with sleep, and agreed to act as a go-between.

He parked his pink-and-white Lincoln Leland—the coachwork had been redesigned by himself—a few yards from a brothel and got out.

"You can come aboard," Candido called.

Ciccio delightedly complied.

"*Do* show me over your great big train, Candido darling. I'm absolutely *dying* to see it."

"Later. Let's hear what they had to say first—and don't call me darling."

Ciccio eased his lemon-yellow two-piece suit into one of Great-uncle Amílcar's second Empire armchairs, which was upholstered in crushed strawberry velvet. He shuddered.

"What a *ghastly* combination of colors. I should have worn pink or white—off-white, preferably. Well, Candido, I saw your Uncles Tristão and Leandro. They were smoking cigars—at eleven in the morning, I *ask* you, and me with my *horror* of tobacco smoke!"

"Ciccio, please!"

"They don't like you much."

"What about Dom Trajano?"

"He wouldn't see me at first. My father had to bend his ear for a good two hours. They're childhood friends, after all. They've bankrupted farmers, evicted peasants and cheated foreigners together ever since they came of age."

"Did you see him, yes or no?"

"I saw him. I must say, you've made yourselves really *snug* here." Ciccio recollected himself and smiled sadly. "The answer is no, my poor Candido. Your father refuses to come here himself or send an intermediary. He won't cooperate in any way."

Candido recalled the terms of his message. He hadn't asked his father for help, merely requested a brief hearing. If only Dom Trajano and his uncles would meet him halfway, he might stand a chance of getting off the hook. He could return the Leopolda to her shed and end the revolution by sending everyone home—by making it clear that revolutions were just a futile, murderous ride on a merry-go-round.

"I'd better tell you exactly what your father said, Candido. He said, and I quote: 'You may inform that criminal who claims to be my son that

I'm here at my desk. If he chooses to open fire on me, let him. I'm not budging.' Sorry, Candido darling, I did my best."

"Thanks, Ciccio."

"*Are* you a revolutionary?"

"He's nothing of the kind," Samantha cut in. "He's just a sweet, gentle man who's been mistaken for someone else."

Candido had risen and was peering through a loophole. He could picture Dom Trajano seated at his desk on the top floor of the big building in the distance. There was a strange, terrible ache in his chest.

"Out you get, Ciccio. We're leaving."

Ciccio hesitated. "You're all going to get yourselves killed," he said. "I can't bear to think of it."

Hastimphilo stepped forward, took Ciccio by the arm and shepherded him out. He secured the armor-plated door and lowered the shutters over all but two of the loopholes, which he left half open. Then he tugged at the cord that ran the length of the train and rang a bell in McAuliffe's cab. The Leopolda's public address system came to life. It wasn't *La Vie Parisienne* this time, but *La Grande Duchesse de Gerolstein*. "*Voice le sabre, le sabre, le sabre de mon père,*" the grand duchess bellowed at full volume.

The Leopolda backed out of São Paulo.

The first blood flowed only nine days later.

The Leopolda was standing some two hundred yards from the frontier post at Jaguarão on the Brazilian-Uruguayan border. After leaving São Paulo, she had traversed the states of Paraná, Santa Catarina and, finally, Rio Grande do Sul, the last stage of her journey to Uruguay.

"We'll return to Brazil," Hastimphilo had insisted, "but not at once. Things are brewing, and we must wait for them to come to a head."

The holdup had already lasted twenty minutes. The Brazilian officer commanding the frontier post returned carrying his white flag, a shirt on the end of a broomstick. He was unarmed, his revolver holster empty. Candido went to meet him for the second time.

"Well?"

"I just received confirmation of my orders by telegraph. I'm to stop you getting through."

The officer was twenty-three at most. At their first encounter he'd introduced himself as Ensign Affonso Lima de Carvalho of Sorocaba, near São Paulo.

"That's a ridiculous order," Candido told him. "How do you propose to carry it out? Have you seen this train?"

"I could dismantle the track."

"It wouldn't do any good. We're equipped to repair it."

"I may have mined the bridge."

"Our scouts would have warned us. Anyway, you didn't."

"I don't have any dynamite, to be honest. Even if I had, I wouldn't know how to use it."

"Do you have any artillery?"

He was an exquisitely courteous young officer. Candido felt sorry for him.

"One small field gun. It hasn't been fired since 1869."

"It would probably blow up in your face."

"True."

"There's only one answer," Candido said. "Stand well clear and fire it at us. That way, your honor will be saved and no one'll get hurt."

"I don't have any shells."

"I'm sorry," said Candido. "Next time we'll come another way, I promise. Would you tell your men to step aside, please?"

Drawn up in two files, right in the middle of the track, were eight ragged soldiers with five rifles between them. The young officer turned to look at them, turned back, thought a while.

"I can't do that," he said at length. "My orders are to detain you. I doubt if my men will obey me, but at least I'll have done my duty."

"You'll get them killed for nothing—*if* they obey you."

"I know, but my hands are tied."

"We're wasting time."

Hastimphilo had just appeared.

"Don't be a fool, Affonso," Candido said. "We haven't the least desire to kill you."

The ensign continued to shake his head. He eyed Hastimphilo, turned about, walked back along the track, turned again for a look at the Leopolda's monstrous snout and set off once more, striding out smartly with the white flag held aloft.

The idiot! He's quite capable of standing his ground.

"Time to go," said Hastimphilo.

"Affonso," Candido called, "out of the way, for God's sake!"

The locomotive emitted a hoarse roar and began to move.

"Come on!"

Hastimphilo grabbed Candido one-handed and hauled him back into the cab.

"They'll get out of the way," he said, "you'll see."

Seven hundred and fifty tons were on the move. Dead ahead, the ensign had rejoined his men. Retrieving his revolver from the sergeant, he stationed himself at their head.

A hundred yards.

Fifty.

Candido put his head out of the observation slit. "Stop!" he yelled.

The Leopolda gathered speed.

"STOP!"

The soldiers loosed off two or three shots and leapt aside. Not so the ensign, who opened fire on the eighteen-foot wall of iron bearing down on him. The frail wooden barrier marking the frontier was reduced to matchwood. The Leopolda's speed increased. Candido withdrew his head, feeling sick. Ezra McAuliffe made an impotent gesture—Hastim-philo had relieved him of his Colt—and pointed to Zé Julio, who was driving in his place.

Minutes later Zé Julio slowed the monster and brought it to a stop, but the looks on the bystanders' faces said it all: Ensign Affonso Lima de Carvalho had been transfixed by one of the ram's teeth. The steel fang had pierced his stomach and was protruding from his back.

"Asleep, Samantha?"

The Leopolda, surrounded by an endless expanse of grassland dotted with granite hills, was steaming slowly through the night. In twenty miles she would reach a junction where she could either head west toward the Argentinian border or continue on her way toward the capital of Uruguay. The Leopolda's band of armed revolutionaries had concluded a nonaggression pact with the Uruguayan authorities: they would refrain from using their artillery, mortars and machine guns to subvert the existing regime or disturb the peace that had been laboriously preserved for twenty-odd years; in return, as long as local rail traffic suffered no disruption, the government of this so-called "South American Switzerland" would totally ignore their presence.

"Asleep, Samantha?"

"Fast asleep."

Candido left it at that. He got dressed and went out onto the platform, which was guarded by two of the men allegedly detailed to protect him.

A fine drizzle was falling. The sound that had alerted him became more distinct: the dull rumble of the train was overlaid by a mechanical hum. He hoisted himself onto the roof of the Love Nest, which was now enclosed by a breastwork of sandbags, fascines and wooden beams. A dozen men were sleeping up there, stoically wrapped in their ponchos.

He didn't spot the car until he'd made his way to the front of the train.
A dark blue limousine was keeping pace with the tender. Perched on the
running board with his head through the window, apparently in conversation with the car's occupants, was a man. Candido crouched down, his
face streaming with lukewarm rain. Ahead of him, squatting on top of the
tender, Hastimphilo was following the conversation with interest. He
caught Candido's eye and smiled.

A minute or more went by. At last the figure on the running board
straightened up, said a few words drowned by the rumble of the train,
gave a clenched-fist salute, and leapt back aboard the train. Candido
recognized him as one of their recent recruits, a man named Leite Abade,
whom even Hastimphilo treated with respect. The limousine slowed and
began to lose ground. Candido identified two of its four occupants as
Stepa Onegin and Policarpo Moravec. The car fell back, little by little,
until it was several hundred yards behind. Then it turned off along a track
leading east and the twin beams of its headlights faded.

Candido joined Hastimphilo on the tender.

"Damned rain."

The former accountant of the Rio Trolley-Car Company shrugged.
"It's the time of year," he said. His tone was amiably sardonic.

Leite Abade had already disappeared into the Leopolda's cabin. Candido followed him down the narrow steel ladder. Zé Julio was at the
controls, Ezra McAuliffe asleep in a hammock with his tam-o'-shanter
over his eyes. Abade turned just as Candido put his foot on the last rung.
A journalist and a qualified lawyer, he was reputed to have been in prison
for political reasons.

"I think we should return to Brazil, Dom Candido," he said.

Hastimphilo descended the ladder in his turn and squeezed in behind
Candido, almost asphyxiating him.

His status was that of a ship's captain who loses control of his vessel
and crew but is studiously treated as if he's still in command. Although,
unlike Captain Ahab, Candido had no desire to hunt a whale of any color,
he was being compelled to sail the seas in search of something utterly
useless and appallingly dangerous. Herr Doktor had put it in a nutshell:
"Revolution, my boy, is the term applied to any movement whereby an
object, having come full circle, ends up where it started."

"According to certain information just received," Abade went on,
"our return is imperative."

Leite Abade was a scrawny, hollow-cheeked man whose ascetic appearance was enhanced by a straggly beard. He always wore a solar topee.

"But of course," he added with a smile, "we're all under Jaguar's
command."

◆ ◆ ◆

Bloodshed was commonplace after that.

They came under attack three times in Rio Grande do Sul. The first and toughest engagement took place west of Cachoeira, when they were crossing a river swollen by the autumn rains of the southern hemisphere. The iron railway bridge had not been blown. The military authorities had simply dismantled the central span and brought up a field battery to deter the Leopolda's engineers from repairing it. The 105 retaliated, making use of its superior range, and destroyed the enemy's main gun emplacement with its fifth shell. After a heavy mortar bombardment, Hastimphilo's two hundred and fifty infantrymen charged the position and captured it. Both sides fought hand-to-hand with the savagery typical of all civil wars.

There were more workers and townsfolk than peasants among Hastimphilo's latest recruits, some of whom were renegade soldiers. At São Gabriel, shortly after they crossed the frontier, a Captain da Silva and forty of his men defected to the so-called revolution. The captain, who was fifty years old and hadn't been promoted for a decade, justified his desertion by citing an argument Candido often heard in time to come: that Brazil was virtually a dictatorship controlled by São Paulo and Minas Gerais. "The president of the republic always comes from one state or the other, and so does everyone else in authority—generals, cabinet ministers, police chiefs. . . ."

Two weeks later the Leopolda passed through Erechim and steamed north for sixty or seventy miles through the mountainous state of Santa Catarina. In some places the track skirted deep gorges, and it was on one of these stretches that the armored train, unable to advance or retreat because of rockfalls brought down by dynamite, was attacked by a column of three thousand men. The revolutionaries were now so numerous that the Leopolda, their focal point, was sandwiched between hundreds of men proceeding on foot or in trucks and horse-drawn carts. Scores of these ragged insurgents were killed in the course of the fighting.

The Leopolda finally extricated herself. McAuliffe uncoupled all the cars and charged the northern rockfall six times until the track was clear. He then hauled the train into more open terrain where the 105, previously rendered useless by the narrow gorge, could be brought to bear on the enemy.

Once these difficulties were behind them they could have headed north across the Paraná to Curitiba or even São Paulo, now less than five hundred miles away, because the Leopolda had proved herself indestructible and unstoppable. Leite Abade and the others vetoed this, however, and pronounced the time not yet ripe. They returned to Rio Grande do Sul, where they steamed around gathering reinforcements.

Then two things happened simultaneously.

The first was the arrival of some news that Abade and Hastimphilo had apparently been expecting for months: a military revolt had broken out at Copacabana. It seemed that part of the army had mutinied and intended to join the revolutionaries.

The second took the form of a figure on the iron bridge spanning the yellow waters of the Paraguay River. This sudden apparition came as no surprise to Candido. It was the man who had been sitting beside Stepa in the limousine—the man who had started it all.

"Samantha, meet Policarpo Moravec."

"I'm dumbfounded," said Policarpo Moravec.

The train was on the move again.

"You haven't changed a bit, Jaguar. You still look as gentle and lethargic—you still have those big, green, boyish eyes and that deceptively innocent smile."

Samantha nodded. "You're right, he looks as if butter wouldn't melt in his mouth. He fools me too, sometimes—especially in bed."

"Amazing!" Moravec exclaimed. "To think that the Jaguar lurks beneath that exterior! Who would credit it?"

"Who indeed?" said Candido.

"I've just come from Moscow. You and Comrade Samantha are much talked of in exalted circles. You're heroes now."

"We're both very flattered, comrade," Candido said. "Precisely who mentioned us to you in Moscow?"

Careful, the madman may have news of Herr Doktor!

It was feeding time, and Samantha was suckling Candida while Eglantina washed nappies. Moravec, with surprising prudishness, averted his eyes from this spectacle.

"You know the price of discretion as well as I do, Jaguar."

"All right, forget it. You speak the language of the Soviet paradise, I presume?"

Switching to Russian, Moravec described the enthusiasm with which certain comrades were following Jaguar's efforts to bring Brazil into the community of socialist republics. They included Bulganin and Bulgakov, Afanasyev and Fyodorov, and—better still—Joseph Vissarionovich Djugashvili himself.

"Never heard of him," said Candido.

A genius, Moravec insisted, a universal genius not only comparable with Vladimir Ilyich Lenin but—incredible as it might seem—actually superior to him in some respects. His sobriquet was Stalin, Man of Steel. Comrade Stalin's lucid intelligence was equaled only by his profound love of humanity.

"With qualities like that he must be worth more than Christ, Muhammad and Buddha put together—not to mention Botafogo's current goalkeeper. Who else, apart from this prodigy, has been taking an interest in us?"

"Oh, any number of people. Felix Dzerzhinsky, for one. What was that name you mentioned?"

"Grüssgott," Candido repeated, his heart in his mouth, "—Herr Doktor Taxile Grüssgott."

No, Moravec replied, looking blank, the name meant nothing to him. On the other hand . . .

"On the other hand, Jaguar, someone asked me to give you his affectionate regards. He wants you to know that he's always with you in spirit. Those were his very words, and he was most insistent that I pass them on."

Alekhin.

"A man of immense courage. A trifle disconcerting at times, but the great and good Stalin esteems him highly. Comrade Alekhin now heads a worldwide organization. No one can cross the Soviet frontier without his say-so. It was the death of Vladimir Ilyich, whom he mourns like the rest of us, that enabled him to rise to his present position." Moravec broke off. "Are you sure that negress can't understand what we're saying?"

"Positive."

"To think you're a personal friend of Comrade Alekhin's! How happy you must be!"

◆　◆　◆

The train had been on the move for weeks. It began by steaming north to strike a blow against the capitalist hyenas of São Paulo in support of some heroic officers who had taken up arms against the corrupt puppet government. The revolt wasn't spreading as quickly as Abade had hoped, however, and the armored train's interventions had become vital to the cause. To the strains of *La Grande Duchesse,* the Leopolda fought several fierce engagements in the highlands of the Serra do Paranapiacaba. Every barricade fell before the steel monster's furious onslaught, but Abade, who was waiting to be reinforced by a column of insurgents, failed to exploit the breakthrough. By the time he resumed the offensive three months later, the enemy had prepared a strong defensive position at the approaches to a small town called Itarare. It proved to be impregnable.

The Leopolda disengaged. She herself had come through almost unscathed, but the rest of the train, crowded with six hundred men of whom at least a hundred were wounded, was a complete wreck. In accordance with Abade's strategic plans, which were steadily assuming the character of a headlong flight, they headed northwest for the Mato Grosso.

The Mato Grosso . . .

Ezra McAuliffe insisted on a prolonged stop for urgent repairs, or he wouldn't answer for the consequences. The Leopolda was in danger of breaking down for good, he said—even of exploding. Not even Zé Julio, who prided himself on his mechanical knowledge, could follow his stream of technical jargon.

The 110-millimeter side members were bent, and they were indispensable. "You want the chassis to collapse before your eyes? Look, they're all buckled, can't you see? It's staring you in the face! The same goes for those crank axles, even though they're made of special carbon steel—gun steel, it's called, with a resistance of 130 kilograms the square millimeter. *You* may not realize they're in bad shape, but *I* do. No, you Brazilian blockhead, of course you can't see it with the naked eye. Do you have to see your innards to be sure you've got the stomachache?"

Other trouble spots included the superheater, the only one of its kind in the world—"It took me sixteen years to perfect it"—and the copper cladding around the smokestack. "I couldn't care less, myself, but sooner or later the old girl will blow up in our faces with a bang they'll hear in Africa. It's up to you, Abade."

Leite Abade gave way. To meet McAuliffe's requirements and give the Leopolda room to maneuver, a small network of track was constructed with the aid of spare rails, cross-ties and points.

"I want to run some trials," McAuliffe announced on the third day. "Shunt those armored wagons and the turret car onto that track there, Zé Julio, but leave the Pullman where it is—we don't need it for the moment. And make sure the tender's chock-full of fuel, I want to see if I've cured those vibrations. What vibrations? What a daft question! When you've spent half a century aboard a locomotive, like me, you'll feel them all right! It was going over those mines that did it. We could be derailed at full speed or rounding a bend."

_____

"Now," said Candido.

He'd just heard the prearranged signal: three leisurely hammer blows followed by two in quick succession. It was three-forty A.M.

"Shut the door behind me."

Samantha's fingers caressed his cheeks and lips in the gloom.

He ducked beneath the Pullman car, unhitched one end of the steel cable that had been secreted there for the past eight weeks and started to unroll it. God, was it heavy! A hundred yards on his back between the rails, hauling the cable behind him, its weight increasing with every yard. On two occasions he froze with his head resting on a cross-tie, hardly daring to breathe because some restless soul in the encampment had got up and was chatting to a sentry only feet away. It suddenly started to rain, *graças a Deus,* and the patter of heavy, tropical raindrops was enough to drown his labored breathing. At last, after what seemed an eternity, he made it. McAuliffe's callused fingers closed around his bleeding hands.

"Come aboard, laddie."

The armor-plated door was ajar. He hauled himself through it, crawled across the steel footplate and was brought up short by the recumbent form of Zé Julio, who appeared to be fast asleep.

"Tuck your legs in, I can't get the door shut. There, that's it. Let's go, laddie—I've secured the cable. Don't worry about him, he hit his head on my hammer. Let's go."

The rhythm of the Leopolda's monstrous breathing scarcely changed, but a tremor ran through her vast frame.

"I bet you she's tucking up her skirts right now, so they don't rustle. She's sneaking off on tiptoe, laddie, like a woman leaving her lover's bed to rejoin her husband."

Very cautiously, Candido poked his head through the trapdoor in the roof of the cab. He could just distinguish the lights of the encampment on his left. No one had reacted yet, but then, why should anyone think twice if the Leopolda, which had been carrying out incomprehensible trials for hours, performed yet another maneuver? How many people, himself included, knew what a vertical tie-rod was, let alone a McAuliffe superheater?

The Leopolda continued to steal away. Nothing moved except the cable, which slithered merrily along the track as if the Leopolda would be in Peru by the time it drew taut. The Pullman, standing beneath the trees with Samantha, Candida and Eglantina on board, remained obstinately motionless. Candido began to think they were towing the wrong car.

Hastimphilo!

It was the big black man beyond a doubt—Candido could see him silhouetted against the glow of a camp fire, obviously puzzled by the Leopolda's stealthy departure.

He'll spot the cable and guess what's happening!

"It's Hastimphilo!" Candido shouted to McAuliffe. "He's after us!"

"What of it, laddie? All you've got to do is shut the trapdoor."

Hastimphilo's long legs quickly ate up the intervening distance. He leapt for the tender, clambered over the tarpaulin-covered logs, hurled himself at the cab. Candido slammed the trapdoor and bolted it.

Two seconds later a slight jerk indicated that they'd taken up the slack at last.

"We're in business," said McAuliffe, glancing in his patent rearview mirror.

Hastimphilo's eyes glared at Candido through a loophole, ablaze with fury and hatred, only to disappear almost at once. He covered the length of the tender in three strides, dropped to the ground and started running back along the track.

"He's going to cut the cable or unhitch it, Ezra. Can't you go any faster?"

"No. We're lucky the damned thing's holding as it is."

The Leopolda was now doing twenty miles an hour. Zé Julio groaned and stirred.

"Dump him."

"Are you sure you didn't fracture his skull?"

"It was only an affectionate little tap—he isn't a bad mechanic for a Brazilian. Go on, laddie, push him out."

The rain had stopped and the moon had emerged from behind the clouds. Visible at a range of two hundred yards, the Pullman car was sedately following in their wake. Not a sign of Hastimphilo.

We've done it! But . . . Why doesn't Samantha open the door? Surely she realizes we've got clean away?

"Let's have a little music, Ezra. And hand me the binoculars, please."

He trained them on the Pullman's door. It was still shut.

Why? She must have seen through the loopholes that nobody's after us.

Only then did it occur to him to look a little higher.

Hastimphilo was standing on the roof of the car.

He was still there three hours later, when the Leopolda steamed into the Mato Grosso to the strains of *La Périchole.* He'd made three attempts to get into the car by the only possible route, a boarded-up shell-hole on the right-hand side.

Candido had fired three times, warning shots only. He deliberately refrained from hitting the black man, terrified by the realization that he didn't want to kill or even wound him. He simply wanted him to go away and leave them in peace.

"Look!" McAuliffe yelled suddenly. "The bastard's as strong as an ox!"

Candido saw what he meant. Hastimphilo had managed to wrench a metal cross-tie off the Pullman's armor-plated roof. He brandished the six-foot length of steel above his head and smiled contemptuously.

"He'll smash those planks, laddie—he'll end by getting inside. If he takes your woman and the baby hostage we'll have to stop and go back. He knows you aren't up to killing anyone. Jesus Christ, I'd shoot him myself, but I'd miss a barn door at ten yards."

Candido had climbed out onto the roof of the cab. He was sitting with his legs dangling over the edge and Zé Julio's rifle across his thighs.

I've never harmed anyone in my life, not deliberately.

"That's two planks he's levered off, laddie!"

Candido swiftly took aim, fired once and threw the rifle overboard. McAuliffe brought the Leopolda to a stop. They jumped down and ran toward the Pullman. There was a sound of bolts being withdrawn and the door opened.

"Candido, oh, Candido!"

He hugged Samantha, took the baby from Eglantina and hugged her too. Then he walked back along the track for a couple of hundred yards.

Hastimphilo was lying face up with his arms out sideways. The bullet had hit him in the left temple.

It had to happen. I've killed someone at last.

"The jaguar," he remembered reading somewhere, "becomes a man-eater only in very exceptional circumstances."

VII

THE JAGUAR HAS ALWAYS BEEN
HUNTED BY MAN. SOUTH AMERICAN INDIANS
USE CURARE-TIPPED ARROWS FOR THIS PURPOSE. IT
CAN ALSO, THOUGH THIS IS MORE DANGEROUS, BE
FLUSHED OUT AND BROUGHT TO BAY WITH DOGS. ALL
THAT REMAINS IS TO WRAP A SHEEPSKIN AROUND
ONE'S ARM AND STAB THE ANIMAL WITH A SPECIAL
TYPE OF DOUBLE-EDGED KNIFE. THE DOGS
ARE THEN LEFT TO FINISH IT OFF.

The days and nights that followed were lovelier than any dream. The Leopolda, now coupled only to her tender and the Pullman car, seemed to amble across the uninhabited wilderness where Candido had once awaited death on his *trombas* in the middle of the Pantanal. Nothing could have been pleasanter than to dawdle through the *floresta virgem,* the virgin forest, while Eglantina and the baby kept Ezra McAuliffe company in the cab and Samantha and Candido made memorable love in Great-uncle Amílcar's outsize bed and the Leopolda relieved the primeval silence by blasting out the "Barcarolle" or, better still, their favorite aria: *"Dis-moi, Vénus, quel plaisir trouves-tu, à faire ainsi cascader, cascader, cascader la vertu. . . ."*

"This is all very well, my bairns," said McAuliffe after eight or nine days had gone by, "but we'll have to make our minds up some time."

The old Scot was growing apprehensive. Every hour of every day saw him peering ahead, behind and sideways in the dread expectation of sighting a detachment of bloodthirsty regulars or—almost as unwelcome—a band of yelling insurgents with Leite Abade at their head, eager to retrieve their nominal leader and figurehead.

"We could always shut ourselves up in the Leopolda, but how long would we last if they tore up the track and our food and water ran out?"

They held repeated councils of war, sawed up nearby trees for fuel, pored over maps. To be on the safe side, Candido cut the telegraph wires at thirty or forty points.

They couldn't go on like this forever, it was true. The army chiefs at São Paulo, or wherever else they were based, must be under the impression that Jaguar was still with his revolutionaries. Sooner or later, however, they would learn that he'd retired from the fray and send troops in pursuit.

Samantha pointed to the map. "What's that country on the other side of the frontier?"

"Bolivia," Candido told her.

The three of them looked at one another.

They felled stacks of timber and sawed it up to keep the Leopolda fed. All was quiet at Campo Grande when they passed it under cover of darkness. The towns that followed were just as peaceful. For some reason Samantha couldn't grasp, Candido found this odd.

"You said it yourself. It won't occur to them that you're heading for Bolivia. Besides, you cut those telegraph wires."

Two days later they came within sight of Corumbá, the last town before the frontier. Some soldiers opened fire on the Leopolda in the derisory hope of stopping her, but the element of surprise proved invaluable. The railway bridge was intact and unobstructed except for a small locomotive and a few freight cars. The Leopolda nudged them gently into a siding and continued on her way.

They were now in Bolivia, much of which, according to the map, consisted of a vast plateau. There was only one city of any note, Santa Cruz, and only one rail junction for hundreds of miles, a place called Boyuibe, where they would have a choice of two routes.

Once across the frontier they steamed serenely along with nothing to do but contemplate intermittent swamps and endless, rain-swept plains dotted with anthills and the occasional totay palm. The wood of the totay was unsuitable for stoking the Leopolda, so they were fortunate in being able to avail themselves of the fuel stored beside the track for ordinary trains. A deal had been struck with the Bolivian authorities at Puerto Suárez, a dreary little town some thirty miles inside the border. They proclaimed themselves run-of-the-mill tourists traveling by private train and armed with nothing but peaceful intentions (five hundred dollars' worth). They would, of course, give way to regular rail traffic if informed of the national network's timetables and the places where one train could pass another.

At Boyuibe they were confronted by a decision: they could either send the Leopolda puffing into the mountains or head south for Argentina.

Ezra McAuliffe, who had sailed to Buenos Aires from Scotland half a century earlier, wasn't unattracted by the thought of revisiting his old Argentinian haunts. Besides, driving several hundred tons of iron and steel over ill-maintained mountain tracks didn't appeal to him in the least.

"Well, I'd like to see Lake Titicaca," Samantha said. "It's such a cute name."

Candido seconded her.

"I haven't seen a sign of the Claws," he said. "I vote we put some more distance between us and Brazil by heading west. That's the best way of keeping them out of our hair."

Titicaca won the day.

An ordinary train appeared, laden to the roof with passengers whose tortoiselike profiles indicated that the local population was almost entirely Indian. They waited for it to pass and then set off. The gradient quickly increased until it seemed impossible that they would ever scale such an awesome wall of rock. The rain had stopped at last, affording a clear view of immense gorges with torrents gushing in their depths.

"We could go to Machu Picchu," said Samantha. "There was an article about it in that *New York Times* Ciccio brought us at São Paulo. I read it while we were waiting for your father to give you the brush-off. Machu Picchu's an Inca site in Peru—an American discovered it ten or twelve years ago."

McAuliffe said he doubted if the Incas had built a railway line to it.

"There isn't one," Samantha said eagerly. "The best thing would be to go to La Paz or even a bit farther. Then we could either put the Leopolda on a raft and ferry her across Lake Titicaca or complete the journey on foot."

"There isn't one," McAuliffe repeated.

"I know, that's what I said."

"I'm not talking about your trip to Macky Picky, I mean the track ahead of us. It's gone."

He applied the brakes.

Stepa Onegin sauntered leisurely up with his hands in his pockets.

"I know you, Cavalcanti," he said in Russian. "You aren't the kind to fight a losing battle. To be on the safe side, however, I should warn you that two of us are inside the Pullman with your daughter and the black girl."

Otto Krantz appeared behind him.

"Where were you planning to go?"

"For a swim in Lake Titicaca," said Samantha.

Stepa shook his head. "That's out of the question, I'm afraid."

"Where's Afonka Tchadayev?" she demanded.

"You'll see him if it's necessary, but it won't be. Mr. McAuliffe? You've got three minutes to get this locomotive moving—downhill, this time."

"You give me a pain," the old Scot growled.

"I could shoot you on the spot, McAuliffe. We don't really need you—one of us could get this contraption going. Do as I say or we'll kill the black girl. Cavalcanti?"

"Please, Ezra," said Candido. "Where to, Stepa?"

"Boyuibe. I was hoping you'd decide to go south. The fact that you chose the mountains compelled us to step in sooner than we planned." The Russian turned back to McAuliffe. "Unless it's running late, a Bolivian train will be starting up this track five hours from now. You've time to reach Boyuibe before that. If you don't, you'll be responsible for a massacre."

Candido and Samantha boarded the Pullman just as the Leopolda set off in reverse. Stepa followed them inside.

"Let's all sit down and take it easy," he said. "We're going to be together for quite a while, so I don't see why we shouldn't make ourselves comfortable."

"Where are we going?" Samantha asked.

"Back to Brazil, of course. Where would the revolution be without its historic leader?"

From Boyuibe they headed south into Argentina. Five more men got on at a small town called Tartagal: three Brazilians, an Argentinian and a Venezuelan from Caracas who introduced himself as Carlos. They were underlings whose principal duties were to stoke the Leopolda, fell and chop wood for the boiler, and act as additional guards. Now nine strong, Jaguar's escorts ensured that Candido never got a chance to speak with McAuliffe, presumably to prevent them from concocting some wild scheme of escape.

Argentina went on forever. After a seven-day wait at Tucumán they set off across the pampa, traversing it at periods when regular rail traffic was slack. Skirting the northern outskirts of Córdoba, they spent one night apiece at Santa Fe and Paraná, where the train was cordoned off by armed soldiers. The doors of the Pullman had been sealed.

On the last evening Samantha broached a forbidden topic—one that Candido wouldn't have raised for the world. She demanded to know what would happen when the Leopolda reentered Brazil.

"My comrades and I will discreetly withdraw," Stepa told her.

"And then?"

Candido caught Stepa's eye and silently implored him to say nothing. But his silent plea was in vain. Stepa gave a thin smile.

"Then? Jaguar will die, of course. A revolutionary leader is often more useful dead than alive. He will be killed in battle or captured and brutally executed by the imperialist regime, one or the other. Even if, by some extraordinary mischance, he were to escape both those fates, he would have to be killed notwithstanding. By whom? By those who know the truth, namely, that Jaguar is a mere fiction. We couldn't afford to let that come out, Comrade Samantha. But never fear, we'll provide your man with an end worthy of his legendary reputation.''

◆　◆　◆

"Time to split up," said Stepa. "We're ten miles from Brazil and our work is done. Other things being equal, you won't see us again.''

"What comes next?''

That was Samantha, of course.

"It's quite simple. You're expected across the border, a few miles beyond an absurd barricade that the Leopolda will brush aside as usual. It won't stop her if she gets up enough speed.''

Samantha looked at Candido and—*graças a Deus*—said nothing. He'd urged her a thousand times to keep her mouth shut, but for Samantha that was next to impossible.

"You'll all remain shut up in here—you two, your daughter and the black girl. The doors will be opened as soon as you've crossed the frontier and linked up with the nearest elements of Jaguar's army. I wish you a good death, Cavalcanti. You deserve one.''

The train had been stationary for several minutes. Matriona and Otto Krantz had already got out.

"How truly heroic," Stepa drawled. "Just when the fate of his revolution hangs by a thread—just when his loyal followers have been almost encircled and thrown back on the defensive—Jaguar, instead of skulking in the safety of a foreign land, returns to share his people's tragic destiny and die with the remnants of his army. Unless, of course, the revolution is miraculously revived by his presence and regains strength. Stranger things have happened.''

He too got out, covering them with his revolver until the last moment. Two motor vehicles had driven up, a truck and a limousine—a black one, this time. Matriona was already installed in the car. At that range, Candido might almost have mistaken her for Samantha.

The Man Mountain had left the Leopolda's cab and was busy helping Otto Krantz to secure the forward door of the Pullman. Candido, peering through a peephole, saw that they were simply threading a length of wood through the big, semicircular handles. They walked to the rear of the car and secured the other door in the same way.

Samantha, who had been silent far too long, couldn't contain herself any longer. She proceeded to tell Stepa Onegin, Matriona, the Man Mountain, Otto Krantz and the rest of their kind what she thought of their past, present and future.

"Please don't, Samantha.''

"I will if I want."

"Not now."

"When, then? Standing over your grave?"

She still didn't understand. They would never let her visit his grave. She knew too much. She'd die when he died. Perhaps it was better that way.

"At least wait till we're on the move."

"Why? Anyway, we're moving now."

The wheels were making a strange, soft, muffled sound. Samantha's eyes widened. She stared at him in surprise.

But her expression was nothing compared to that of Stepa and his acolytes. They looked thunderstruck, and at least two seconds elapsed before they reacted. The Man Mountain leapt for the rear platform and hung on, the others jumped into the limousine or the truck and sped in pursuit of the Pullman, which was gathering speed.

"What's that?"

"We're moving on our own. We couldn't hear the sound of the wheels before—the Leopolda always drowned it."

"Where's Ezra?"

"He's deserted us. Listen."

She strained her ears.

"Dis-moi, Vénus," a distant voice was singing, *"quel plaisir trouves-tu, à faire ainsi cascader, cascader, cascader la vertu. . . ."*

"He knows it's our favorite tune, so he's playing it for us. It's his way of saying good-bye."

"Forever, you mean?"

"I'm afraid so. He talked about it that first night at Bragança Boa Vista. I never said anything—I didn't want to alarm you. He's the only person capable of destroying the Leopolda. If I'm right, he'll send her sky-high in one blinding flash."

The Pullman was beginning to slow. The Man Mountain, still clinging on outside, was cranking away at the brake handle with all his might. Candido hoped he'd burst a blood vessel—Ezra had dismantled the brake shoes months ago. The car would stop, but only of its own accord.

It did so a couple of miles down the track.

"Out," said Stepa.

Candido smiled at Samantha.

"I'll be back."

He got out. The Leopolda was stationary, a mile away.

"Into the car, Cavalcanti."

He squeezed into the front seat of the limousine between Stepa, who took the wheel, and the Man Mountain. The others, including Otto Krantz and Matriona, remained beside the Pullman.

They approached the Leopolda, which promptly spat steam and withdrew a hundred yards. The limousine followed, and again the Leopolda backed away like a ninety-foot cat determined to keep its distance.

"I know Ezra," Candido said. "He's stubborn. I'd better go and talk to him on my own."

"Out of the question," said Stepa.

"Then he'll wait—for weeks, if necessary, and I'll miss my prearranged date with those idiots across the border. Think, Stepa: you've got Samantha and the baby. My hands are tied."

I've scored a point for once. He doesn't know what to do. He's just a machine, and not a particularly sophisticated one. He carries out Alekhin's instructions, but that's all.

It's our only chance.

Stepa opened the door and swung his legs out.

"Stay where you are," he said in Russian to the Man Mountain. "Cavalcanti, come with me."

"He won't let you near him, believe me. See for yourself."

Stepa took ten paces. The Leopolda withdrew ten yards.

A pause.

"All right, Cavalcanti. You know what to say?"

"Yes. If he doesn't come back and pick up the Pullman and take us across the frontier as planned, you'll kill Eglantina."

"And your daughter."

"And my daughter. But I'll never convince him, Stepa. Alekhin didn't order you to murder my daughter—or Eglantina, for that matter. I give you my word: if you touch either one of them, I'll kill myself. You'll have lost Jaguar and wrecked Alekhin's plans. He won't be pleased."

Stepa's eyes clouded over again.

Got him. I've got him.

"Try all the same," he said, "and don't forget I'll be listening."

"Ezra?"

No reply.

"Ezra, can you hear me?"

Silence. Finally:

"That you, laddie?"

"Didn't you see me coming?"

"Too plastered, laddie, can't see much of anything. Had to do it so they wouldn't catch on. I drank so much they got careless. Four whole bottles—never drunk so much in my life. God, am I tight!"

"What have you done with the men who were with you?"

He was talking deliberately loud so Stepa wouldn't miss a word.

McAuliffe mumbled something about them hitting their heads on his hammer.

"You mean they're dead, Ezra?"

"Aye, they're out o' the running. And now, laddie, I'm going to send the Leopolda to kingdom come. It'll be the bang of the century."

"But Ezra, if you do that they'll kill Eglantina and the baby."

"Can't be helped, laddie. Too bad, can't be helped."

Candido looked back at Stepa.

"I beg you, Ezra. They'll kill my daughter."

" 'Sno use, laddie."

"So why did you stop here?"

"Dizzy spell, not feeling too good—they broke a couple of my ribs. Like some more music?"

He isn't quite as drunk as he makes out, but he won't give way, I know it.

"Ezra, I implore you, open up and let me in."

The only response was a volcanic eruption of steam and smoke as the Leopolda got under way. Her huge wheels spun a little, then gripped and turned more slowly. Ten yards, twenty yards . . . Candido broke into a run, Stepa Onegin followed suit. The Man Mountain brought the limousine level with the cab. Half leaning out of the window, he tugged in vain at the heart-shaped, armor-plated door before letting go and grabbing the wheel in time to avoid a collision.

Candido had squatted down between the rails to get his breath back. Stepa caught up and remained standing behind him. The Leopolda was half a mile away by now, her prodigious, hurried breathing a sign that she was accelerating fast.

"Without a load, laddie, I bet you she'll still do a hundred or even a bit more. . . ."

A mile. With the loudspeaker system operating at full volume, the music was clearly audible even at that range: it was the overture to *La Grande Duchesse de Gerolstein.*

Four minutes.

Five.

An almighty explosion, then silence. The Leopolda was no more.

No tears, not now of all times.

"You may not believe me, Stepa, but I will kill myself unless you come up with another plan."

"I don't have another plan."

"I have one. No one gets killed. Leave them all alone and I'll join those men across the frontier. I'll stay with them at least a month, I give you my word."

Another silence. A huge column of smoke was rising above the skyline. *Don't cry, damn you.*

"Listen, Stepa, you're going to follow us anyway—you can kill them any time if I break my word. At least you'll have completed the assignment Alekhin gave you. I'll still die according to the plan."

All right, cry a little if you must.

It was three hours since they'd abandoned the limousine and the truck. Candido, with Samantha just behind him, was carrying the little girl. Then came Otto Krantz and the Man Mountain, then Eglantina. Matriona and Stepa brought up the rear. The others were strung out ahead and on either flank. It was a dark night.

Crossing the frontier at Santana do Livramento had proved impossible. A man sent to reconnoiter the place reported that it was in turmoil. In preparation for the armored train's arrival, several wagons laden with stone had been parked on the track to form a barricade covered by a whole battery of field guns. There was nothing there now but an enormous crater. The army had kept its distance in case the Leopolda came armed with her own artillery, so the wounded far outnumbered the dead. Everyone had been stupefied by the monstrous explosion, whose exact cause remained a mystery. It was rumored that Jaguar had committed suicide by cramming his famous locomotive with dynamite.

"Hear that, Cavalcanti? They think you're dead."

Candido didn't reply, content for the moment to have warded off the threat to Candida and Eglantina. The truck and the limousine had driven north for a hundred miles or so, Stepa's intention being to ford the Quaraí, which marked the frontier. Compelled to proceed on foot because the water was too deep and the current too swift, they were thereafter restricted to rough tracks known only to the scout in the lead.

They walked for hours and hours. At daybreak Stepa finally called a halt and leaned against a tree with his finger on the trigger of his automatic.

"I need some water for the baby," Samantha said.

Stepa ignored her, then stiffened a little: he'd heard the rustle of movement that Candido's ears had caught at least thirty seconds earlier.

Whistles and recognition signals followed. The Jaguar's Claws melted into the undergrowth just as some men appeared. They numbered around thirty and included the familiar figure of Vivaldo Maria, Clovis's brother, who appeared to be in command. He came forward, smiling.

"Good to see you again."

"Speak for yourself," said Samantha.

"I'm glad all the same," he said. "But we must leave at once—it isn't safe here. There are hordes of soldiers looking for you an hour away— they don't know for sure if Jaguar died in that explosion. We've got some carts waiting not far away. Let me help you with the child."

"Drop dead," said Samantha. "Keep your paws off her."

Candido looked round.

Stepa and the others had vanished.

"Is your brother still alive?"

"Clovis was wounded in the battle beside the Santo Anastácio, but he's all right. Jorge's dead, and so are Celso and João Alberto. Edson was taken prisoner—they'll have shot him by now. As for Hastimphilo and Zé Julio, we don't know what became of them."

"Zé Julio had a fractured skull the last time I saw him—he hit his head on McAuliffe's hammer. Hastimphilo's dead. He fell off the train while it was moving."

"You're sure he's dead?"

"Sure is an understatement."

"He seemed so indestructible. . . ." Vivaldo Maria shook his head sorrowfully. "But you did well to take off when you did. Right after you left, the soldiers launched a surprise attack. They couldn't have failed to capture the Leopolda if she'd still been there. Did you smell a trap, or what?"

"Pure coincidence, that's all."

"Hastimphilo was a hero. I'm sure he'd have preferred a soldier's death. He must have died with rage in his heart."

Candido nodded. "I've seen people in better moods."

It was late afternoon, and the carts had been making their way along rutted tracks for hours. Samantha, Candida and Eglantina were asleep in spite of all the jolting. Lookouts stationed on the nearby hills had been flocking in from all directions to reinforce Vivaldo Maria's column. A general retreat was in progress, it seemed, and this detachment, now a hundred strong, formed the rear guard.

"What are you doing so far south, Vivaldo Maria? The last time we met you were on the outskirts of the Mato Grosso."

"We heard that Jaguar and his armored train were about to reenter Brazil by way of Uruguay."

"Who spread the word?"

"One of your secret agents, Jaguar."

"Secret agents?"

"Please. Everyone knows you have them."

"Don't call me Jaguar. My name is Candido. And my name is just about all I have left."

"Well, to cut a long story short, Abade and the other commanders decided to come and meet you. Clovis was supposed to welcome you as soon as you'd smashed through that barricade—I and my detachment were merely covering the flank—but you took everyone by surprise as usual and crossed the border farther west."

Candido had declined a place in one of the carts. He felt he ought to get back into top condition. Much later, in the Great Silence, he would cherish a wry recollection of his insistence on walking that day, the very first day of the Long March.

Vivaldo Maria's column, having meantime joined forces with Clovis's detachment, linked up with the bulk of the rebel army after a series of forced marches lasting six nights and five days. The main body was more numerous than Candido had foreseen. No less than five thousand men were encamped on a chain of hills watered by tiny streams that fed tributaries of tributaries of the Paraguay River.

He was taken to headquarters. His original intention was to say nothing, but he changed his mind. He explained that the old locomotive had been on her last legs, so he'd had her blown up rather than let the army take credit for her destruction. Leite Abade and Tasso Aranha, another commander, believed him, more or less, but they were almost as much prisoners of the Jaguar myth as he was himself.

Abade and Aranha—ex-Captain da Silva was an utter nincompoop who didn't count—had no idea what to do next. Their entire strategy had been centered on the Leopolda. Without her, they were completely at a loss.

"If I were you," Candido told them, "I'd go north."

North? What for?

He had a very specific destination in mind: the Mato Grosso, the *floresta virgem,* the impenetrable wilderness. Samantha had refused to hear of it, but he felt sure he could talk her into it. His chances of getting there with two women and a young child would be improved if they traveled under the protection of an army on the march.

"The north is wild and unexplored," he said. "No army will follow us there. We can get to the Amazon, capture Manaus and set up a provisional government there while waiting for the tide to turn."

It would mean a march of over fifteen hundred miles, admittedly, but that was just the point. Who in São Paulo or Rio would think them likely to embark on such an extraordinary venture? It would be the best way of eluding the troops sent against them.

Above all, they would go down in history.

History . . .

They're going to fall for the idea. God knows how, but I've pressed the right button. I'm becoming—what's the word?—well, cynical. Perhaps that's what it takes to be an anarchist. Or a general. Or Jaguar.

"That you, Clovis?"

"Everything all right, Candido?"

It was the thirteenth night of the Long March, and they'd bivouacked on the northern edge of Rio Grande do Sul.

"Thanks for not calling me Jaguar, it makes a nice change."

"I know you don't like the name."

"You really think I'm the jaguar type?"

"I'm not sure."

"You know me. Your great-grandmother knows me. I was quite good to old Domitila—you saw that for yourself when you sent her the money I gave you."

"That proves nothing. A person can be good to any number of people and still be good at all kinds of other things."

"Like what?"

"Running fast, reacting quicker than most, knowing how to shoot. We talked about you while we were at Bragança Boa Vista. One old servant told us you were very handy with a gun, even as a boy."

The servants there had known him since childhood. Was that the image they'd preserved of him? Could he be wrong about himself?

"I don't know whether you're Jaguar or not, Candido," Clovis went on.

"I've never cut anyone's throat in my life, I swear it on my mother's grave."

Clovis stared at him, then looked away. "If you say so," he said.

People are odd. Clovis will mourn me when I die, if he's still around himself. He likes me a lot, but it doesn't prevent him from hoping I'm Alekhin's creation, the mythical cutthroat. He actually wants me to be Jaguar. Perhaps he needs me to be Jaguar.

Candido produced three letters.

"Could you get these delivered for me?"

"That depends."

"I'd appreciate it if you did. Pick a man you trust—three men, preferably."

"To make sure at least one of them gets through?"

"Exactly. These are three copies of the same letter addressed to three different people."

They were João Pessoa, Ciccio Vaz Vasconselos and Aristides Dantas, an exattorney of Dom Trajano's.

"I'd like you to read it, Clovis. It's the story of Candido the Jaguar the way it really happened."

"If you want me to."

"Thanks."

Clovis pulled the dark lantern closer and began to read, silently mouthing the words. Candido watched him. From time to time the former trolley-car conductor raised his head and stared as if to reassure himself that the Candido Cavalcanti in question and the man facing him were one and the same. Then he read on.

An hour went by.

Clovis had finished. He sat quite still and gazed at the nearby river with the last sheet in his hand, too deep in thought to add it to the others and refold them. At last he said, "It certainly isn't an ordinary story."

"Do you believe it?"

Another silence. Clovis wasn't uncertain how to answer, just spellbound by what he'd read.

"Yes," he said, "I believe every word. I'll send your letters, Candido, and I'll pick the very best runners I've got. I'll be damned if one of them doesn't make it."

He replaced the letter in its rubberized pouch, which he secured with a piece of string.

"At least they'll stand a chance," he went on. "As for the rest of us, we're going to die. There were ten of us trolley-car conductors when we left Rio with you. The only ones still alive are Vivaldo Maria, Teotônio, Lindolpho and myself. That's four out of ten. I read what you wrote to your friends about our wives and children. Thank you."

"I think they'll do as I ask. Dom João and Dom Ciccio will, certainly. I don't know about the other man."

"We're all going to die," Clovis repeated. "We haven't done four hundred miles yet. There are still a thousand or more to go, and we've already lost plenty of men. None of us will ever reach the Amazon."

"The forest can be beaten," Candido said. "I've done it before and I'll do it again."

Clovis contemplated the three waterproof pouches.

"That letter," he said, "—it's like a last will and testament."

◆　◆　◆

The first engagement took place on the seventeenth day. It was a pure miracle they hadn't had to fight sooner, but the military authorities had never expected several thousand men to march due north—insofar as the terrain allowed—and were taken by surprise. If Candido had entertained any doubts about Clovis's skill as a tactician, this first brush with the enemy dispelled them. His battalion, which formed the advance guard, bore the brunt of the fighting. The Iguaçú, a river enclosed by banks the color of blood and flowing through a snake-infested jungle, lay in the rebels' path. Having managed to get half his men across, Clovis wheeled right and dug in to check the advance of some twelve hundred federal troops. Meanwhile, the bulk of the rebel army passed behind him and made its way westward along the Argentinian border.

Clovis stood his ground for forty-eight hours, and although he took his walking wounded with him, he left at least fifty corpses behind.

The retreat turned into a nightmare. The forest was dense and stifling, trackless and impenetrable. Every branch, every root that plucked at one's foot or leg might be a snake. The wounded hobbled along with fear and despair in their eyes, not daring to ask for help because the choice that confronted those who could go no farther, though threefold, was limited: to die by their own hand, by that of a comrade, or by that of an enemy soldier.

A halt was called.

Candido let go of the man he was supporting and sank to the ground. If he was weary, those around him were exhausted. Some of them were vomiting blood, and the smell of vomit mingled with that of excrement.

Clovis lay sprawled on his face, pale as death. Candido got up and went over to him.

"Are you wounded?"

An almost imperceptible shake of the head, eyes closed. Leaving him to rest a while, Candido made his way back to the Iguaçú and sat down at the top of the bank.

A snake was eyeing him from nine or ten feet away. "No point in glaring at me like that," Candido said. "I'm not going to bite you. You stick to your territory and I'll stick to mine. You've got reddish-orange skin ringed with black and a skull as thick as a sergeant-major's—you use it to dig tunnels with and knock other snakes on the head before you eat them. Well, why not, that's your affair. Hey, I've had an idea—tell me what you think of it: soldiers should be made to eat all the soldiers they kill. That would soon cool their blood, and I think help make their breed extinct.''

The snake acted up. It flattened its body by spreading out its ribs, raised and curled its tail to show off the underside, which was handsomely variegated.

"You don't impress me one bit," Candido told it. "That's just a waste of energy."

Annoyed, the snake went off for a swim in the river.

Clovis is wrong. I will *get out of the* floresta virgem *alive, and so will Samantha and Candida and Eglantina.*

The forty-sixth day. They had to have covered seven hundred miles, but their rate of progress was slowing. Crossing the Paraná, the Ilha Grande and Ilha dos Bandeirantes had been a terrible experience. Most of the carts and wagons got bogged down and had to be abandoned. All they had left now were two carts and three horses to pull them.

"I'll get down and walk," Samantha said, speaking Russian to foil potential eavesdroppers.

"Stay right where you are. Don't worry, you've got plenty of walking ahead of you."

"Why, are we going to make a break for it?"

"Not yet."

"How many of them are left, would you say?"

"Three thousand or so, maybe less."

"Watch out for snakes."

"Jaguars aren't afraid of snakes."

"My eye."

"It's a very pretty eye. What's the matter with it?"

"Nothing."

"Are you crying?"

"No."

"Then what . . ."

"It's nothing, Candido. I told you." Samantha took a deep breath and wiped her eye with the side of her hand. "It's nothing."

The fifty-ninth day. Clovis's advance guard was down to sixty men out of the five hundred he'd started out with, but then, it was his job to blaze a trail and beat off attacks, of which there had now been nine in all.

"You're still alive, though," Candido pointed out, "and so are your brother and Lindolpho."

"I don't know where Lindolpho is. I don't even know where *we* are."

"Lindolpho's with Samantha and the child, and we've just crossed the Serra de Maracaju."

"But we're in the Mato Grosso, aren't we?"

"Right in it," said Candido.

Well, nearly, but there's no point in depressing him even more.

The sixty-first day. They were descending the slopes of the Serra de São Jerônimo, and Clovis's scouts had pushed west toward Cuiabá, the only sizable town for hundreds of miles. A motorized column ambushed them but failed to pursue them very far. The rebels' tactics were unvarying: the remnants of their army simply melted away into the jungle.

Candido's relative strength surprised him. He felt tired, but not exhausted. He hadn't been reduced to eating worms or leaves or baby caymans, like so many of the others. He was still on a diet of rice and beans. The next township they came to was Cáceres, namesake of a Spanish wine that Dom Trajano used to import in barrels from La Rioja. Here they halted for four days and Candido spent the last of his dollars on a meager stock of provisions. As soon as scouts reported the approach of some soldiers, possibly those that had held the road to Cuiabá with such determination, they moved on.

The map indicated that the Chapada dos Parecis, a highland plateau, lay some hundred miles due north. Any survivors who managed to surmount that obstacle should then be able to locate one of the tributaries of the Saceruiná.

"Have you been that way before, Candido?"

"No," said Candido, surprised by the question. He thought he'd made that clear when recounting his own trek through the Mato Grosso.

Leite Abade was a walking skeleton. Even his skull seemed to have shrunk; his topee rattled around on his head.

"Isn't there any other possible route?" asked Aranha, who was in little better shape.

"We could head west along the Bolivian border. Then, as soon as we come to a river flowing north, we could follow it to the Rio Guaporé. There are villages on the Guaporé—Indians who spoke a few words of Portuguese sometimes turned up at the army post where I was stationed. They might help us to build some rafts."

"Which route would *you* take, Candido?"

Just the question I've been waiting for.

"The Guaporé," he said. "It's longer, but at least we'd stand a chance."

A chance, yes, except that it would mean traversing several hundred miles of jungle so dense that no one had ever ventured into it except the Indians and one legendary Portuguese expedition three centuries ago. . . .

Abade and Aranha bent over the map. Many areas were simply blank.

"And after the Guaporé?"

"There's an army post at Guajará-Mirim—fifteen men at most, you wouldn't even have to fire a shot. From Guajará-Mirim you could head downstream to Pôrto Velho, a hundred and fifty miles northeast, following the Rio Madeira—"

"Which joins the Amazon only a hundred miles from Manaus," Aranha put in.

"It's up to you," said Candido, as he left the shack where the joint commanders of the rebel army had set up their headquarters. Samantha, Candida and Eglantina were aboard the one remaining horse-drawn cart, and for the past week he'd been allowed to walk alongside it. Having lost their distrust of him, the rebel leaders no longer thought it necessary to separate him from his family.

"Everything all right?" he said to Samantha.

"Couldn't be better." She smiled as best she could. "Are we getting near?"

"Very near. Did you have a word with him?"

They were speaking Russian. "Him" was Lindolpho the telegraphist, who drove the cart.

"He's all set."

They'd been on the move again for a week now, and the column was more compact than it had ever been since leaving Rio Grande do Sul. Discounting several dozen individuals whose continued survival was little short of miraculous—though not, unfortunately, destined to endure—an inexorable process of natural selection was taking place. Candido had observed it before, and every passing day confirmed Herr Doktor's theory: size and stamina weren't synonymous. Toting a lot of muscle around was more of a handicap than an advantage, and women were better than most at withstanding privation.

The first river they crossed flowed south. Two days later they encountered another, but that one, apart from being full of caymans, was also flowing in the wrong direction. Only a few miles farther on they came

to a third river which, by some quirk of nature, flowed north. Scouts sent
out by Clovis returned with the news that it was the Rio Alegre.

Although Candido wouldn't have gone so far as to say that he recognized every tree or bend in the river, something about the area struck a
chord in his memory.

"I think it's over on the right," he told Samantha in Russian, "maybe
two hours' march from here. See that mountain? I remember thinking it
looked like my father lying on his back with his nose in the air."

"Mountain? It's only a rock, and there are fifty of them exactly like it.
You're starting to worry me, Cavalcanti."

"Farther on, where the river makes a hairpin bend, there's a little
valley with a lake the size of a pocket handkerchief and a waterfall
cascading down a huge wall of rock."

"You're making things up as usual."

"What do you bet me?"

If I'm wrong it'll be the last mistake I ever make.

Far ahead, Aranha and his detachment had gone to reinforce Clovis
and his men, who were laboriously hewing a path through the jungle with
axes and machetes. The column was now strung out for nearly two miles,
with Lindolpho bringing up the rear as instructed. A good hundred yards
separated them from the end of the column, and the vegetation was so
dense in places that it hid all signs of life. They might have been alone
in the wilderness.

Candida, Lindolpho's only remaining passenger, was bedded down on
the rebels' last few sacks of rice and beans. Samantha and Eglantina had
dismounted and were now proceeding on foot.

Another two miles, and Candido's prayers were answered: the bend in
the river came into view, and there on the right were the lake and the
waterfall tumbling down its wall of rock.

"You've won yourself a memorable night in bed, Cavalcanti."

"Now, quick!"

They all set to work. Samantha and Eglantina unhitched the horse,
Candido and Lindolpho loaded the beast with four sacks. The machete-
hewn path ahead of them was already silent and deserted. With the
caution now habitual to him, Candido had carried out several experi-
ments: whenever Lindolpho deliberately got stuck and lagged behind, it
took an average of ten minutes for elements of the rear guard to double
back and extricate them. Now that the column was so strung out, Candido
estimated that it would be at least a quarter of an hour before anyone
noticed their absence and came back for them.

Abandoning the cart in the middle of the track, Candido hoisted the little girl onto his shoulders and set off. He turned to look after ten laborious yards. The other three were following in his wake and the wall of vegetation had closed behind them, but their tracks would be detectable. Lindolpho joined him and took the lead, hacking away with his machete.

"Keep to the shallows."

The lake water was silty and rust-colored. Their feet disappeared into it as though cut off at the ankles.

No caymans around? Amazing. Snakes, though, and plenty of piranhas. I hope they aren't the carnivorous kind. Only one in a hundred is, according to the Indians.

"You may think I'm being kind of a coward," said Samantha, "but I'm not too fond of snakes."

"They're more scared of you than you are of them."

"In that case I pity them."

Shouts could be heard in the distance. The others were looking for them, but their first thought would be that the Indians had kidnapped them and stolen the horse.

"Hurry!"

They were now only thirty yards from the waterfall.

"What do you expect us to do, Cavalcanti, swim up it?"

Samantha was puffing and blowing like the Leopolda, Eglantina almost swooning with exhaustion. Lindolpho had taken the horse's bridle and was trying to coax it over the smooth, wet boulders, which would retain no trace of any footprint or hoofprint. Candido peered upward, wondering how he'd manage to surmount this obstacle. And then he saw it just above: a diagonal cleft about three feet wide. The sides dropped away almost sheer, he remembered, but the fallen soil and stones in the center were drier than they'd been the first time.

"Up there, quick, but watch those bushes. Don't snap any twigs."

The rocky corridor climbed for nearly three hundred feet. Samantha and Eglantina preceded him, not stopping once till they reached the top and slumped down on the boulders there, which were as smooth as the ones at the bottom. The little cave where he'd hidden for two days was on the left, out of sight but only fifty yards away.

He paused to catch his breath while Candida burbled at him in her own special language, asking him to sing her a song. Eglantina lay sprawled on her back a few feet away, eyes shut and arms outspread, her black face

tinged with green. Samantha, who didn't look too fresh either, was cursing—inarticulately for once.

"The cave's over there," he told her. "Don't go inside, though, it may
be swarming with snakes. You take Candida, I'm going down again."

Lindolpho and he spent the next forty minutes wrestling with the
horse, which was definitely disinclined to make the climb, with or without
its load. In the end, when pricking it with the machete had no effect,
Lindolpho resorted to a more drastic method: he singed the beast's rump
with a makeshift torch of twigs.

Success at last.

Only then did Candido take stock of their surroundings. An astronomi-
cal telescope would doubtless have revealed the Andes on their right, the
Atlantic on their left, the Caribbean in the north and Tierra del Fuego
in the south. They weren't very high up—no more than two thousand
feet—but that was enough to give them a panoramic view in all directions.

"No snakes in the cave," Lindolpho reported. "There were two, but
they're dead now. We can light a fire."

The next morning they lazed a little for the first time in almost four
months.

"Which way did you go, Candido?"

As far as he could recall, he'd headed due south across the plateau for
four days.

Samantha had become anxious. What were they doing, perched on this
plateau above the Mato Grosso? It would make a perfect observation post
if there was anything to observe, but there wasn't.

That night they bivouacked at a spot where *mangabeira* fruit were
plentiful. Candido found it idyllic; Samantha didn't. She refused to let
Candida touch the manga-whatsits—they might be poisonous—and she
was fed up with snakes and bugs and mosquitoes.

"You don't need mosquito boots in this country, you need a diving
suit. I've been bitten all over. And have you looked at your daughter
lately? She's an absolute pin cushion, the poor little darling! Of course
she isn't crying, but what does that prove? She's inherited her father's
easygoing temperament, that's all."

Samantha continued to grouse and grumble when they moved on the
next morning. She must have walked halfway across Brazil by now, didn't
he realize?

"I'm sick of it, Cavalcanti. We're getting nowhere fast—I'm sure
you're lost. That story of yours was pure hokum. You made it up just to
talk me into coming along. A track? That? Don't make me laugh! A
rhino's the only thing that ever came this way."

"There aren't any rhinos in Brazil."

"Says who? Who ever set foot in this godforsaken spot aside from you? What about that Conan Doyle book—the one where prehistoric animals roam around on top of a plateau just like this? We could bump into a triceratops or a gigantopithecus any minute!"

Jesus, where does she get all these long words?

"This isn't a man-made path and those aren't boundary stones, they're dinosaurs' droppings. If you ask me, a fifty-foot tyrannosaurus let fly here and those are the fossilized remains. And as for that building there . . ."

Ahead of them stood a Gothic edifice constructed of well-dressed stonework. Its gateway resembled the portals of certain churches in Ouro Prêto.

"May I offer you something to drink?" the hermit inquired.

"I heard your shots," said the hermit. "They intrigued me a little, so I went to look. Did you spot me?"

"You kept under cover about twenty yards to our left. You must have been following us ever since we entered the trees."

The hermit smiled.

"Precisely. Two women, two young men, a child and a horse."

"And one of the women talked the whole time," Candido added.

"Is that a dig at me, Cavalcanti?"

Candido, delighted to find the hermit there, ignored Samantha and smiled back. He really was a picture-book recluse: tall, emaciated, white-bearded and quite old—sixty at least. It would have been nice if he'd washed his feet occasionally—once a year, say—but that was secondary. Herr Doktor was on the grubby side too, but that didn't prevent him from being omniscient.

They were ushered into the *reducción,* a mission station built two and a half centuries earlier by Jesuits from Paraguay. Once installed there, they had rounded up the local Indians, made them cultivate the soil, and taught them all kinds of things. The Jesuits' reward for this selfless activity was a crop of Christian converts and ownership of the entire plateau—or so Herr Doktor had said, but he was rather anticlerical.

"You aren't Brazilian."

"Bolivian," said the hermit. Forty years ago he'd been something of a bandit specializing in attacks on trains and banks. Having killed a number of people including three or four policemen, he'd fled in company with his wife. After losing her while crossing the Llanos de Moxo, he was so overcome with remorse that he'd taken refuge permanently in the *reducción.*

"Did you know Butch Cassidy and the Sundance Kid?" asked Samantha.

"Never heard of them."

"They were in your line of business."

The hermit took them on a guided tour. The great gateway, twenty-five feet high, led to an inner courtyard flanked on one side by a chapel with stalls sufficient to accommodate sixty monks. They toured the refectory, the kitchens, the father superior's study, which still contained some moldering books, a row of cells, three large workshops, a stable and a well-tended garden with a sandstone fountain fed by a spring.

"Do you like my hermitage, Dom Candido?"

"It wasn't true, was it, that bandit story?"

The hermit burst out laughing.

"Not a word of it. I came across this place by chance while prospecting for gold and fell in love with it. One fine day I decided to stay here for good. That was thirty years ago."

"Did you find any gold?"

"It doesn't matter much any more. You're very young to see through a liar so easily. I've had three or four Indian wives in my time, but I do without women these days. Does gold attract you?"

Candido stared into the sandstone basin. He didn't reply at once.

"I doubt if you're even Bolivian," he said eventually. "You speak Spanish, but not like a Bolivian—or an Argentinian, for that matter."

The hermit explained that he was an Englishman who had studied geology at Oxford before going in quest of his personal Eldorado, which took the form of mineral specimens, not gold. He'd clambered around the Andean cordillera for years without making any discovery of interest.

Candido recited the first few words of a poem.

"'Resolution and Independence' by William Wordsworth," the hermit said with a smile. "How the devil many languages do you speak?"

They sat down on the edge of the basin. Laughter drifted across the courtyard. Samantha and Eglantina were bathing the little girl. Candido was overcome by a strange, almost painful sense of tranquillity.

He proceeded to tell the story of the Jaguar from start to finish. There was no hurry—they had all the time in the world.

Till tomorrow, anyway.

"That was quite as good as my bandit story," the hermit commented, "if not better."

"I think so too," said Candido, and he went on to explain what he proposed to do—subject to the hermit's consent, of course.

The hermit digested this in silence for a moment.

"Personally," he said at length, "I don't see any objection—in fact I'd welcome the chance to speak a little English again—but the first problem is, do you trust me sufficiently? Solitude may have driven me insane."

"There are more madmen in the outside world," Candido said. "What's the second problem?"

"Your lady friend. I overheard her talking while I was following you here. She isn't the type to let herself be pushed around."

"You can say that again." Candido paused. "Do any Indians ever visit you?"

"Now and then."

"What language do they speak?"

"Bororó. Do you know it?"

"A smattering."

"They may help you," said the hermit, "—if you can coax them out of their hammocks. And now it's my teatime. I hope you and your little party will join me. I make some quite acceptable muffins with manioc flour, and my *mangabeira* jam isn't too nauseating."

They rose and walked back across the big walled garden.

"Just before leaving England," the hermit resumed, "I suggested to a certain Miss Alicia Thompson that she might care to climb the cordillera with me—and marry me as well, of course. She said no, but I ought to have insisted. Have you ever experienced a difficulty of that nature?"

"Absolutely not," said Candido, "but I've never known why."

The hermit tugged at a rope hanging down the wall.

"I always ring for tea. If it isn't an indiscreet question, how are you going to broach the subject to her?"

"It isn't indiscreet at all. I've been asking myself the same question for the last two days, ever since I made up my mind. On balance, I've decided to leave without saying a word."

"Meaning that I'm to have the dubious privilege of breaking the news to her?"

"I'm afraid so."

The hermit winced. "I hope I survive," he said.

Run and walk, run and walk . . .

Two thousand strides at a jog trot, a thousand at walking pace, and so on *ad infinitum*. Counting occupied his mind and prevented him from picturing her face too clearly. He'd heard the mission bell a moment ago, just as he was taking his four-thousand-three-hundred-and-somethingth stride, but it might have been the hermit ringing for breakfast, not Samantha calling him back.

They'd taken a good two days to traverse this part of the plateau; he planned to cross it in six or seven hours. He'd slipped away before dawn—Samantha was still fast asleep—feeling vaguely, irrationally remorseful and apprehensive. He trusted the hermit, so why be apprehensive? The mission's whereabouts were known to no one but himself, its occupants and a few Indians whose language was unintelligible to outsiders. He was panicking for no good reason.

In mid-afternoon he reached the boulders at the top of the waterfall and slithered down the cleft in the rock face. No one had followed them; the markers he'd left were still in place.

The little lake. Here, by contrast, footprints were visible in the silt. A number of men had trampled around near the approaches to their upward route, failed to spot it and departed.

He found his way back to the machete-hewn path through the jungle. The cart was gone, together with such supplies as it had still contained.

By dusk he reckoned he'd done another three or four miles. They had a three-day start, but he, by taking advantage of their trail, could travel four times as fast.

I'll catch up with them by tomorrow night—unless I opt for the other solution. All right, I'll try it.

The Guaporé, whose right bank he was skirting, was less than a hundred feet wide at this point. He should be able to cross it almost dry-shod by way of those rocks and banks of red sand.

Quicksand!

He spread his arms and legs in a reflex movement, one eye on a lurking cayman. He wasn't even carrying a rifle. The caymans of the Mato Grosso would end by thinking he despised them and take offense, especially as he'd eaten three or four of their young.

He extricated himself by crawling, then hauled himself into a mango tree where he spent the night as well as he could with several caymans in conference below him. He munched some manioc muffins and slept a little, attached by one wrist to a branch. As soon as dawn broke he set off again, and another hour found him making his way along what was undeniably a path—even Samantha would have conceded that—on which the imprints of bare feet were clearly visible.

Toward midday he came out in a riverside village inhabited by some thirty Bororós, all as naked as the day they were born.

"I'm Jaguar," he announced. "Tapi, the big chief who lives in the south, is a friend of mine."

They were dumbfounded to hear him speak their language. Two hours of discussion followed. Yes, of course they'd seen the rebels' column, but why worry, none of them would leave the jungle alive. They, the Bororós, had spitted three or four with their bows and arrows and eaten a few choice slices of them, but the rest were too numerous to tackle. Candido, who didn't care for the way the Indians were looking at him, played his last card: the Hermit, who would lay them low with his death ray (a telescope) if they failed to help him.

Five minutes later he was in a dugout canoe, feeling somewhat reassured but sitting where he could keep an eye on his two-man crew.

They didn't have to exert themselves much because they were paddling downstream—north, in other words. At least, he hoped so.

"No, Clovis! It's me, Candido. Please don't kill me."

The erstwhile trolley-car conductor stood there openmouthed for several seconds. At last he lowered his machete.

"How on earth did you get here?"

Candido had heard them coming for over an hour. The sound of their slow progress appalled him when he reflected how much farther they had to go. The very rhythm of their machete strokes was eloquent of exhaustion.

Other men appeared. The word traveled from mouth to mouth, all down the column: Jaguar was back.

"Where are Samantha and your daughter, Candido? Where's Eglantina?"

Candido smiled. He'd been waiting on the banks of the Guaporé for nearly six hours. Having overtaken the rebels' column during the night—their camp fires were only too visible—the Indians had put him ashore and paddled back upstream without eating so much as a morsel of him. The old traditions were dying fast.

At least he'd been able to wrap himself in his poncho and snatch some sleep, snug in the hammock in which he still reposed. His nonchalant manner was a trifle exaggerated, he had to admit, but it tickled his vanity to see how flabbergasted the others were to find him swinging comfortably between two trees, right in their path, when they'd lost track of him four days ago.

The column had come to a halt. Bearded faces flushed with exertion, eyes bright with fever, all the men in sight flopped down on the ground.

"Tell them to take care where they sit, Clovis, they'll get chiggers."

"They've already got them, and so have I. How did you manage it?"

A skeletal figure tottered up. It was Leite Abade, so consumed with fever that he didn't look long for this world.

"What are you doing here, Cavalcanti?"

"I'm back, that's the main thing."

"Where have you been?"

"We jaguars roam the jungle as we please."

"What about the women and the little girl?"

"Safe in my lair. At this rate, Abade, none of you will ever get out of here alive."

Abade, who had been leaning against a tree, slid down it into a squatting position. His hands, cut to the bone in several places, were bleeding profusely.

"What happened?" Candido asked.

"One of the men went berserk and started laying about him with a machete," Clovis explained. "We had to kill him."

Candido pointed to a nearby bush.

"Tell one of your men to gather some of those leaves. They must be chewed and applied to those wounds like a poultice, otherwise he'll get gangrene." He turned to Abade. "Well, do you want my help, or shall I go and leave you to it?"

"We'll make it without you."

"You've still got five hundred miles to go, and the worst is yet to come. How many of you are left?"

"Around eight hundred."

"Let's get one thing straight: I've no wish to be your leader, Abade. I came back to offer you a helping hand, that's all. I'll make no decisions— I'll simply tell you what I think and leave it to you."

"All right," said Abade.

"A mile downstream you'll find some trees. I suggest you build some rafts. The caymans are less dangerous than the jungle—at least they're killable."

"Where are they, Candido?"

"I must keep it a secret, Clovis, even from you."

"Is Lindolpho dead?"

"Why should he be dead? He was fine the last time I saw him."

"Do you really have a place of your own near here?"

"In a manner of speaking."

"Couldn't we all go there?"

"It's only a little lair, Clovis, there wouldn't be room for everyone. Is your brother still around?"

"I saw Vivaldo Maria yesterday—he's in command of the rear guard. *Meu Deus,* who are those fellows?"

"Friends of mine," said Candido, "—Bororó Indians. They're going to help us build some rafts. I'll come with you as far as Guajará-Mirim or Pôrto Velho, Clovis, depending on circumstances, but then I'll have to leave you."

"And go back to your lair?"

"Exactly."

It took five days to build enough rafts. Some of the men succumbed to snakebite, many to sheer exhaustion. Poor food, fever, festering sores, dysentery, nausea and, last but not least, despair at the prospect of never regaining the outside world—all these had weakened them to the point of nonresistance. Most of them died because, in their heart of hearts, they had given up. Lucidity wasn't necessarily an advantage. Herr Doktor was right: the men with the greatest endurance were almost always those with the least intelligence. They had an animal's gift for survival.

Or were they all inventions of his own, these precepts he ascribed to Herr Doktor whenever he became too introspective? If he didn't stop, he would wind up believing that Herr Doktor had never existed, or else that he was another version of himself.

It's all in the mind. Well, maybe not all of it. Just eighty percent.

He'd lost count of the days. The Bororós had left them long ago, ostensibly because they were no longer on home ground and the other Indian tribes were hostile. Men continued to die like flies, either drowned like the dozens who deliberately committed their bodies to the river, or bitten by snakes, or eaten by caymans. Some died all alone, others were done to death by Indians. They walked off into the jungle or lagged behind and never reappeared. There was no point in going to look for them; all it did was exhaust one a little more.

Somewhere between the thirtieth and thirty-fifth day the Guaporé merged with another large river. The embryonic map, with its big blank spaces indicating unexplored or uncharted territory, suggested that it was the Rio Mamoré, which rose in Bolivia. Flotsam in the shape of old crates adorned with faded lettering proved that there must be villages upstream not exclusively inhabited by Indians.

"Are we getting close, Candido?"

"We're nearly there."

"But we're still on the Guaporé."

"The Guaporé has become the Mamoré. Guajará-Mirim can't be more than a hundred miles away."

They had to disembark again because two of the rafts were breaking up and in need of repair. Abade could scarcely walk now. His machete wounds had healed, thanks to the poultices, but he was infested with ticks like most of the others, and his abscess-encrusted body was burning up with fever.

"You're looking pretty fit, Candido."

"I am pretty fit."

I've lost a bit of weight—I must be down to a hundred pounds—but I'm feeling quite bright and cheerful. My training's pretty good too. I don't know what my time would be for the ten thousand meters, but I might give the Finnish champion a run for his money.

Clovis and he had just counted the survivors. They numbered five hundred and nine including seven women and two children. Roughly ten percent of the original force—more than he'd dared to hope. . . .

Through binoculars he watched a jaguar, a real one, fishing from the opposite bank. The animal was stretched out on a fallen tree trunk overhanging the river. Its eyes, which looked yellow or green depending on the light, glowed in the shadows that enhanced the dappling of its fur. The head was gracefully inclined, the ears were pricked. Frozen in an attitude that denoted infinite reserves of patience, it might almost have been asleep. It had dipped one paw in the water and was gently moving it this way and that to create a little eddy.

Too greedy for its own good, a plump fish came to investigate. The paw moved like lightning, the claws gripped in a tenth of a second, the wriggling fish flashed through the air.

The jaguar ate daintily, one mouthful at a time. Still lying at ease on the tree trunk, it paused now and then to raise its head and survey the opposite bank. The tapetum, the membrane that sheathed the retinas of the animal's eyes and improved its night vision, looked fleetingly phosphorescent in the gloom.

It can't see us across the river. It can't see colors either—its world resembles a black-and-white film. It can't see us, but it knows we're there. Something other than its nose and ears is at work.

A sixth sense.

Guajará-Mirim: a landing stage high enough to avoid periodic flooding, a few shacks, a bare esplanade sloping gently down to the water's edge, some yellowish, dusty banana trees, a handful of idlers, an army post flying the Brazilian flag.

There were only half a dozen soldiers, not fifteen, commanded by a sergeant who looked thunderstruck at the sight of so many people flocking ashore. He'd never heard of the revolution or Jaguar.

"You mean you crossed the Mato Grosso on those rafts?"

He couldn't believe his ears. Abade and da Silva answered his stream of questions and put some of their own. What was the best way of getting to Pôrto Velho, the Amazon and Manaus, or, failing that, Santarém?

"Are you going to leave us now, Candido?" asked Clovis.

"Yes."

"We'd never have got this far without you."

"Decent of you to say so."

"I mean it."

Very decent, but I'm not so sure I've done them a good turn.

"This river should get you to the Amazon not far from Manaus. What you do then is your affair, not mine, but you haven't got there yet."

"There'll be villages on the bank and steamers going in both directions. It won't be like the last stretch, Candido. Will we meet again?"

Who knows? I rather doubt it.

He would grab a night's sleep and then return, but not by the same route. Drifting down a river was one thing, paddling upstream another. He would take to the hills instead. Sooner or later they would lead him back to the Chapada dos Parecis. And Samantha.

Who won't be best pleased. It'll take me a good ten days to pacify her.

"Dom Candido Cavalcanti?"

The sergeant had come up to him in the local store, while he was buying two shirts and a pair of trousers with a little money lent him by Clovis from the revolutionary war chest.

Oh God, it can't be true!

The sergeant handed over a crumpled, mildewed envelope that had been entrusted to him weeks earlier by two men in a motorboat.

"Can you describe them?"

Their names won't mean a thing, I know.

The sergeant did his best. One of them was very tall—a formidable-looking type. The other was of medium height, with fair hair, glasses, and—

"And hands that move by themselves," Candido interposed. "He never looks at them. They do things—like whittling a stick with a big knife, for instance—and you'd swear they had a life of their own."

The sergeant nodded eagerly. "That's him all right."

The Man Mountain and Otto Krantz. From one angle, their faith in me is flattering. They took it for granted I'd make it across the Mato Grosso.

He opened the letter and read it.

It's sheer madness. Don't go!

◆ ◆ ◆

You're an utter lunatic.

Maybe, but shut up and paddle. You've got to finish it once and for all—you can't spend the rest of your life wondering where the Claws are and what they're up to.

He wasn't really paddling, just dipping his paddle in the water occasionally to keep the stolen dugout heading downstream. He'd sneaked out of Guajará-Mirim in the middle of the night, without even telling Clovis. Although they were bound to notice his absence in the morning, they would put it down to his eagerness to get back to his lair and Samantha. Besides, Jaguar's reputation would gain added luster from yet another mysterious vanishing trick.

Do I like being a legend? No, not really. I'd sooner be in bed with Samantha—not that the one thing precludes the other. I can be a legend and still make love. The trouble is, I don't want to be a legend; I simply want to be left in peace.

He'd briefly considered asking Clovis and Vivaldo Maria to come with him. They would gladly have lent him a hand, he knew, but it was better this way.

The dugout glided silently down the dark river.

No one could have seen him leaving Guajará-Mirim and no one could see him now. No one knew where he'd gone, either, unless the sergeant had opened the letter and read it, but that seemed unlikely. The sergeant hadn't looked like a reader of letters or anything else.

At daybreak he concealed the dugout beneath some overhanging vegetation and breakfasted on the hardtack he'd bought at the store. He spent the day half dozing, half watching out for river traffic.

Nothing.

Nothing the next day either, except for one small steamboat chugging up the Madeira towing a dinghy laden with supplies. He scanned the passengers through binoculars, but their faces meant nothing to him.

A little before dawn on the third day, just as he was looking for another place to lie up, he spotted a fire and heard voices. Without a moment's hesitation he paddled swiftly out into midstream. Crossing the Madeira despite the current, which was very strong in places, he grounded the craft seven or eight hundred yards down river and concealed it in a nest of foliage. A man would have had to trip over the canoe before he spotted it.

Then he dived into the trees, many of which were hevea rubber trees growing wild. At the first sign of a path, some two hundred yards from the river, he stopped and hid in the undergrowth. It was light by this time. Minutes later a couple of dozen Indians, men and women, filed past carrying gouges and buckets of the kind used by rubber tappers.

There were too many heveas around for safety. He withdrew, obliterating all traces of his presence, and finally found a quiet spot to sling his hammock. Wrapping himself in his poncho, he tried to sleep.

It was pointless to reread the letter for the umpteenth time—he knew it by heart. One of the two sheets was a sketch map, the other was in Herr Doktor's handwriting but undated:

Come at once, I implore you, Candido my boy. Only you can save me.

Just that and a signature.

There was equally little point in telling himself, over and over again, that it was a trap. There wasn't the faintest chance that Herr Doktor would be waiting for him at the plantation.

The rifle Clovis had given him was a No. 1 Mark III Lee-Enfield with a magazine capacity of ten rounds (he would have to make do with only six). The barrel had been shortened, the handguard and trigger pull modified. It was a compact, heavy weapon.

He hugged it to him.

At nightfall the rubber tappers returned to their village. He gave them a minute's start and then followed, keeping out of sight.

Thirty yards from the fires he got out his binoculars. The Indians, who numbered around fifty, had no weapons of any kind, not even bows or blowguns. They looked glum and dejected, spoke little and in low voices. They might have been prisoners serving a life sentence, devoid of hope and resigned to their fate. He wondered why they didn't make off into the jungle.

Slowly panning the binoculars, he brought them into closeup. Naked bodies bearing the marks of the lash, some of them still oozing blood, arms that ended in stumps . . .

Stumps?

He counted six men and two women with one hand severed at the wrist, three men and one woman with no hands at all. Certain *fazendeiros* employing Indian rubber tappers laid down a scale of penalties for the encouragement of those who failed to work hard enough: one hand for a first offense, two hands or death for a second. Dom Venancio Carneira, owner of the plantation on the sketch map, was obviously one of these charitable souls. Candido couldn't wait to meet him.

He set off again, keeping to the track this time. A mile farther on he came to the *estrada,* the road that linked the various hevea plantations.

The house came into view. He circled it once at long range to be on the safe side. It was a relatively modest establishment comprising half a dozen rooms, all on one level and raised above the ground on six-foot piles. Beside it stood a shed containing the vats in which the latex was smoked, a bunkhouse for overseers and servants, and a stable.

Later on, and especially in the Great Silence, he would regret not having given up and returned to the river, but he was too intrigued by what he could see through his binoculars: a lamp-lit veranda, and on it, peacefully drinking and chatting among themselves, five figures.

Take your time.

He focused on the faces one by one. It was them sure enough: Stepa Onegin, Matriona, the Man Mountain, Otto Krantz and someone who could only be Venancio Carneira, a corpulent man in shirt-sleeves, with his riding breeches tucked into high boots. There was a horsewhip within arm's reach of him and a revolver in the holster on his belt.

Afonka . . . Where's Afonka Tchadayev?

An Indian maidservant was shuttling back and forth between the veranda and the interior of the house. He followed her movements for a while, then turned his attention to the windows. They were simple, unglazed apertures, and through them he could dimly make out beds shrouded in mosquito nets.

He changed position again, very cautiously, until he had a three-quarters rear view of the house including Stepa Onegin and part of the veranda. There was no trap that he could discover.

This is almost too easy.

Yard by yard, with the Lee-Enfield tucked in the crook of his arm, he stole over to the stable. It took him some time to check it out—the only occupants were half a dozen horses—and even longer to cross the gap that separated him from the house itself. He could now hear what was being said. Stepa Onegin, in his drawling voice, was describing a torrid affair he'd had at Belém two months ago.

Candido hauled himself up and in through a window, carefully feeling his way in case he triggered an alarm of some kind. He was in a bedroom: a bed, a crude chair with a suitcase on it, a woman's skirt hanging up to dry on a line. Suspended from a nail in the wooden wall was an elegant toilet case in Russian leather bearing the initials M.R. It had to be Matriona's room.

He emerged into the passage, glanced to his right. Otto Krantz was standing only five yards away with his back turned, a cigarette between the fingers of his left hand.

Candido eased one door open, then another and another.

He tiptoed into the living room just as the maidservant left it. He heard her go out onto the veranda, then withdrew again. That completed his tour of the premises. Nothing to report, no sign of Herr Doktor. Although he'd never really expected to find him there, he couldn't suppress a pang of disappointment.

Now for the bunkhouse.

A good two minutes to open the door, which had a tendency to creak. His ears caught the sound of deep, regular breathing. The cramped interior contained two bunks separated by a curtain suspended from the ceiling to create an illusion of privacy. One of the bunks was empty, the other occupied by a mestizo and an Indian girl, both naked, both snoring openmouthed. The girl's hand was cupped over her bedmate's genitals.

Candido's rifle butt smashed the mestizo in the middle of the forehead. Almost simultaneously, he trained the Lee-Enfield's muzzle on the Indian girl's face.

"Ssh!"

He waited for some reaction from the veranda. Two minutes went by, but he could have waited for hours if necessary.

"Tie him up," he whispered, miming for the girl's benefit.

He tried again in the five or six Indian dialects he knew. No reaction at all. Either she didn't understand or she was a complete imbecile. She had very pretty breasts and couldn't have been more than fourteen.

He smiled at her when she finally understood and complied, and signed to her to lie face down on the bunk. Then he tied her up too, stuffed a scrap of old shirt into her mouth, and gagged the man as well. He hoped he hadn't killed him, not that it would be any great loss to the world.

There were now only four of them on the veranda—Venancio Carneira was missing. A few moments later he returned with another bottle of _cachaça_ and picked up the thread of some incomprehensible story about two mulatto girls who were as alike as a brace of coffee beans and who . . .

Candido withdrew to some bushes a hundred yards from the house. Once under cover he squatted down to watch. There they sat like well-fed, law-abiding citizens, peacefully chatting and swigging the national drink of a country—_his_ country—to which they'd pursued him from halfway across the world. Why? Simply because Alekhin had ordered them to. No point in trying to add up how many murders they'd committed and laid at his door—it would have taken him all night, even discounting the ones he didn't know about. They must be delighted to be idling in Brazil. They had to cut the occasional throat, of course, but the rest of their time was pure relaxation. They were certainly better off here than in Russia, where they would already have been imprisoned or shot for one reason or another.

So be it.

He straightened up, took aim and fired as quickly as he could.

Stepa Onegin first.

Now Otto Krantz.

Now the Man Mountain . . .

Damn, he's only wounded—he moved too fast for me and hit the ground. Smart of him. Now he's up and running—blazing away, too.

Venancio Carneira had also drawn his gun and opened fire.

This is for those severed hands, Dom Venancio. . . .

The fat man took his fourth shot full in the face like Stepa Onegin and Otto Krantz.

Now Matriona.

No, you can't!

Something hit him in the left side, knocking him off balance for a moment. The Man Mountain had just made a hole in him—he'd been firing at him all the time.

Now only twenty yards away, the colossal Russian dropped his empty gun and charged.

Candido's fifth shot hit him in the throat. He covered another few yards, then crashed to the ground like a felled oak. Candido started walking. He sidestepped the inert form without giving it a glance. His eyes were fixed on Matriona.

She was holding a small automatic. He walked on. Twenty yards short of the veranda he halted.

"Where's Herr Doktor?"

She stared at him impassively.

"Where is he?"

"I haven't the faintest idea," she said at last.

"Is he in Brazil?"

"Not that I'm aware."

"In Russia?"

"I don't know."

"Who does?"

"Stepa knew."

Careful, she only said that to distract your attention.

He didn't move.

"Why not take a shot at me?" he said.

"You've only got one round left."

"Correct."

"Afonka warned us you were an outstanding marksman, but Stepa didn't believe him. He said you might be able to shoot but you'd never be able to kill. He was wrong."

Kill her. The fact that she's a woman makes no difference—she's one of the Claws. KILL HER!

Ten seconds went by. Matriona dropped her gun. Still covering her with the Lee-Enfield, he walked the last twenty yards and mounted the veranda steps.

Forget she's a woman. Search her anyway.

"Face down in the doorway with your arms and legs spread."

She complied.

How beautiful she is!

He proceeded to turn out the dead men's pockets.

Otto Krantz was carrying three passports—German, Austrian, British—and a thousand-odd dollars in cash. The leather sheath that held his knife was strapped to his thigh. The blade was eight inches long and razor-sharp. Nothing else of note.

"Is this Carneira?"

"Yes."

Carneira's pockets yielded some small change and several nude photographs of mulatto girls in complicated poses.

Next, Stepa Onegin. More money—nearly ten thousand dollars' worth—plus four assorted passports, one of them Russian and made out in his own name, letters of credit on sundry banks in major Brazilian cities, a copy of Gogol's *Tales of St. Petersburg,* and a small black leather notebook, which Candido pocketed.

There was also a *muiraquita,* one of those mysterious pieces of jade, roughly carved into the shape of a fish, that collectors believed to date from the time of the South American Amazons. Candido wondered where Stepa could have found it. Uncle Ulisses used to say they were worth more than the finest emeralds.

"Did you know I was coming?"

"Stepa did."

"On your feet and come with me, but don't make any sudden moves."

Matriona set off along the passage. Her stylish shoes would have looked more appropriate in a Paris salon.

"I won't," she said.

Something in her tone alerted him. He spun around and regained the veranda in two strides.

Uniformed figures were closing in on the house from all directions.

He'd never run so fast. Still clutching the Lee-Enfield, he'd dived over the balustrade and rolled across the luxuriant grass, then sprinted for the trees like a madman.

Three hundred yards, five hundred. He could hear sounds of pursuit, but who cared? They would never catch him—it was silly of them even to try.

A barbed-wire fence. He ran straight into it, bounced off it, fell over backwards.

That's why they're chasing me—they knew about the fence all along. Your reconnaissance wasn't thorough enough, you fool!

The soldiers were now only fifty yards away. He struggled up again, face and chest bleeding. The bullet wound in his side was starting to hurt badly.

He sprinted along the fence. No time to get through it, no point in trying. Another thought struck him: the river. He would head for it and dive in. On balance, piranhas and caymans were preferable to capture. He would swim downstream under water, come up for air every five minutes, and sooner or later reach the Amazon. No problem.

It's strange they haven't hit me, though, after blazing away all this time. Are they missing me on purpose, or what?

They were.

They want me alive.

Another few yards.

I'll make it, Samantha, I promise.

He went on running in his head, but his legs had failed. He collapsed.

Someone's standing over me—someone in shiny boots. They remind me of something.

He crawled away, digging the Lee-Enfield into the ground like an ice ax. What really annoyed him was that it should be this particular man, with his shiny boots and ridiculous mustache.

All right.

He turned and leveled the Lee-Enfield. It was the colonel from the Mato Grosso, now wearing general's insignia.

Not him again! He's got me on the brain—it's a positive fixation.

His finger curled around the trigger. He aimed between the eyes, then in the air. The bullet sped skywards.

They've got you, Candido.
I know.
Give up?
No.

He now knew how a real wild beast must feel when deprived of its freedom by a zoo collector.

They shipped him down the Rio Madeira in a motorboat escorted by other motorboats laden to the gunwales with soldiers. "I always knew I'd get you in the end, Cavalcanti," said the one-time colonel of the Mato Grosso, prodding him with his shiny boots from time to time.

After the Rio Madeira, the Amazon. Exhibited on landing stages for the edification of sometimes silent, sometimes muttering crowds whom the soldiers kept at a safe distance from his cage, he stood—or rather, crouched, because the cage was too small—and growled for fun.

"Grrr."

They kicked him repeatedly to shut him up, but the more they kicked him the more he growled. Not loudly, softly, just to annoy them.

It's one way of showing that I haven't given up.

"Grrr."

What's that revolting stench?

Christ!

He was disgusted with himself for doing it in his cage.

It's not my fault. They never let me out of here.

You repulse me, I tell you! You've given up.

No, not that, not ever. I've become an animal that never surrenders because it doesn't know the meaning of the word.

He threw up his arms to shield his face from a jet of water so powerful that it pinned him against the bars. It hurt a bit, but not as much as all that. Anyway, he needed a good hosing down.

Through a town in the back of an open truck. The streets were flanked by soldiers facing away from him—facing the crowds that lined his route.

"Grrr."

A prison—they've put my cage in a prison, the dumb bastards.

"Grrr."

More kicks.

I'm going to sleep a while.

Sleep, I said, not give up.

No, never give up.

Never.

"Cavalcanti?"

"Grrr."

"Can you hear me, Cavalcanti?"

"Grrr."

"I know you're awake. Open your eyes and look at me. Stop playacting."

"Grrr."

"Let him out," said another voice. "It's inhuman, keeping him shut up in there."

They're taking a risk. If they let me out I'll pounce on them.

"He won't answer you while he's in that cage," said the other voice, which sounded vaguely familiar. "Let him out or you can kiss your chances of promotion good-bye, believe me. Let him out and bring him something to eat and drink. At once!"

Not interested. Going to sleep a bit longer.

"Candido?"

"Grrr."

"It's Aristides Dantas, Candido. You sent me a letter."

"Grrr."

"You've got to eat and drink. You're committing suicide by refusing."

Don't listen to him, it's just another of their traps. Go on sleeping—growl at them and go on sleeping.

"There, they've let you out. That's what you wanted, isn't it? You've no reason to refuse their food and water, not any more. Are you listening, Candido? I'm Aristides Dantas, the attorney from Rio, the one you wrote to, remember? If you want me to help you, you'll have to help me a little too."

He opened his eyes, which were instantly, agonizingly stabbed by the light. The fact was, he couldn't see too well. He managed to raise one hand. The figure bending over him understood and drew closer still.

Aristides Dantas?

Careful, it may only be someone who looks like him.

No, it's him all right.

My letter! It got through. It really got through!

"Do you recognize me, Candido?"

"Yes."

"Will you take some food and water now? Please do."

He felt a trickle of water on his lips—lips he half opened for the first time since . . .

Since I can't remember when.

———————

"Feeling better?"

"I'm fine, really."

"You're to have some soap and a towel, and I persuaded them to allow you a shave and a haircut. I've also brought you some clean clothes."

"Thank you."

"The doctor who examined you this morning will be back soon. Your thirty-day hunger strike posed some problems. And a bullet went straight through you. Other than that, all he had to do was set three fractures—cracks rather than fractures, actually—and clean up your cuts and sores, most of which had been healed by themselves. He's quite amazed by your progress. You're blessed with an exceptionally strong constitution."

"Any news of Samantha and my daughter?"

"I don't know where they are. Nor does anyone else, it seems. The army hasn't captured them, if that's what you mean."

Say nothing.

"Is there anything I can do for them, Candido?"

"Not really. What about the revolutionary army?"

"I presume you're referring to the rebels led by Leite Abade and Tasso Aranha. No news of them, either—they're still being hunted by the army. I can try to find out more, if you like."

Candido shut his eyes, partly because he was feeling drowsy after his first intake of nourishment—a kind of milk soup—and partly to evade a conversation that was going too fast for him. If Samantha and Candida hadn't been captured and nobody knew where they were, they must still be at the mission station with Lindolpho and Eglantina. In other words, safe.

Thank you, God.

The next day:

"You're looking better, Candido, no doubt about it. I'll get you some different clothes—those are a bit too big for you. The doctor came, I gather?"

"Yes, I'm doing fine."

That morning a barber had shaved him and cut his hair under the supervision of an officer who forbade them to exchange a word. He was then handcuffed and chained to a ring in the wall.

He contrived to stand up during the night. He even managed, after three or four fruitless attempts, to take at least three steps, holding the chain in his hands to stop its rattling.

"Yesterday, Candido, we were talking about your American lady friend
and your daughter. The authorities believe they entered the Mato Grosso
with you and may still be there. I appreciate your caution, but perhaps
I can help them in some way."

"No."

"Are they still alive?"

Candido turned his face to the wall.

"I understand," said Dantas. "That is to say, I sympathize with your
reluctance to speak, whatever the reasons. For their sake, however, I trust
you never regret your failure to confide in me."

He continued to stare at the wall.

"As for Leite Abade, Tasso Aranha and the rest, my inquiries have
yielded very little. If there are any survivors of that incredible trek, their
whereabouts are unknown, though there's talk of Guajará-Mirim. The
soldiers ventured as far into the Mato Grosso as they did for the sole
purpose of hunting you down. They were tipped off, I gather. It seems
that the general in command of your two hundred and fifty pursuers had
personal reasons for wanting to capture you. He's the man you had
trouble with in the old days, isn't he?"

The wall.

Oh, Samantha!

The next day:

"You haven't asked me if I'm acting on your father's behalf, Candido."

"You'd have told me if you were."

"I paid a visit to São Paulo before leaving Rio for Belém—that's where
we are now, incidentally. He declined to see me, but I did have a word
with some close associates of his. According to them, he's being rather
obstinate." Dantas smiled. "No need to ask where you get your remarkable strength of character."

He's only trying to butter me up. I'm not like Dom Trajano, not a scrap.

"Don't you want to talk, Candido? I'll be defending you at your
court-martial, but I'll leave if you prefer."

*Keep your temper. You've never given in to anger or despair before, so don't start
now.*

"Please forgive me," said Candido, "and thank you for being here.
You say I'm to be court-martialed?"

"Yes, as an army officer formerly stationed in the Mato Grosso. You were sentenced to death and pardoned once before, but circumstances have changed since then. Let's not go into the indictment, the list of charges is too long. Just tell me what criminal acts you've committed. It's your own version I want."

"I've killed five men: Hastimphilo, who was one of the revolutionary leaders; a man called Venancio Carneira; Stepa Onegin; and another two known to me only as Otto Krantz and the Man Mountain."

"The last three being those whom your letter referred to as the Jaguar's Claws?"

"Yes."

"And Carneira?"

"He hadn't harmed me personally. He *tried* to shoot me. And he chopped off the hands of some Indian forced laborers."

"Carneira was a civilian with a notorious reputation. A military court won't be too concerned about him. Anything else?"

"I explained it all in my letter."

"Did you at any time, not being under duress, willfully and knowingly render assistance to the revolutionaries?"

"I helped them get through the jungle. I'd have done the same for anyone."

Even for the Mato Grosso colonel who's now a general, and that's saying something.

"What do you know of the woman Matriona Reczak?"

"Reczak? Is that her last name? Only that she's one of the Claws. Where is she?"

"She's sworn a damning affidavit against you, and not only in respect of the four men you killed at the plantation. She claims you're Jaguar, the instigator and leader of the so-called revolution."

"Has she any proof?"

"It's her word against yours. If I accept the truth of your statements, which I do, it's clear that she can't pursue her accusations very far without implicating herself."

"Where is she?"

"No charges have been laid against her. Officially, she was just a Swedish national visiting Brazil. At Belém she made the acquaintance of a Russian émigré and two Germans with whom she went for a trip up the Amazon."

"You still haven't told me where she is."

"The woman has connections. They helped get her out of the country."

What's come over you? You aren't giving up, you're more determined than ever.

The only trouble is, you're as cold as ice—you aren't yourself any more. Who are you? Jaguar?

"Who else has taken an interest in my case?"

"Ciccio Vaz Vasconselos and his family. Whatever my opinion of young Ciccio, I'm bound to say that his defense of you has been positively fanatical."

"No one else?"

I shouldn't have asked that question—he's obviously embarrassed. I was wrong about him.

"I owe you another apology," Candido said.

He didn't utter a word when the court-martial sentenced him to death. His one regret was that he had nothing to read, and that his request for a guitar and writing materials had been denied.

It makes no difference, I'm already dead inside.

Well, not really dead. More patiently than anyone could possibly have imagined, he was watching and waiting for the least little mistake, the smallest chance of escape. For the present, that was his only thought.

I'll never, ever give up. Cling to that—keep believing it up to the very last moment.

He received no visit from Dantas or anyone else. No one came to see him.

Until they burst into his cell in the middle of the night. Not one of the ten soldiers and two officers dared to meet Jaguar's eye as they hustled him outside. Once in the courtyard he staked everything on a final bid for freedom. He managed to run a few yards in spite of the shackles on his wrists and ankles, but they bore him to the ground. Even then, with half a dozen men holding him down, he continued to lash out and struggle for at least two minutes.

They've knocked me out. If they hadn't, I'd have made it.

Candido was being wheeled along on a metal stretcher when he regained consciousness. He tugged at his chains, but they didn't budge an inch. He started to sing "The Jaguar," "The Ballad of Ezra McAuliffe" and the rest of his repertoire.

A vista of white corridors.

I'll never give up.

A door opened. The light beyond was blinding. He struggled more fiercely than ever when they released him from the stretcher. It took a lot of them to restrain him.

"This'll calm him down. Hold him tight, he's a regular wild animal, this one."

He glimpsed the face of a white-haired man in a surgical gown.

They got the needle in despite his convulsions.

"You can let go of him now."

He started struggling again as soon as they removed his shackles. He struggled, but in slow motion.

"Cavalcanti? My voice is the last you'll ever hear. The very last."

"I'll never give up."

No reply. He crawled along the floor, unable to open his eyes and resist the leaden onset of sleep.

The Great Silence engulfed him.

VII

When a jaguar displays exceptional ferocity, the natives believe it to be a magical or imaginary being, not a real animal. They may also regard it as the incarnation of some long-dead and particularly evil man.

won't give up.

He was pacing to and fro. Eleven paces one way, eleven the other. It was square.

It was also white. White tiles covered the floor, ceiling and all four walls—identical tiles without the smallest scratch to differentiate them. If he looked closely, really closely, he might be able to find a speck of dust the size of a pinhead.

That would be better than nothing.

The cell's utter featurelessness was, however, relieved by seven things.

Item one: the overhead light, a disk of thick glass embedded in the middle of the ceiling. Ten feet up and completely inaccessible, this sole source of illumination never varied in intensity, never went out.

Item two: a ventilation duct four inches in diameter. The air that issued from it was just as unvarying, neither too hot nor too cold, and the circular outlet was equally inaccessible.

Item three: the latrine facility. A funnel-shaped cavity twelve inches across at floor level, this was connected to a sunken wastepipe. The water, which was dispensed by a slit in the wall, gave off a lemony odor, faintly antiseptic but not unpleasant. Flushing took place at regular intervals, every six hours or possibly four.

A couple of hours are neither here nor there.

Item four: a small, circular depression into which water for drinking and washing flowed straight from the wall.

Item five *(The most exciting):* a hatch. This, too, was tiled, but when the flap was raised it revealed a niche at the bottom of a miniature elevator shaft. At regular intervals a small cardboard meal tray was lowered on the end of a string. The food, which wasn't bad, included meat cut up into squares to enable him to eat it with his hands.

The string's pretty thin, but I might just manage to strangle myself with it. I'll have to see.

Items six and seven: a foam-rubber mattress four inches thick and a small pillow of the same material, both white.

If I tore them up with my teeth I could choke myself with the bits. No hurry, though.

He was stark naked. Apart from the mattress, the pillow, the cardboard tray and the string, he had nothing.

He'd spent a long time, he didn't know how long, looking for a door. His final conclusion was that there wasn't one at all. They must have dumped him inside and walled him up, but there wasn't an iota of difference between one wall and another. All four were identical.

He was entombed with two mortal enemies: time, which he had no means of measuring, and silence.

The Great Silence.

There was nothing to be heard: no footsteps, no muffled voices, no rattle of keys, no creaking doors, no gnawing of little teeth or mandibles, no mice, ants, cockroaches, fleas, spiders.

A silence fit to burst the eardrums.

To drive a man insane.

Which is what they want.

All right, let them try.

I won't give up.

He cracked at last, possibly struck down by a bout of the fever that had carried off so many of his companions while crossing the *floresta virgem.* The shivering fits became more and more protracted, more and more painful, until they convulsed his whole body and froze him to the marrow. Steel bands seemed to be compressing his chest, crushing his skull. Then came hallucinations: a gloomy Mongolian forest full of trees oozing blood; soil that palpitated like a gigantic heart; a stone fortress approached by a dank flight of steps; dark depths from which corpses floated to the surface in unending succession, all with their throats cut from ear to ear, all with Samantha's face.

Having more or less controlled himself till then, he was suddenly overcome with panic. He could remember screaming—screaming again and again and banging his head against the walls.

It can't have lasted more than an hour or two. Now it's over. I'm back in control. Everything's all right again.

He was lying curled up in a corner. If he could have embedded himself in the tiled wall, he would have done so. His knees were drawn up beneath him, his arms folded against his chest, his shoulders hunched: a fetus. The cell looked immense—an infinity of whiteness.

Yes, yes, I'm fine—just shaking it off, that's all. These things take time.

He played tag with his mind, but it kept eluding him. Just when he thought he'd caught it, it slipped through his fingers.

Count: one, two, three, four . . . What is seven times seven? Forty-nine. See? You're getting there. How about the opening words of the Grimmelshausen, just to see if you can remember them?

"The present age (which some say will be the end of time) has witnessed the outbreak among common folk of a singular epidemic. . . ."

Good, excellent. Now a passage at random—Book II, Chapter 16: "By all appearances, matters were going from bad to worse with me. Indeed, so parlous was my predicament that I felt I had been born for naught but misfortune. I had put only a few leagues between myself and the Croats when I fell into the hands of some bandits. . . ."

That's right, you've got a grip on yourself, so don't let go. How are you feeling, Candido Cavalcanti?

I'd rather be in bed with Samantha, but it's only a matter of time. I'm not giving up.

That was a close call, you realize? You were within an inch of going crazy.

I know, but I made it. By the way, there's only one of me in this ceramic cesspit. I'm talking to myself. Better stop it.

He surveyed the cell. The tiled floor was a revolting mess—worse than an animal's cage.

It must have lasted more than an hour or two. Much more.

The rubber mattress was in several pieces and most of the pillow had been gnawed away. The floor was littered with broken bits of string, one of which ended in a running noose.

I must have tried to hang myself, but from what?

I'm hungry. Thirsty, too.

All right, but first you can damned well clean the place up. I want to see those tiles shine.

That was when he noticed his nails. The ones that weren't broken had grown at least a couple of inches.

Hair and beard?

Likewise. His hair, which had been cut at Belém, was now below his shoulders, his beard long and matted.

It had definitely gone on for some time—months rather than weeks.

Another gust of panic smote him. The red and black monster in his innermost depths was struggling to lift the lid, preparing to burst forth with bared teeth and rend him. . . .

One nine is nine, two nines are eighteen, three nines are twenty-seven, four nines are . . .

Slam the lid and sit on it. Sit tight.
Got you!

He swabbed the place from top to bottom and washed himself again and again. The floor was clean enough to eat off. If the tiles had been of a different texture, he could have seen his face in them.

The rubber mattress he repaired as best he could with bits of string. It was comfortable enough, but one little romp with Samantha would have dismembered it again in no time.

That's enough, drop the subject. Get back into shape. Force yourself to eat—the food could be worse. You need exercise, too. Start with a hundred circuits of the cell in one direction and a hundred in the other. Yes, I know it's tough, but keep going.

He attacked the remains of the pillow, purposefully this time. Using his teeth, he detached a piece about six inches square and carefully, delicately, nibbled it into a sphere.

A ball.

You're playing center forward for Botafogo. The goal is four tiles deep by six tiles wide, and you're up against Flamengo in the Rio Cup Final. Flamengo is leading six-one, so you've got a lot of work to do.

Before long he reduced the area of the goal. It was becoming too easy to score, even left-footed. He could now have killed a fly at fifteen feet.

For variety's sake he played Basque pelota, striking the ball with the flat of his hand for want of a chistera.

And tennis.

And checkers, imagining that every other white tile was black.

And chess, though his knowledge of the rules was hazy. Herr Doktor had made a dozen unsuccessful attempts to teach him, so he devised a version of his own in which Samantha was the white queen and the knights were jaguars.

He played a hundred games, then stopped because it was getting on his nerves.

He could now run three thousand circuits of the cell. A more dangerous form of exercise was to run at the opposite wall, climb it with the aid of his own momentum, perform a backward somersault and land on his feet. He could do it every time these days, but he'd taken a few nasty falls on the way.

He also practiced jumping in place—five thousand consecutive jumps without a break.

Plus gymnastics.

Plus holding his breath.

Plus musical composition. He composed "The Prisoner's Song," "The Ballad of the Great Silence," "Floresta Virgem" and several more, picturing the staves, notes and fingering in his mind's eye.

His mental library was another standby. *Der Abenteuerliche Simplicissimus Teutsch* he read and reread nine times in succession without forgetting a single word. The interminable sentences of *Du Côté de Chez Swann* and *Les Jeunes Filles* were harder to recall, especially in French, but Edgar Allan Poe made a pleasant change.

Sometimes, though, his mind wandered off and he had the devil's own job to recapture it.

Take care, my friend, take care! Run, jump, play games. Tennis, pelota, billiards—anything. Try heading the ball five hundred times without letting it touch the ground.

Take care!

Help me, Samantha, please help me. Don't forget me—don't desert me. Oh God, I can't take it anymore, I can't, I can't . . .

He was crawling back and forth on all fours.

"Grrr."

It was almost incessant, this toing and froing on his hands and knees.

"Grrr."

He growled softly. *The jaguar is a silent creature. A low growl is the most it ever utters.*

"Grrr."

Sometimes he would rise on his hind legs and scrabble at the wall with his claws, his twisted two-inch nails. At first he used to growl at the circle of light overhead, but not any more.

"Grrr."

He cocked his leg to urinate, defecated wherever he happened to be, ploughed through his own excrement, resumed the interminable, mesmeric pacing typical of a caged but untamed beast.

"Grrr."

Sometimes he would sink down exhausted and curl up with his chin resting on his forepaws, fangs bared and green eyes blazing.

"Grrr."

He didn't eat, he thrust his muzzle into the food and devoured it.

He didn't drink, he lapped.

"Grrr."

Some men in boots appeared. They stuck a needle in him.

"GRRR!"

He bit and clawed. His feline throat emitted hoarse, inarticulate sounds expressive of the utmost ferocity.

They put him on a leash and led him out.

I've done it, by God! I've fooled them!

He was tied to a bed by the wrists and ankles. They'd washed and shaved him, cut his hair and nails.

"Grrr."

"Phenomenally tough, this boy," said the white-haired man. "I've never known such stamina. No one ever survived more than two months in there. It's quite incredible."

"Will he ever become human again—regain his own personality, I mean?"

"His dementia is complete and irreversible, I'm afraid. You made me do this thing. The responsibility is yours, I told you that in the first place."

They fed him on raw meat and milk, the only diet he would accept. Although he still growled when spoken to, he was showing signs of domestication. He even contrived a kind of purr at the approach of one particular nurse, who was very proud of their relationship. "You see," she said, "he recognizes me. The poor boy behaves like a great big pussycat. He's quite gentle now."

He waited.

On the eleventh night, after washing him, they retied his left wrist with insufficient care.

He freed one hand, then the other, then his ankles.

Everything went like clockwork after that—he'd had ample time to plan each move, God knows. At first the slightest noise had made him jump and almost ruptured his eardrums. Now, after this ten-day interval, his sense of hearing was not only normal but better than normal. His ears were keener than they'd ever been.

The male nurse on duty had retired for a smoke, locking the steel door behind him as usual.

Hurrying to the bathroom, Candido inserted the plugs in the bathtub and washbasin, wedged the lavatory ball cock open, blocked all the overflows, turned the taps on full.

Now wait. Be as patient as that jaguar fishing in the river—except that you aren't a jaguar, you're Candido Stevenson Cavalcanti de Noronha, and you're going to escape from this prison hospital and find Samantha.

The water in the bath, basin and cistern rose until it overflowed. He perched on a chair and watched it creep across the tiled floor.

I fooled them. They thought I was crazy, but I'm not.

The water continued to rise until it was a couple of inches deep. *Now!*

He called "Help!" at the top of his voice, three times.

Somebody started hammering on the bathroom door. A voice demanded to know what the matter was.

Candido's fourth yell sounded like that of a dying man. Moments later—when he'd already immersed the bare electric wires in the water—the door burst open.

A single scream, then silence.

He withdrew the wires and draped them over a towel rail. His movements were swift and sure—even his mad jaguar act in the cell had been designed to keep him in fighting shape.

Corridors, offices, an outside staircase, a garden. In the background, a square building enclosed by barbed wire: the Great Silence.

I'd like to bump into that white-haired doctor and demonstrate the effects of his therapy.

Shouts came from the hospital as he headed for the garages. Armed guards could be seen running in the opposite direction.

He cranked a Fiat Sedanca 519 into life, got in behind the wheel and drove off. Shots rang out, but by that time the range was too great. The Fiat smashed through a pair of wooden gates. The dirt road beyond was quite drivable. He flattened his foot.

No signs of pursuit.

Jaguar's at large again.

Four hours later he abandoned the Fiat among some other cars outside the Teatro da Paz on Belém's Praça da República. With a bit of luck its presence wouldn't be reported for several days. The only spoils yielded by the trunk and glove compartment were a camera, an instrument case containing a stethoscope, some clothes in a suitcase of very fine leather— superbly tooled cayman skin—and a silver and enamel toilet case.

He raised the price of a steamer ticket by selling everything except the shirts and underpants, which he jettisoned. They weren't his size anyway.

Some musicians were playing on the bandstand in the square while trolley cars rattled past, acetylene lamps flaring. An old man tried to sell him a twelve-foot boa constrictor. Caryatids supported the chandeliers at the top of the theater's grand staircase. He could picture Samantha ascending the steps in an evening gown, eager to see the place where Pavlova had danced.

In Ver-o-Peso market he bought a toothbrush, ate a plate of *maniçoba,*

an Amazonian dish of pig's head and manioc leaves, and made friends
with some buskers who were practicing in a corner strewn with rotting
fish and vegetables. It was fourteen months since he'd plucked a guitar
string.

"That's a lovely touch you've got."

"Thanks. I haven't played for ages."

He launched into "Candido-Candida" and "The Ballad of Ezra McAuliffe." His newfound friends loved the tunes and asked who had composed them. He had, he said, and played on. "Samantha's Song" was
followed by "The Jaguar," "The Girl from Berlin," "The Prisoner's
Song," "The Great Silence Samba," and others, but he didn't sing the
words.

There were fifty of them around him now, all plying him with food and
drink. He wolfed another plate of _maniçoba,_ some _pato no tucupi_—duck
in a hot sauce—and an assortment of Amazonian fish: _tambaqui, pirarucu,
curimoto._ A couple of buskers asked if they might hawk his compositions
around. Of course, he told them, be my guest.

He was bound for Manaus? He'd already bought a ticket? The composer of such melodies shouldn't have to pay for his passage. The captain
of the river steamer, who was a cousin, would be only too pleased and
honored to have him aboard.

He used the refund to buy himself a guitar, though his fans did their
best to present him with one.

He steamed up the Amazon to the melancholy strains of "The Jaguar"
and "The Great Silence Samba." And sometimes, when darkness fell and
he was alone, to "Samantha's Song."

On the landing stage at Santarém, an intermediate port of call, Candido
passed two or three of the men he'd guided through the Mato Grosso.
He refrained from accosting them, much as he would have liked to
inquire after Clovis and Vivaldo Maria. Many days later he reached
Guajará-Mirim, where he ventured ashore with some Americans who had
engaged him as a guide and interpreter. "Simplicio," he told them when
they asked his name. "My father's a _fazendeiro,_ a rubber planter."

At dawn the next day, having explained to the Americans that his father
had been taken ill, he set off in a tropical downpour, alone and unarmed
except for a machete.

He began by following the Madeira downstream to Venancio Carneira's plantation, which was now deserted. Here he retrieved his satchel
from the spot behind the stable where he'd buried it beneath a scattering

of soil and leaves. Inside were his binoculars and the jade fish and black leather notebook he'd found on Stepa Onegin. He leafed through the notebook. It contained no names, just a string of figures.

The bullet struck the stable wall three inches above his head. He dived through the door.

"I could have killed you," said a familiar voice.

"I believe you, Afonka. You only missed me because you meant to."

Candido burrowed beneath some old fodder transformed into a stinking mass by Amazonian heat and humidity. He might be able to get out the back way if only he knew where Afonka had fired from and where he was at this moment. The next shot would be on target.

"How long have you been here, Afonka?"

"Ever since I heard you'd managed to escape from the Great Silence. I never thought you'd make it—not without going crazy."

"But *he* did, didn't he? He knew I'd make it."

"Yes."

As soon as the news reached him, Afonka had taken the first steamer to Santarém, where he'd rented a small motorboat for the journey to come.

"I didn't think you'd have the nerve to get off at Guajará-Mirim. Logically, you should have come straight here. Stepa's notebook was never found and you didn't have it on you when you were arrested." Afonka chuckled. "You're full of surprises to the end, Candido. Have you got the notebook?"

"Yes."

"I must have missed it by inches. I looked everywhere."

"Would you have gone away if you'd found it?"

Another chuckle.

"I'm not here for the notebook."

"Where's Samantha? Where's my little girl?"

"I said it would be a girl, remember?"

"What have you done with them, Afonka?"

"I don't even know where you hid them."

"You didn't answer my question."

"I answered it well enough. How can I have done anything with them if I don't know where they are?"

Candido paused, trying to decide if the man was lying.

"Are you planning to kill me?"

"I'm afraid so." There was a hint of laughter in Afonka's voice.

"A legendary death, is that it?"

Afonka laughed aloud this time.

"No, no more legends. He wants me to kill you once and for all. You'd have done better to go crazy in that cell of yours. What was it like?"

"Restful. No noisy neighbors." Candido paused again. "Is he as jealous of me as all that?"

"Jealous?"

"Think, Afonka. He can't have any other reason for wanting me dead."

"He isn't the emotional type."

"He is when it comes to me and Samantha. He's jealous of our relationship."

Silence.

"It's conceivable," Afonka said eventually. "I'd be surprised, but it's conceivable."

"I'll go back into the jungle and never come out again. Tell him you've killed me. What's the difference?"

More laughter.

"The difference is he told me to kill you and I'm going to."

Afonka was still speaking when Candido made a dash for the door. He avoided the barbed-wire fence—*never make the same mistake twice*—and headed straight for the *estrada,* the rubber-tappers' path.

He stopped short just in time: it had been fenced off. Frantically, he squeezed under the lowest rail. The path was overgrown but still passable. He made his way swiftly along it for a couple of hundred yards and then paused. Afonka was somewhere on his right.

"Can you hear me, Afonka?"

"Perfectly."

"This is the *floresta virgem.* Don't try to follow me—you haven't a chance, rifle or no rifle. We jaguars are unbeatable in the virgin forest."

"You're always good for a laugh, Candido. Hunting is my favorite occupation. One time in Siberia I stalked a bear for over five weeks. Just for the hell of it."

Candido was sheltering behind a tree trunk. The bullet hit it fair and square.

"The bear—did you get it?"

Afonka chuckled.

"Of course," he said.

All I have to do is keep enough distance between us. Not too little or he'll put a bullet in me, not too much or I'll lose him. And that I don't want.

The chase had been going on for several days. Afonka would give up first, he felt sure. He was luring the Russian to a place of no return. The Mato Grosso wasn't Siberia. It couldn't have been more different, and besides, Afonka didn't have Samantha and Candida as an incentive.

The following night he decided to get some sleep. To prevent the former bear hunter from taking him by surprise, he laid a barely discernible trail that petered out in an evil-smelling swamp thick with wild orchids and decaying tree trunks.

I mustn't underestimate him whatever I do. A snapped twig on the right bank and an almost invisible footprint in some moss thirty yards farther on. That'll be quite enough.

He retraced his steps, making no more noise than a falling leaf, and secreted himself in the bushiest tree he could find.

A minuscule sound at nine o'clock, maybe fifty yards away. He froze. The sound was repeated twice, no louder than that of a match snapping in half. And then, with startling abruptness, Afonka Tchadayev came into view.

Damn it, he's as light on his feet as I am!

Scared?

Of him, yes.

Afonka took a few more steps, then froze in his turn.

He can sense I'm not far away. This foliage isn't thick enough—if he looks up I'm a dead man.

After twenty interminable seconds, Afonka set off again. A minute later came the subdued sound of water lapping against mud: he was wading through the swamp. Silence returned, the light faded.

Candido lashed himself to a branch and dozed off.

He didn't stop once in the next two days, maintaining a pace that seared his lungs. He sighted Afonka twice through the binoculars, just as Afonka undoubtedly sighted him.

Be honest, you never thought he'd keep it up this long. He doesn't look too fresh, but perhaps he's bluffing.

The jungle, *o mato impenetrável,* was becoming more impenetrable still. No one could have come this way before, not even an Indian. Candido hesitated. Prudence counseled him to bear southeast and head for the hills.

No, forget the hills and stick to the jungle. You may leave your bones here, but so will he—unless he's a superman.

He no longer tried to cover his tracks or lay false trails that might delude Afonka into making futile, exhausting detours; he hadn't the energy. He toiled on night and day for forty-eight hours without a break, most of the time compelled to carve out a path with the machete. On two or three occasions he narrowly avoided snakes nestling in foliage, monstrous anacondas peacefully suspended from branches, or veritable cities teeming with voracious red *marabunta* ants. At last, having just dodged a wild boar whose ferocious visage reminded him of Dom Trajano, he could go no farther and treated himself to a brief rest.

Stay alert, though, I'm sure he's still behind me. It doesn't seem possible, but he's there, I know it.

He set off again. Although he sometimes went astray in the aquarium twilight that filtered down through the forest canopy, he continued to make progress. Suddenly, at dawn the next day, the ground underfoot began to rise.

If these aren't the foothills of the Chapada dos Parecis, I'm lost.

Some hours later the wall of vegetation finally parted, flooding him with sunlight.

It was the Chapada dos Parecis beyond a doubt. The mission station was about a hundred miles away. Another four or five days' march.

He scrambled to the summit of the nearest hill and got out his binoculars.

If Afonka's made it this far, he's bound to emerge at the spot where I did. After all, I've blazed a trail for him.

One hour.

Not a sign.

Afonka was lost—he had to be.

Wait a bit longer, you never know. Think: do you want him bursting in on you, grinning all over his evil face, just when you're back in her arms? The sun says it's around eight A.M. Wait till noon.

Still no sign.

Go back and make sure he's dead. Finish the job.

Afonka Tchadayev emerged from the jungle just before nightfall, crawling along on all fours and towing his rifle behind him on a rope. He'd lost his hat, his green shirt was in tatters and there was a big, bleeding gash in his right thigh. Twice he fell on his face and twice, after an eternity, he struggled up. Twenty yards clear of the trees he collapsed and lay inert.

What now?

I'll wait till tomorrow morning. If he hasn't budged by then . . .

❖   ◆   ◆

Afonka was lying where he'd lain the night before, his position almost unchanged, his rifle a rope's length away. Candido crept nearer.

It's a trap—he's leading you on, pretending to be dead or dying. As soon as you show yourself he'll put a couple of bullets into your head. You've seen him shoot—you know how good he is.

The sun was climbing into the sky. Ants were greedily advancing on the motionless mass of flesh, flies buzzing around the cuts and sores that adorned it.

Candido pounced. With the machete in his right hand, he snatched up the rifle left-handed and leveled it.

Idiot, he must have unloaded the thing. It's a trap, don't you see?

No reaction.

He put the point of the machete to Afonka's throat. One of the Russian's hands was out of sight beneath his body. On the alert for any sudden movement, Candido turned the body over with his foot.

"You won't have time to fire, Afonka."

He tossed the rifle aside, gripped Afonka's wrist and gently withdrew it. A revolver came into view. He detached the fingers that were gripping it.

"Not dead yet?"

The features were hideously bloated, the lips cracked, the nostrils pinched. A vein was still pulsing in the throat. Candido sent the revolver to join the rifle.

"No one could call you an easy man to kill, Afonka."

He took the gourd he'd filled at a mountain stream and trickled a little of the contents between the dying man's lips. Afonka opened his eyes and looked up, one little black insect motionless in the center of each off-white iris.

"Water," he muttered.

Candido gave him another drink. Then, taking Afonka's machete with him, he squatted down a few feet away.

"Good hunting, that," said Afonka.

"Except that this time the bear came off best. What's the matter with your leg?"

"Snake."

The dried blood on the machete's blade had already told its story. Bitten by a snake, Afonka had slashed his thigh in an attempt to prevent the venom from invading his bloodstream. The wound was at least three days old.

"Think you'd have got me if it hadn't been for the snake?"

"No."

"You mean I beat you?"

Childish of me to want him to admit defeat.

"Yes. It wasn't the snake—you went too fast for me."

"You towed the rifle behind you hoping to get me with the revolver when I made a grab for it?"

"Yes, but I was too tired."

Afonka's eyes closed.

Kill him right now. He was one of the Jaquar's Claws—the most dangerous of the lot. You weren't as scared of Stepa Onegin, Otto Krantz and the Man Mountain, yet you killed them. Besides, you'd be doing him a favor. That leg of his is gangrenous. He won't survive, he'll only die in agony. Kill him.

Candido, with Afonka Tchadayev on his back, had been toiling up the slopes of the Chapada dos Parecis for two days. He tended him as best he could, washing his wounds and poulticing them with leaves.

Another rest, the sixth in half a mile.

I'm crazy, lugging him around like this when he's bound to die anyway. It's not only holding me back, it's using up the last of my strength.

He put Afonka down, almost vomiting at the stench that rose from the Russian's suppurating wounds. Afonka was burning up with fever and raving in Russian. He gave him some more cool water. Afonka's eyes fluttered open and finally, after a considerable time, focused on him.

"It's pointless, what you're doing."

The voice was very faint.

"Where are they, Afonka? Where are Samantha and my daughter?"

Afonka was lucid for the first time in two days.

"You know where they are, don't you?"

No reply. Afonka closed his eyes again.

He's going fast. I could have saved myself the trouble.

"Matriona," said Afonka, "with Matriona." He mumbled a few unintelligible words, then: "Not the child."

"Just Samantha, you mean? Is she a prisoner?"

"Yes. Good hunting, Jaguar."

Candido tried to revive him, but it was over. Afonka was really dead at last.

Candido got to the *reducción* four days later. Having failed to spot even a wisp of smoke rising from it, he knew in advance that his fears were well founded. He walked through the gateway, crossed the courtyard, toured the rooms one by one. They were neat and tidy but deserted.

The letter had been left in a conspicuous position on the study table. He read it.

He was stunned for a while—how long he didn't know—but at last he got up and went outside. The Jesuit burial ground was situated behind the main building. Most of the graves were very ancient and marked with decaying wooden crosses, but one was quite recent, not yet even filled in. Bending over, Candido saw the hermit's corpse stretched out at the bottom with his hands folded on his chest in an attitude of repose that not even the worms and ants, whose work was already far advanced, could destroy. Candido took the spade lying next to the grave, filled in the hole and erected the slab of stone that was lying ready, complete with inscription. The hermit had thought of everything.

Candido made himself an omelette with some fresh eggs from the henhouse and forced it down in spite of the nausea that constricted his throat. Unable to weep although he knew that tears would be a solace, he lingered in the study for hours, forcing himself to read a book Samantha had bought in Rio. According to the author, a certain E. M. Forster, life was sometimes life and sometimes pure theater; to confuse the two was inadvisable.

He spent the night in the bed he'd shared with Samantha fifteen months ago. It still retained a trace of her perfume.

Late the next morning, having slept far longer than he intended, he set off in the direction of Cuiabá and Rio.

Though Rio, he knew, would not be the end of the road.

João Pessoa was transfixed by the sight of him sitting in the lamplit library with all the curtains drawn.

"My God, I'd abandoned all hope of seeing you again."

He barely gave Candido time to put the question. No, he hadn't seen Samantha. He knew no more than Eglantina and Lindolpho had told him. After three months at a Jesuit mission in the depths of the Chapada dos Parecis, Samantha had decided to wait no longer. Hundreds of miles farther on, having extricated themselves from the Mato Grosso and stolen a car, the four of them were stopped by a detachment of soldiers and escorted to the little town of Jatai in the state of Goiás. The officer and his men had been strangely reticent. They simply announced that Jaguar was dead and called down curses on his head for having led them on such a dance. At Jatai, Lindolpho and Eglantina were imprisoned in separate cells. Two weeks later, without explanation, they were released and told to take the little girl with them. Of Samantha there was no sign.

"Lindolpho and Eglantina came to see me as soon as they reached Rio.

I knew even less than they did—I thought you'd been executed at Belém, and so did Aristides Dantas. And then, some months ago, when I was battling yet again with your father's attorneys, one of them shook his head and stated that it was out of the question for your daughter to inherit before you were officially dead. I asked what he meant by 'officially dead'—hadn't you been executed at Belém? It wasn't as simple as that, he said, but he wasn't authorized to say more. . . ."

The little lawyer threw up his hands.

"But I'm getting ahead of myself. I've so much to tell you, the most important thing being that your daughter is here in Rio, alive and well. She's so attached to Lindolpho and Eglantina, I thought it best to leave her in their care. I should have told you that at once, old fool that I am, but I'm still half asleep. I'll have my chauffeur get the car out and we'll go there right away."

João Pessoa lived on a quiet *ladeira* overlooking the city, one of the steep, winding streets in the Santa Teresa quarter. Dawn was breaking when his chauffeur drove down it and headed south toward the sea.

"I bought the house they occupy, Dom Candido, using your money but not—for safety's sake—your name. Apart from me, no one knows of its existence except Aristides Dantas and your little girl's companions: Eglantina and Lindolpho, of course, and an English governess personally engaged by myself. There are also six bodyguards, whom I trust insofar as I trust anyone in this life."

Candido pondered the reference to "his" money. He didn't have any, but he would need some if he was going to find Samantha, and he could guess where she was—or rather, where she wasn't, namely, Brazil.

"What's this money you mentioned?"

"You've forgotten, Dom Candido, but that's understandable. You asked me to make inquiries and, if necessary, initiate proceedings for the recovery of your great-uncle's estate. It was a hard fight, but most of your claims have been met. We finally agreed, your father's attorneys and I, that a settlement would be preferable to a lawsuit—which we would doubtless have won, but only after years of legal argument."

"I'm going to need at least ten thousand dollars."

"The basic settlement amounts to four million dollars, if I've converted the sum correctly, plus the fazenda at Bragança Boa Vista, the summer residence at Petrópolis and a certain number of paintings and pieces of jewelry."

Meu Deus!

"All these assets are now held in trust by a private corporation formed by me in accordance with the discretionary powers you assigned me at our last meeting. I'll spare you the legal niceties, but the said corporation is wholly owned by you, the usufruct of its capital and other assets being enjoyed in equal shares by your daughter and Miss Samantha Franck. Should you have failed to reappear within nine years and five months of today's date, all rights of ownership would have passed to your daughter and her mother."

"You did well, Dom João. I can't thank you enough."

There are tears in my eyes. Not because of the money—I couldn't care less about that—but in memory of Great-uncle Amílcar. . . .

"Here we are."

They were carefully checked by two guards on duty at the wrought-iron gate, beyond which lay a drive flanked by bougainvilleas, mangoes, flame trees and jacarandas whose foliage met overhead to form an archway. Lindolpho emerged from the house, and the two men exchanged a silent *abraço.* Eglantina was sobbing.

"She's still asleep, Dom Candido. If I'd known you were coming . . ."

"Don't wake her."

He went alone to Candida's room, quietly pulled up a chair and sat down beside the little bed.

I didn't weep at the mission because, for some reason, defeat leaves me dry-eyed. But now . . . She's the image of Samantha—except for her eyes, so they tell me. No need to be ashamed of your tears, they aren't a sign of weakness. You're weeping for joy, and that's different.

"There's something I should tell you, Candy: I'm crazy about your mother. You call her 'Mummy' and I call her 'Samantha,' but she's one and the same person. I don't quite understand how she can be the woman I've held in my arms and the woman who used to feed you at her breast, but still. I've never been jealous of you—well, maybe a little bit, but don't hold it against me. I'm only twenty-three, that's my one excuse, and twenty-three is still pretty young, so they say.

"My love for your mother, as I see it, is final. Ever heard of E. M. Forster? He's one of her favorite authors. According to him, a once-in-a-lifetime love diminishes a person. Know what I think? I think it's possible to be a great writer and a total idiot.

"That's not the point, though. I'm very much in love with your mother, but I'm far from convinced she feels the same about me. Occasionally I'm rash enough to imagine she loves me. The rest of the time I tell myself I'm only her lover, and that she accepted me as the father of her child—you, in other words—just because I happened to be around.

"She's gone, Candida, but she wouldn't have left you behind unless she'd been forced to. She must think I'm dead, or she'd have left me a message. Alternatively, they may have told her I was still alive, and that I'd be executed unless she went away. But that I can hardly believe. She would have had to love me a lot to give in to that kind of pressure.

"No, you must have been the lever they used: either she went away with them, or they'd kill you. Remember Matriona? Beautiful, isn't she? I ought to have killed her on the banks of the Madeira, but if I had, He would have sent someone else.

"I'd better make something clear, Candy. If she's back with Him I'll kill her. No, I could never do that, I'd kill myself instead.

"Anyway, He'll kill me. It was a miracle I got Afonka Tchadayev. With Him I won't stand a chance. I'll have to go and find Him in Russia, you realize. Can you see me roaming round Moscow with a gun, playing Jaguar?

"I'm going there come what may, of course, but this time it'll end in death.

"Of course, everything seems to end in death for Jaguar."

"Vivaldo Maria's dead," said Clovis. "They executed him at Manaus with several of the others, but he only had himself to blame. He wouldn't come with us."

"Where were you going?"

"Iquitos in Peru."

Iquitos, where Leite Abade and da Silva might still be hiding out. Clovis hadn't heard from them for some time, nor did he want to. It was all over now.

He'd spent only two months at Iquitos. Weary of dreams, battles and revolutions, he made the long journey to Lima and then, with two companions, sailed from Callao. His return to Brazil had passed unnoticed.

"I'll never leave Rio again, and I never want to see another gun in my life. I suppose you know my great-grandmother's still alive?"

"It was Domitila who told me where you were and what name you were using."

"She must be at least a hundred."

Candido smiled. "As old as I feel, you mean."

Clovis, now known as Anacleto Paciência, was living in the slum district of Cachambi. He hadn't gone back to work for the trolley-car company, where he would have risked exposure, but was somehow managing to support his pregnant wife and their two children—not to mention his sister and her five children by Hastimphilo—on the meager wage he earned as a bus driver on the Rio–Belo Horizonte run.

"How are things with you, Candido?"

"Couldn't be better."

"And Samantha and your daughter?"

"They're fine too. I'm happy to have seen you again, Clovis. I'd like you to do me one last favor. Tomorrow, or as soon as convenient, please call on Dom João Pessoa, the lawyer. You know where he lives. He'll give you some papers."

"What am I to do with them?"

"Keep them for me—for Samantha, Candida and me."

They were two documents, one giving ownership of the bus company for which Clovis worked to his alias, Anacleto Paciência, the other underwriting the purchase of a house for the said Anacleto Paciência, which transaction was to be effected by Pessoa in consultation with the future owner. Clovis's expressions of gratitude were the last thing Candido wanted to hear.

"I really thought you were dead, you know, but I kept these just the same—to remember you by."

The balalaika was as mildewed as the Grimmelshausen.

"Thank you," said Candido. "May Nossa Senhora protect you, Clovis. I doubt if we'll meet again, but you never know. Samantha wants to tour Europe. We'll be gone for a considerable time."

"I'm glad to hear that. You're in danger here. In Europe you'll be able to relax."

"Exactly," said Candido. "Relax."

He spent his last night in Brazil at Ciccio's Rio mansion. The rear windows afforded a view of the Corcovado and the Rodrigo de Freitas lagoon, the front of the house faced the beach and the Atlantic rollers.

"Sure you won't have some champagne, Candido?"

"Quite sure."

"I watched you from the car this afternoon, running in Tijuca Forest. You're a terrific long-distance runner. You ran for two solid hours, but you weren't a bit tired afterward."

"I was. It didn't show, that's all."

"You never show a thing, Candido. You look the way you always did, a boy of eighteen with smiling eyes. Me, I've already got wrinkles—in spite of all the face creams I use, or because of them, I'm not sure which."

"Don't make me laugh. We're the same age."

"It must be because I'm dark-haired."

"Definitely."

"Do *you* think I've aged, Candido?"

Meu Deus!

"There, at least I've made you smile. Did you read those Prousts I gave you?"

"They were absolutely brilliant," Candido tried to remember them, "—in parts."

Beaming with pleasure, Ciccio went on to reminisce about their boyhood and adolescence. Silence had descended on the residential quarter in which Ciccio's house stood, and it was past eleven when Aristides Dantas finally turned up.

"Everyone thinks you're dead, Candido. You succumbed to multiple injuries sustained while attempting to break out of your cell, that's the official version."

"What news of my father?"

Dantas's hesitation was revealing.

"I haven't seen him."

It's infuriating, this ability to guess when people are lying or concealing part of the truth. Lucky I'm destined to die young—it would become unbearable in the long run.

"I didn't visit you in your prison at Belém, Candido, because I was in São Paulo. I went on trying, right up to the last minute."

Wait for it.

"Your father stepped in, Candido. I'd given up hope—he was your last chance."

"He got my sentence commuted?"

"He woke the president in the middle of the night."

"Were you there at the time?"

"No, I was on my way back to Belém. Unfortunately, they'd already removed you by the time I got there."

"So he had me sent to the Great Silence."

"From which no one but you has ever emerged alive, much less sane. He had no choice."

"I see," said Candido. "Does he know I'm out?"

Dantas shrugged. No idea—he'd never seen Dom Trajano again.

"Are you leaving Brazil, Candido?"

"Yes, under my name," said Ciccio, opening his mouth for the first time since Dantas's arrival. "I got hold of a passport with Candido's photograph in it instead of mine. It'll be rather fun, being in two places at once: Rio and London, Paris, Rome or wherever."

Dantas hesitantly inquired after Samantha and Candida and got the same reply as Clovis. He wasn't fooled, Candido felt sure, but he said no more, just took his leave with a cordial *abraço*.

Why does that man leave me cold? I feel absolutely nothing for him, yet he's done so much for me. But for him I'd be dead.

Candido left the next morning in Ciccio's limousine with Ciccio himself at the wheel in the guise of well-trained chauffeur. He reveled in the part. Ciccio's sense of fun, coupled with his intelligence and his love of music and books, had always formed the principal bond between them despite their dissimilar attitudes toward the opposite sex.

"You didn't play your balalaika for me yesterday, Candido."

"You didn't ask me to."

"I did, but you didn't hear. Pity."

"Keep it for me."

"I'll do no such thing. Take it with you—you'll be needing it. You won't be your old, adorable self till the day you start playing again."

"My old, adorable self is a thing of the past."

They got through the checkpoints, Ciccio flaunting his candy-pink peaked cap and uniform to distract the policemen's attention.

"There's no need to come aboard with me, Ciccio."

"Ah, we chauffeurs insist on attending to the comfort of our respected employers. Besides, in a sense the cabin's mine. Why don't I come along too, as your valet? I promise not to peek at you in the bath."

"Get going now, that siren's for you."

Ciccio burst into tears.

"You'll never come back, Candido, I know it. Or rather, I know you don't intend to. I'm sad, really I am. Try to play your balalaika."

"I will."

"Promise?"

"I promise."

Ciccio had provided him with enough books to last the voyage: Marcel Proust, of course, from *Le Côté de Guermantes* to the recently published *La Prisonnière,* but also Thoreau's *Walden, or Life in the Woods,* a selection of Melville and Poe, and a slender volume of Ciccio's own poems bound in pink leather, published privately at the author's expense, and dedicated in the most compromising fashion to "my adorable Candido, in memory of our nights together." Candido couldn't help laughing.

He didn't leave his cabin throughout the voyage, pleading seasickness, and took all his meals there. As soon as he landed in England he sought out a London bookseller specializing in original editions of the Russian classics.

"Do you have _Tales of St. Petersburg_ by Nikolai Gogol—in Russian, of course."

The bookseller, who knew Russian, asked if he spoke the language or only read it.

"Neither. I want to make someone a present of the book, that's all."

"A magnificent work," the bookseller enthused. "Dostoyevski used to say that the whole of Russian literature stemmed from one of the stories in this collection, 'The Overcoat.' "

"What a shame I don't know Russian. Never mind, I'll get hold of an English translation and read it. Is yours a complete and unabridged edition?"

It was an _original_ edition, the bookseller said stiffly. More complete than that you couldn't get.

Candido returned to his hotel in Carlos Place, the Connaught, whose impressive staircase delighted his eye. Once in his room he locked the door, sat down at the desk and placed Gogol's _Tales_ and Stepa Onegin's little black notebook side by side.

Stepa Onegin in the depths of Amazonia, reading a collection of novellas by Gogol, who wasn't even one of the classics approved by the regime. It wasn't impossible, but it seemed improbable.

Anyway, I've nothing else to go on.

He set to work, mindful of certain articles by Edgar Allan Poe, who had claimed that any secret code could be broken.

After a good two hours his first hypothesis collapsed: the first figure wasn't the number of the page, nor the second that of the line, nor the third that of the word.

It was too simple, but the Gogol had to be of some use.

The information in this notebook must be vitally important. Afonka wasn't joking when he asked what had become of it. The answer's in here somewhere.

He tried starting from the back of the book. No luck.

He tried counting the lines from foot to head. No luck again.

The words from right to left? Still no luck.

He ruled out any form of cipher based on the title, the author's name or that of the publisher.

He went out and bought three books on cryptography at a bookshop next to Fortnum & Mason in Piccadilly. Poe's articles were fresh in his mind, but techniques had improved since 1840.

He referred to the table compiled by Blaise de Vigenère, the inventor of modern cryptography. You wrote down the alphabet first horizontally and then vertically, using A as a touchstone twice over. This gave you twenty-six horizontal and the same number of vertical boxes. There were never more than twenty-six possible solutions.

He had all his meals served in the suite and ran around Hyde Park three times a day, closely watched but left in peace by puzzled London bobbies.

Vigenère's table yielded no results at all, or none that he could discern.

I suspected as much. If Stepa had had the table with him, I'd have found it when I searched him. Too bad, forget it.

Next, Kasiski, the German cryptographer whose guiding principle was that combinations of two or three letters recurred frequently in all languages, and that it was impossible, except in the briefest messages, to avoid repeating them.

Still no luck.

The Chinese cipher, so called because it was written and read vertically, not from left to right, proved equally unilluminating.

Numerical substitution? Double numerical substitution? Transposition and numerical substitution?

He'd been closeted in the Connaught for over a week, not counting his circuits of Hyde Park. "I'm studying for an exam," he explained to the staff.

How about a specially devised cipher with JAGUAR as the keyword?

I know you're tired, but too bad.

First, all on the same line: J A G U A R followed by those letters of the alphabet not contained in the word, that is, B, C, D, E, F, H, I, K, L, M, and so on.

So much for the top line.

Immediately below it, the normal alphabet: A under J, B under A, C under G. There were two A's in the keyword, but that was just too bad. Or could the second A in *jaguar* be replaced by an E?

J A G U E R B C D F H I K L, and so on.

Now the normal alphabet underneath.

Now write I LOVE YOU SAMANTHA substituting the letters in the top line: D IMVE YMT QJKJLSCJ.

Try saying that and see how it sounds. You're going crazy, man, really crazy. Calm down and think, you hear? All right, don't get mad.

The first keyword had to be JAGUAR, but there had to be a second as well. A short keyword that Stepa Onegin wouldn't forget.

USSR?

Otto (Krantz)?
Isba?
Nyet?
NYET, for God's sake! JAGUAR-NYET, the non-Jaguar. Alekhin was making a little joke. I'm sure that's it!

He pounced on the black notebook, ignoring all hyphens and punctuation marks. They were just traps.

It worked like a charm. The very first row of numerals—once he'd eliminated the first of them, which was itself a trap, though it took him five hours to grasp the fact—produced a name and address: "Warszawa (Warsaw), Adam Lipovski, 54 Bednarska."

As a final precaution, Stepa had listed all the addresses in reverse alphabetical order.

Other addresses appeared one by one, dozens of them situated in major cities throughout the world excluding Russia, where Stepa and his acolytes had needed no backup. Brazil was represented by São Paulo, Rio, Belém, Manaus, Recife and Pôrto Alegre, Europe by London, Dublin, Edinburgh, Paris, Monte Carlo, Rome, Geneva and Zurich.

One thing's for sure: the Gogol stories were no use. Improbable as it may seem, they were simply Stepa's bedside reading.

Forget Gogol. You're on the right track now.

He'd spotted Harvey Bloggs, their garrulous companion in Petrograd, Moscow and the train to Nizhni Novgorod.

For a week or more, Candido had been keeping watch near the entrance to 49, Rue de Bellechasse, one of the Paris addresses in Stepa's notebook. The ground floor was occupied by a certain Louis Grosjean, a tall, fair-haired, blue-eyed man who ran a bookshop on Avenue George V. Grosjean, who seemed convinced of the benefits of physical exercise, walked to work every morning and walked home every evening. Not having any special reason for dogging his footsteps, Candido almost gave up and went on to the next name on his list. He'd already wasted a week in London watching the comings and goings of one Paul Jupp, an apparently blameless lawyer, before impatience finally overcame him.

And then, one Sunday, Grosjean emerged from number 49 in the company of a woman. She was almost as tall as Matriona, and thus Samantha, but her blue eyes and broad cheekbones hinted at Slav blood. Candido tailed the couple to a concert hall, where he overheard them talking. The woman spoke French with a Russian or Polish accent. It wasn't much to go on, but it was all he had.

For the next few days the bookseller continued to walk to work at his usual brisk pace, heels beating out a march rhythm on the pavement, shoulders swinging freely, lithely, in a characteristic way.

One evening, he pulled down the shutters, switched off the lights and locked up, but instead of turning into Rue François Iᵉʳ as usual he walked back up Avenue George V and sat down at a café table on the Champs-Élysées.

The table was already occupied by a talkative man with buckteeth and huge horn-rimmed glasses: Harvey Bloggs.

Candido waited. Although the evening was warm, he was wearing a light raincoat made to measure in London. A reversible in beige and dark brown, like his cap, it enabled him to transform his appearance at a moment's notice.

After half an hour the bookseller rose, shook hands and walked off down the Champs-Élysées. Harvey stayed put, taking his ease. He ordered a beer and eyed the female passersby with a complacent half smile on his face.

I'm warning you, Harvey: I'll tail you to the ends of the earth—for a year if necessary. You're my only hope.

Harvey loafed around for the next five days, striking up conversations with strangers, slapping them jovially on the back, buying them drinks. On two occasions he repaired to his hotel on Avenue de Messines with some woman he'd picked up in a café or on the street.

Toward eleven on the morning of the sixth day he went to the Place de la Concorde and exchanged a few words with the porter of the Hôtel Crillon. Candido couldn't get close enough to hear, but there was no mistaking the significance of the porter's gestures: the person Harvey had asked for was out.

I'm getting warm, I can sense it.

Candido felt tempted to stop tailing Harvey and transfer his surveillance to the Crillon and its environs—Maxim's, for example, whose cuisine Samantha had often dreamed of sampling some day—but Harvey was off again.

He strolled jauntily along Rue Royale and Boulevard de la Madeleine to boulevard des Capucines, where he dined alone, casting languorous but ineffectual glances at a pair of simpering young women.

Two hours later, having lubricated his meal with three cognacs, Harvey set off once more.

I knew it: he's going back to the Crillon!

Harvey entered the hotel while Candido loitered outside for fear of being spotted.

She turned up half an hour later, as exquisitely elegant as ever. The car that dropped her outside the hotel was followed by another filled with expensive luggage.

It was Matriona.

"You needn't believe me," said Candido, "but I used to be the sole owner of a locomotive weighing all of two hundred and fifty tons. Even with her skirt off she tipped the scales at two twenty-five. Quite an armful, she was."

The girl looked away to hide a smile and went on walking down the Rue de Rivoli arcade. It was six in the evening.

"I've also eaten caymans raw," he pursued, "but that was when I was down on my luck. I'm now worth four or five million dollars—not that you'd be interested in a minor detail like that, I'm sure. It's just a conversational gambit. My main assets are a kind heart and green eyes. Have you noticed my green eyes?"

She won't hold out much longer. At a guess, another forty-five seconds.

"Another thing: I can imitate an anaconda. You wrap yourself around someone and apply gentle pressure. It feels delicious."

She's cracking.

He leaned toward her in the nicest way. Would she care to join him for a bowl of soup at some modest restaurant or take potluck in his humble student's garret?

Ten minutes later her hazel eyes were sparkling with amusement as they surveyed her surroundings.

"Some garret!"

They were in Candido's suite at the Ritz. Closely supervised by a maître d'hôtel, two or three waiters were preparing dinner in the smaller of the suite's two sitting rooms.

"Some bowl of soup!"

The waiters discreetly withdrew, pocketing their tips.

"I honestly thought you were just a student."

Her surprise was genuine. She hadn't believed a word of his stories about the locomotive, the anaconda and the caymans, still less about his millions of dollars and the great-uncle who, seventy years earlier, had pursued every Parisian *midinette* in sight. She herself was no *midinette;* she was Juliette Maizoué, senior sales assistant at the prestigious fashion house of Molyneux, 14 Rue Royale, and she spoke both English and Spanish. She was also, coincidentally, ravishing to look at.

He'd been keeping tabs on Matriona for four days now, breaking off only to snatch a few hours' sleep, and even then his duties were taken over by one of the three Parisian cabbies whose services he'd engaged by the day. Matriona always lunched or dined in the company of some man or other. On three such occasions her host was an American with an easy manner and extremely amorous disposition. It seemed clear to Candido that, having wound up the Jaguar affair, Alekhin had entrusted her with some new assignment.

Matriona spent the rest of her time shopping. She paid four visits to Edward Molyneux, but she also patronized Coco Chanel, Lucien Lelong, Maggie Rouff and Jacques Heim. Her other ports of call included shoe-makers', milliners' and perfumers' establishments, lingerie boutiques and Boucheron, the jeweler's in the Place Vendôme. But that wasn't all. She spent hours at an English bookstore on the Avenue de l'Opéra and an equal length of time in shops selling phonographs and records. More intriguing still, Candido tailed her to the Paris offices of various film production companies, almost all of them American.

Parcels *had* been delivered to her at the Hôtel Crillon, admittedly, but they were few in number. Her frenzied shopping spree had yielded pretty meager results. Candido was baffled.

Unless . . .

A crazy idea, perhaps, but it's the only possible explanation.

Candido became Juliette Maizoué's lover with an ice-cold efficiency which even he found surprising. Juliette had lost her heart to him, so now he could use her. To account for his interest in the lovely Madame Matriona Reczak he invented a story: she was the second wife of his father, who had remained behind in Brazil.

"We're made of money, Juliette, so I don't give a damn how much she spends. From what you tell me and what I've seen, however, a lot of the stuff she buys never gets delivered to her suite at the Crillon. I want to know why. She must be hoarding it somewhere, perhaps because she's planning to run off with another man, and that I won't stand for. . . ."

This yarn, with which he carefully spoon-fed Juliette at suitable moments, paid off. She not only swallowed it—his green eyes looked so innocent, dismayed and helpless—but readily consented to do a little undercover work.

Though long inured to the whims of their wealthy patrons, the staff at Molyneux had been puzzled by Madame Reczak's behavior. She often bought two copies of the same model—suits, gowns, coats—and paid for them without a murmur, always in cash. When she did buy garments of which only one specimen existed, they were a little too large for her. This was surprising, because she normally had impeccable taste and a precise idea of what suited her.

"She never has the identical or ill-fitting models delivered to the Crillon. They're put aside for delivery abroad—she says she'll notify us of the address in due course. We aren't the only ones, either. I've got a friend at Lelong—we all know each other in the trade—and she does the same thing there. I could check with Chanel and Maggie Rouff as well, if you like."

"Please do."

Candido found it hard not to tremble, so fierce was his sense of exultation.

"Does she buy shoes the same way?"

He got his answer the following day. Juliette's discreet inquiries at several of the best shoe shops in Paris had left her dumbfounded. The answer, of course, was yes.

"She's bought dozens of pairs, Candido. Some of them are definitely for herself, but the ones she's had put aside are much too big. Madame Reczak takes size 6, which is big enough already, but what can she possibly want with the others? I mean, there aren't many women around with size 9 feet!"

Not many, but Samantha was one. Her feet had been a sore point in the old days.

"Will you do me one more favor, Juliette? It's about the things she's sending abroad. . . ."

The wheels began to turn. Juliette called on Madame Reczak at the Crillon accompanied by one of Molyneux's best delivery men, Georges Dieudonné, whom she'd selected because his age and build approximated Candido's. She suggested that all the purchases made at Molyneux and elsewhere should be accompanied to their destination by Dieudonné. A consignment of such value deserved an escort, and the house of Molyneux was prepared to . . .

Madame Reczak approved of this idea. She agreed, subject to one proviso: that, on reaching his destination, the escort should wear livery and recite a message whose wording would be given him when the time came.

"My goodness, Candido, I thought she was going to refuse for a moment. The things you make me do! That woman's eyes send shivers down my spine. She's very beautiful, but if I were a man . . . Well, are you happy now you've got what you wanted?"

Yes, very happy, except that . . .

"If you're really going to take his place," Juliette went on, "I'd sooner not know how you arrange it. As far as I'm concerned, it's the real Dieudonné who's going. I don't want any trouble."

It was all quite simple. Dieudonné obtained a Soviet entry visa without delay, thanks to Matriona, and Candido would travel on his passport. All that remained was to switch photographs with the connivance of a clerk at the passport office, who was given enough money to enable him to retire to Morocco.

As for the real Dieudonné, he quietly pocketed a small fortune. It was arranged that he should quit Paris for an Italian honeymoon the day Candido left.

From now on Candido was Georges Albert Dieudonné, aged twenty-three years and eleven months, born at Fontenay-aux-Roses. Employed by the celebrated house of Edward Molyneux for seven years now, he had often delivered gowns to desperate Riviera socialites by way of the Paris-Lyons-Mediterranean express. He had even made several emergency trips to England, Switzerland and Germany, and had a working knowledge of English, German and Spanish.

Candido's departure was scheduled for the following Wednesday. An entire freight car had been reserved for him and his merchandise, first stop Vienna.

He paid a visit to Boucheron, where he purchased a necklace, bracelet and ring for a sum approaching forty thousand dollars in cash.

"For Mademoiselle Juliette Maizoué, here's the address. I'd like them delivered next Thursday evening—she's bound to be home by seven— and please enclose this letter."

He strapped up his bags and left them behind at the Ritz, but not before emptying his pockets into them. Everything went: his passport in the name of Ciccio Vaz Vasconselos, Stepa Onegin's black notebook—even the jade fish, though this he hesitated to part with for some superstitious reason he couldn't identify. He kept nothing on him that mightn't have belonged to a fashion-house delivery man.

To avoid bumping into Juliette he spent his last two days in Paris at a small hotel near the Gare de l'Est, reading.

Are you scared—scared that Matriona may have laid a trap for you?

Yes, but not of that. Nor of being killed by Him, even though it's a foregone conclusion.

No, I'm scared of what I'll find. Scared that she went with Him of her own free will.

At Vienna the Austrian customs officers showed little interest in him, given that the various containers had been sealed before they left Paris and were only in transit. Faithful to his new identity, Candido flatly refused to be parted from his treasures and insisted on sleeping in the freight car itself.

"My employer, Monsieur Edward Molyneux, has instructed me to guard them, and guard them I will. I've been entrusted with this consignment by all the big couturiers in Paris. It's worth millions, in case you didn't know."

A Westbahnhof forwarding agent introduced himself.

"I've merely got to check the destination of your trunks and packing cases. I don't even know what they contain."

"If you don't know, it wasn't thought necessary to inform you."

" 'Personal effects'—that's all it says. Will you be accompanying the consignment all the way to its final destination?"

"I'm in no hurry. I'm a salaried employee."

The real Georges Albert Dieudonné was more of a snob than the customers he served. Being replaced by an "amateur" had distressed him greatly.

After a two-day wait in a siding the freight car was coupled to another train and hauled into Czechoslovakia. At Bratislava it was coupled to yet another train and subjected to a further delay. Candido broached the supplies Dieudonné had chosen for him and exchanged three bottles of wine for half a dozen demijohns of bottled water. The train's departure took him by surprise. He'd been asleep, and it was still dark.

Next stop Russia. He'll be waiting on the platform, smiling.

The train pulled into a station crowded with men whose threadbare uniforms told Candido that he'd just crossed the frontier. Two civilians boarded the freight car.

"Monsieur Dieudonné, Georges Albert Dieudonné? Kindly come with us. We've reserved you a more comfortable carriage."

"This merchandise is my responsibility," Candido retorted, speaking German with a strong French accent like the real Dieudonné. "There's no question of my leaving it unattended."

Ah, but their orders related to his consignment as well.

The two plainclothesmen, who seemed to inspire deference and even fear in their uniformed colleagues, barely glanced at his passport while the goods were being transferred. He was soon installed in a second-class carriage from which every seat had been removed except the two reserved for his personal use. A man in a smock belted at the waist brought him some tea and two mess tins of hot food.

"Welcome to Soviet Russia, Monsieur Dieudonné."

The train pulled out. He was alone in the carriage with his trunks and packing cases neatly stacked beside him.

I could have half a dozen rifles and a couple of machine guns stowed away in there, not to mention a bomb or two.

He wasn't there, but that means nothing. Why would He come hurrying to meet me on the doorstep of His own country? He knows where I'm going, just as He's always foreseen my every move. This time won't be any different. He'll be waiting for me at the end of the line, keeping my hopes alive to the last.

He must be smiling at this very moment.

Ivano-Frankovsk. It was nightfall again, and the train had been dawdling dejectedly across the northern Ukraine. Three men in civilian clothes tapped on the window and politely inquired if they might join him. They were smiling in spite of their self-important manner.

"Far be it from us to intrude, Monsieur Dieudonné. We merely wish to satisfy ourselves that you aren't traveling in too much discomfort. Would you like us to replace one of these seats with a bed?"

His French is pretty good. They're amusing themselves at your expense, don't you see? They know exactly who you are.

"Actually, yes, a bed would be very nice. Many thanks."

One of the plainclothesmen went to the door and shouted an order in Russian. Some soldiers ran off.

"Anything else? Please don't hesitate to ask."

"Something to wash with?"

"Of course, forgive me for not having thought of it. At Kiev a more comfortable carriage will be placed at your disposal. Meantime, let us try to improve this one. We shall simply delay the train's departure."

"Would you have any reading matter? Anything in French, German or English would do."

Another order in Russian, uttered in the quiet but commanding tones of a man accustomed to instant obedience.

"Ivano-Frankovsk is somewhat short of books, especially foreign books, but we'll do our best."

What else? A balalaika? No, stop acting the fool!

"I'd appreciate a guitar," he said. "I strum a bit in my spare time."

You're crazy.

"A guitar might be a little difficult. Do you play the balalaika?"

"I'm afraid not."

"I don't know much about music, but I believe they're not dissimilar."

"You're too kind."

"My pleasure."

The train pulled out four hours late.

They really had equipped the carriage with a bed. Likewise two armchairs *(Why two? Is one of them for Him?)*, a carpet, a small table, an oil lamp and some books: three by Balzac and two by Jules Verne. Likewise a bathtub ready-filled with hot water and a small bar of soap. If he wanted another bath later, the engine driver had been instructed to provide the wherewithal.

It's crazy but logical. He's amusing Himself. He always did have a very special sense of humor.

Three baths later he reached Kiev. Seen from his bed, the left bank of the Dnieper didn't look too exciting, so he turned his attention to the right bank: the hill of St. Vladimir, the lower city, the parks and gardens, the monument erected in honor of Vladimir by the city's inhabitants, the cathedral of Santa Sophia with its bell tower, the ruins of the Golden Gate, Kiev's principal access during the eleventh century, the various museums. It was impressive, Kiev.

"I'm from Kiev myself," remarked the secret policeman.

"A beautiful city," said Candido.

This new secret policeman, a charming man, had installed Candido-Dieudonné in a "soft" or first-class carriage. No more stopping at every telegraph pole. He was aboard a passenger train and traveling at a reasonable speed, but every door of his special carriage bore a notice stating that to enter or even approach it was strictly prohibited. Even stray dogs gave it a wide berth.

The Red God has me firmly in his grasp.

After Kiev he expected the train to head northeast for Moscow, but it didn't. They were now heading southeast. South-southeast, in fact.

A monotonous routine became established. At Kharkov he was visited by another two secret policemen. They had his "soft" carriage uncoupled but did not make him get out. They smiled at him but offered no explanation, presumably because they thought he knew no Russian. Soon afterward the special-destination carriage was coupled to another train, gave a couple of jerks and started off again.

When he awoke the next morning an attendant brought him hot tea, little buttered rolls and some smoked fish.

"Spasibo."

"You speak Russian?"

"*Nyet,* me no speak Russian, me only know *spasibo nyet.* We go Caucasus and Black Sea?"

The attendant shook his head.

The Volga showed up on the left. Very wide at this point, it described a sweeping bend and turned east.

"Until very recently, the city where we are now used to be called Tsaritsyn. It has now been renamed Stalingrad in honor of the Comrade Genius and Little Father of the People."

"Ah," Candido said simply.

"You'll soon be making your delivery, Monsieur Dieudonné," said the secret policeman. He'd changed faces again, but he was still essentially the same man. "You must be eager to reach your destination."

His English was impeccable, his eyes were those of a hunter on the alert. He could only be one of Alekhin's men.

"Have arrangements been made for my return journey?"

"You're in a country where constant attention is paid to the welfare of every individual. I'm sure you've been thoroughly provided for."

"That's nice to know."

Some caviar? A little later, perhaps, he wasn't very hungry. Some vodka, then? No, he didn't drink vodka or hard liquor of any kind. And he didn't smoke either, thanks.

He settled back in his "soft" carriage. The Volga, just visible in the distance, was now on his right.

Astrakhan . . . Candido hadn't even known of its existence; he'd always thought it was a kind of fur.

The end of the road. It won't be long before I know. Strange how calm I feel—almost serene.

"Welcome to Astrakhan, Monsieur Dieudonné."

In English. Four men, three of them obviously underlings. The fourth, the one who'd just spoken, was fresh-complexioned, fair-haired and little older than himself.

"You can't often make deliveries as far-flung as this."

The smile was affable, even cordial.

"I've never been farther than London and Berlin," Candido replied, not even bothering to mangle his English. "Am I there?"

"Nearly. Have you brought a uniform?"

Of course. Tight pants with twin strips of braid down the sides, matching dolman, cap, white gloves.

"Should I get changed?"

"Please do. Meanwhile, my comrades will start unloading."

I see it all now. He wants to keep up this farce to the bitter end. I'm going to die beside the Caspian, wearing the livery of a Paris fashion house. Which reminds me: Goldilocks's comrades have faces like slaughtermen.

"I'm ready."

"How smart you look," said Goldilocks.

A chauffeur was waiting for them beside a car of which one wing was adorned with a pennant in a black leather sheath. The trunks and packing cases had been transferred to two trucks.

"Did you find the journey tiring?"

"I was anxious to get here."

"How do you like my country?"

"It's magnificent."

Goldilocks lit up but didn't proffer his wooden cigarette case.

He knows I don't smoke.

"Is it far?"

"Twenty miles or so. In the time of the czar, now so happily dead and gone, the house belonged to an aristocrat. It's very beautiful. The climate's pleasant, too—not up to Crimean standards, but the autumns are nice and mild, as you can see."

The road out of town was flanked by astrakhan tanneries. The farther the convoy progressed, the more often isolated trees could be seen jutting from the coastal plain. The sea, which was on the right, looked choppy, its surface ruffled by a stiff breeze.

"Can one go swimming?"

"In summer, certainly, but the season is nearing its end."

Like me.

Goldilocks had announced that his name was Grigory Kirilenko, for what it was worth. He was now asking questions about Paris. Candido found it hard to concentrate. A kind of fog had descended on him.

Scared? Now, yes.

The trees became thicker. The rocky coastline bore a resemblance to photographs he'd seen of the French Riviera, except that the pines were of a different variety.

"Almost there."

The garden, in which statues could be glimpsed among the trees, was enclosed by a wall of pinkish stone. Candido spotted three armed guards, one with a dog on a leash. The shady drive, paved with big slabs of white stone, looked like his idea of Italy.

Another guard. That makes four, damn it. How many more?

The car pulled up. So did the trucks.

"Here we are. And now, if you'll come with me . . ."

The portico had a double colonnade. He followed Kirilenko through it into a spacious hall with a staircase in the background.

"This way. Wait here, please."

He stood motionless in the middle of a vast room that must have been a ballroom in the old days. Three servants appeared, two women and a man. The slaughtermen were already unloading the trucks under the supervision of Kirilenko, who seemed to be enjoying himself.

"Anything special you want me to do?" Candido inquired.

"Nothing. Just give her this when the time comes."

A sealed envelope. He took it, held it in his right hand. Before long the contents of the trunks and packing cases were spread out on tables running the full length of the room: gowns and suits, skirts and blouses, shoes, furs, hats, daintily wrapped items of lingerie. The pieces of jewelry were displayed on a central table under two large silver chandeliers, the perfume bottles arrayed on an inlaid secretary.

"I think that'll do," said Kirilenko, surveying the room. "What do you think, Monsieur Dieudonné?"

"The lady will be delighted, I'm sure."

"I agree. Stay where you are, please."

Ten minutes went by. Then he heard a car pull up outside. And footsteps—familiar footsteps.

She was alone. Quite unhurriedly, she came in and shut the door behind her.

"Well," she said, "what took you so long, for God's sake?"

I don't feel like laughing. Anything but.

He held out the envelope.

"Open it," she said, "since you're itching to know what's inside."

He did so. The handwritten inscription was in English:

To Sam with all my love, Aliochka.

"All right," she said, "it's quite simple: get out of here and make a dash for the garage—it can't be more than four hundred yards. They'll shoot you down like a rabbit before you make it to the cars. They shoot everything that moves, but don't let that put you off."

Why not?

"Is he here?"

"Aliochka? Not that I know of." She stared at him. "My daughter, Candido, where is she?"

"Safe. She's fine."

She still calls him Aliochka.

Footsteps. Kirilenko entered, smiling as broadly as ever.

"Well, what do you think?" he asked Samantha in Russian.

"I'm most impressed. I couldn't have chosen better if I'd gone to Paris myself."

"There aren't ten men in this country capable of doing what he's done for you."

"I believe you. I'm overwhelmed—words fail me."

She proceeded to tour the room, pausing before each item of the extravagant wardrobe, trying on a coat here, a jacket there, holding gowns up against her the way women do.

"I need a mirror," she said.

"I've already sent for one."

"Thank you, Grigory, you're always so considerate."

Candido just stood there with Alekhin's note in his hand.

I can't move. Even in the Great Silence I never had this feeling of utter bewilderment, this inability to string two ideas together. Maybe I'm still in my tiled cell. Maybe I only think I escaped—maybe I'm imagining the whole thing.

"Monsieur Dieudonné?"

Someone was shaking his arm.

"Are you feeling all right, Monsieur Dieudonné?"

A young man with golden hair swam into view.

"I'm afraid the journey was too much for him." Samantha's voice. "It must be all those days and nights in the train. He can't be used to traveling for so long."

"Come with me," said the young man with golden hair. "You've earned a rest. I'll hand you over to Oleg—he speaks a little French."

Some men had come in with one of those big swing mirrors on legs.

"Everyone out," the young man said in Russian. "Oleg, look after the delivery man, he's asleep on his feet. Give him something to eat and put him to bed."

In the doorway, Candido turned and looked back. Samantha was at the center table, rapturously admiring the jewelry. She held a diamond necklace to her throat, inspected herself in the mirror, full face and profile, smiling. Her eyes sparkled.

He was outside in the hall.

"You come," a voice said in French.

Up the stairs, along a passage, up some more stairs.

"This room here. You eat?"

He shook his head and sat down on the bed. The foam-rubber mattress was all in one piece—they must have replaced it. Someone helped him to undress. He stood there, quite docile, then stretched out and closed his eyes.

When I open them again I'll see white tiles.

"You sleep. Eat tomorrow."

Oh sure, keep talking, you don't exist.

He was standing at the open window. Below him, the garden sloped away in a series of rose-arbored terraces to the Caspian Sea, whose waters, faintly lit by the moon, began not more than a hundred yards away. Here and there, whitish statues floated in pools of shadow beneath the pine trees. Something angular projected from a cluster of rocks on the left, possibly the bow of a boat.

Pretend you aren't mad. Even if you are mad—raving mad—why not go all the way? What have you got to lose?

NO.

Act as if everything's normal. She told you He wasn't here, so take advantage of His absence. Again, what can you lose? If you're crazy and hallucinating, nothing at all.

That settles it.

He removed his shoes and tiptoed out of the room. The door wasn't even locked.

A chorus of snores could be heard as he crept along the passage on the servants' floor, hugging the wall to minimize the risk of a creaking board. He descended the narrow staircase in his stockinged feet as stealthily as a cat.

No, not a cat, a jaguar. If you're going to hallucinate you may as well do it properly.

The hall was in semidarkness, lit only by a candle on a console table. He crept over to the door on the left, which was ajar. A light was burning at the end of the suite of rooms beyond it.

Someone must still be awake. What was his name? Yes, I remember: Grigory "Goldilocks" Kirilenko. "You're always so considerate, Grigory. . . ."

Jaguar's turning vicious at last.

He made his way back across the hall and, with infinite care, turned the gilded china doorknob. The ballroom was in darkness, so it wasn't easy to find the blue crepe de Chine dress he'd bought and put with the others, having chosen it because it matched Samantha's eyes to perfection.

Where is the goddamned thing?

Bundled up and tossed onto an armchair.

The dress, complete with matching belt, was still on its hanger, which consisted of an inverted wire V attached to a hollow wooden tube padded with silk and adorned with little ribbons. He removed the wire and discarded it, then left the ballroom and crept back across the hall.

Once outside in the garden he crouched down and waited, green, feline eyes scanning the gloom, keen ears alert for any sound.

Thirty yards away at one o'clock: a muffled cough, a scraping of feet on stone.

That's one of them.

He got ready, taking his time. Carefully opening the slim rubber case in his hand, he removed the six little wooden darts, each of them tipped with curare. Then he inserted a dart in the hollow tube, plugged both ends with the hem of his shirt, and shook it to see if the projectile moved as freely as the Indians of the Mato Grosso recommended. He hoped their curare was still effective—they'd assured him it would be. If they knew he'd padded one of their blowguns with pink silk and adorned it with blue ribbons, they would split their sides.

All set?

Yes.

He started crawling at a snail's pace on his knees and elbows.

I've got the whole night ahead of me. He's only three yards away, if that. Any farther and I'll wind up between his legs.

He readied his first dart.

I don't have too many of them. I'd better aim carefully and hit him in the right spot: the neck. I practiced for hours on end—I can't have lost the knack completely.

A faint hiss of escaping breath. Instantly, the guard clapped a hand to his neck.

And fell dead.

Now for the next one. Let's hope there aren't more than six. I can't retrieve the darts—the Indians made that very clear. They're so brittle, the slightest impact snaps them.

He killed another three.

Only two darts left now, one of which seemed to have been damaged in transit. It felt broken.

The second and third guards were hit in the neck and wrist respectively. The fourth heard him at the last moment, alerted by the rustle of a dead leaf. He turned, one hand on the holster of his Nagant.

Pfff! Full in the face.

How about that? Really vicious of me, wasn't it?

Yes, but there may be others asleep inside the house. Anyway, I mustn't forget about Goldilocks and the three servants.

And Him.

Where He's concerned, I'll have to see. It may seem odd, but I've no intention of trying to kill Him without letting Him know that, thanks to all His efforts, the harmless little kitten has turned into a jaguar—the Jaguar of His own devising. No question of ambushing Him, just the two of us face to face.

He can't be more than a foot taller and eighty pounds heavier.

I'll simply have to climb on a chair and strangle Him.

He searched the garden, the garage and the guards' bunkhouse. He even ventured as far as the little creek where the cabin cruiser was moored. Then he returned to the house.

A guard was asleep in the first room on the left, comfortably stretched out on a silk-upholstered sofa. It occurred to Candido that he'd passed within a few feet of the man earlier on, without either seeing or waking him. He must have been even quieter than he thought.

The fifth dart sped into the guard's half-open mouth at point-blank range.

The ground floor was deserted. Candido paused long enough in the kitchen to filch a length of clothesline and fashion it into a noose.

The layout of the first floor spoke for itself. Three handsome mahogany doors, two double and one single, led into what was clearly a large suite of rooms. Samantha's? He tried the handles without success. The doors were locked. From the inside?

He made his way along the passage. Eight more rooms, none of them locked. In the fifth he heard the regular breathing of someone asleep—man or woman, he couldn't tell which in the darkness. He withdrew and tried the last three rooms. Empty. Returning to the fifth, he went inside again and was brought up short by a four-poster bed. He froze, straining his eyes in the gloom.

There was someone in the bed, alone.

He lit the lamp.

"This is a sarbacane, a blowgun, and the dart in it is tipped with curare. You'd be dead in less than two seconds. Are you going to be good?"

"Yes," said Grigory Kirilenko.

"I've just killed five of your guards," Candido went on in Russian. "You can open the window and call them—I doubt if they'll answer you. Go on, try, but keep your voice down. I don't want to have to kill you right away, neither you nor the three servants."

With one end of the blowgun jammed against his cheek, Kirilenko gingerly got out of bed and opened the window.

"All quiet?"

A predictable lack of response.

"Now shut it. Hands flat against the wall, legs spread."

Candido slipped the noose over Kirilenko's head and pulled until he was on the verge of strangling him.

"Don't worry, I'm not going to kill you—yet."

He wound the clothesline around each ankle in turn.

"Face down on the floor. How many guards?"

"Five," Kirilenko gasped. "Four outside, one in the house."

"Hands behind your back."

Candido laid the blowgun aside and bound his wrists with the rest of the rope. Kirilenko was lying on his stomach, bent backwards like a bow as he tried to relieve the pressure of the noose on his neck.

"There'll be more guards arriving tomorrow, won't there?"

"No."

"If I leave you like this you'll throttle yourself, and it won't be a pleasant death. Who's coming tomorrow?"

"No one."

"What about supplies?"

"No more consignments, not for three days at least. Who are you?"

"Jaguar."

Candido gagged him by stuffing a piece of soap into his mouth. He repeated this operation a few minutes later with the manservant, who confirmed what Kirilenko had said. The two women were also gagged and tied to their bed, ankles together, arms above their heads.

Good. Now for her.

"You idiot," she called through the door, "how am I supposed to let myself out? Grigory's got the keys."

"He didn't have them on him."

"Look again."

"Anyone in there with you?"

"Only the Red Army choir—they're keeping me company till He gets back. Like them to sing you something?"

Kirilenko's eyes flashed him a despairing appeal when he returned to the fifth room. Having made sure the fool wasn't too close to asphyxia, he finally found the bunch of keys under a heap of clothes on a chair.

"I've killed nearly everyone, Samantha."

"Open this goddamned door."

He tried several keys before he found the right one.

She drew herself up in the doorway and glared at him.

"Where's my daughter?"

This time he told her in detail.

"You saw her? Is she really all right?"

"She couldn't be better."

This reply, which was tactless to say the least, earned him an immediate reprimand.

"She'd be better still if she had her mother with her," Samantha retorted icily, pushing past him into the passage. "Who exactly have you killed?"

"The guards."

"Who else?"

"Stepa Onegin, Otto Krantz, the Man Mountain, a *fazendeiro* named Venancio Carneira. And Afonka."

"Afonka? You killed Afonka?"

She obviously hadn't thought he stood a chance against Afonka. He felt tempted to tell her about the bear hunt but decided against it.

"Afonka's dead, you can depend on that," was all he said.

She stared at him. His fury was quite undiminished by the sight of her looking gorgeous in a lace nightgown and a negligee that must have cost the world. The flimsy garments were symbolic of His extravagance, and she was wearing them without so much as a blush. . . .

"What about Grigory, did you kill him too?"

He led the way to Kirilenko's room.

"Untie him," she said. "He's been kind to me—very kind."

"No."

He hustled her out of the room, locked the door and put the bunch of keys in his pocket.

"You're insane."

"True," he said with a smile. "I didn't kill the servants either, want to make sure?"

"Grigory will choke to death."

"Possibly. I haven't decided yet."

He set off up the narrow staircase leading to the top floor. She hesitated, then followed him.

Don't be distracted by anything or anyone, least of all her. Shut her out.

He allowed her a glance at the three bound and gagged servants.

"Liova—that's the younger one—she's been like a sister to me. I'd have gone crazy here without her."

"How touching."

"Untie her. She won't try anything."

"No."

"Untie her, I said!" She raised her hand, as if to strike him, but he smiled at her again.

"I've been hit a good few times in the course of my life, and I can't say it's done me much good. You may be bigger than me, Samantha, but I'm stronger. Believe me."

He shepherded her downstairs to the kitchen, where he searched around for something to eat. Dawn had just broken, and the light was already strong enough to disclose the body of one of the guards lying not far from the house. Samantha walked out into the garden and knelt beside the corpse. He saw her reach for the dart. He hesitated for a split second, then hurried to the door.

"Don't! There's curare on it."

Incredible to think I almost let her go ahead.

Samantha's hand froze.

"There were five guards," she said. "They usually took it in turns, two and two. Grigory must have ordered them to stay awake last night, on account of you. Did you really kill them all?"

"Yes."

"How did you get here?"

"It doesn't matter, does it? I'm here."

I may as well inspect the garden by daylight while I'm out here. Yes, the other three bodies are still here. The Indians were right about those darts, they all snapped off.

Discounting the color of his face, the fifth guard might still have been asleep. He was lying full length with his head resting on the arm of the silk-upholstered sofa.

"Pleased with yourself, Candido?"

He didn't answer, just went back into the kitchen and drank some milk. Then he returned to the room in which Samantha had been imprisoned for the night.

So she says. I won't even speculate on the whys and wherefores of what she's been doing—it doesn't matter for the moment. If I start thinking about that, everything will get mixed up in my head.

Two more rooms led off the first, one of them a vast bathroom. The suite was luxuriously appointed and decorated. It lacked for nothing, from English books to a large table covered with games of all kinds including several jigsaw puzzles.

And a bed—an outsize one.

It would have to be, naturally, for someone His size.

"I'd like you to come with me now, Samantha," he said.

"What'll you do if I don't, kill me?"

"I'd like you to come with me, that's all."

"What for?"

He was feeling like a swim in the Caspian.

He swam and dived for two hours. The water was cold but bearable. Several times he clung to a submerged rock and counted, just to see.

Fine, I'm in good shape.

He hauled himself on to the little concrete platform that served the cabin cruiser as a landing stage. Samantha was sitting there with her legs tucked under her.

Don't look at her too much.

"Has your swim calmed you down, Cavalcanti?"

"Not really."

He was wearing his underpants with the bunch of keys on a string around his waist.

"The Caspian Sea," said Samantha, "is ninety feet below sea level and covers an area of a hundred and sixty thousand square miles. Its average depth is approximately six hundred feet, its maximum depth three thousand. As I'm sure you've noticed, the water is saline."

Candido stretched out in the sun, which was almost hot enough to melt the ice that seemed to be clogging his veins.

My teeth aren't chattering, but I bet I could pick up a red-hot coal without feeling a thing.

"It goes without saying," Samantha went on, "that the Caspian varies in width. At this point, for instance, it's a hundred sixty miles across. A good swimmer could make it with ease in three or four days if he didn't get cramps and drown on the way, and anyhow, there's a garrison at Fort Tsevchenko on the other side. Assuming he did make it without being spotted, he would then be confronted by hundreds of miles of desert. Crossing that would only mean a few weeks without food and water. All he'd have to do then would be to climb the Himalayas."

Don't go to sleep whatever you do.

No fear of that.

"But to revert to the Caspian," Samantha pursued. "Your swimmer might consider going down it instead of across. In that case he'd only have to swim five or six hundred miles to reach the shores of a country that doesn't form part of the Union of Soviet Socialist Republics. He'd then be in Persia, capital: Teheran."

I'm still hungry. I feel like some meat.

"Candido, the keys of the boat are in that bunch you're guarding so jealously. I think you need one to start the engine and another two to open the padlocks. It's chained to the landing stage."

There must be some meat in the supplies Kirilenko mentioned.

"Mind you, I don't know if it's capable of doing six hundred miles without breaking down. I asked Grigory, but he only laughed. Besides, there'd be patrol boats to dodge."

He rose and began to dress.

"But we could try," she said. "We might stand a chance if we traveled at night and lay up by day on the eastern shore—it's almost uninhabited. Even if the engine did break down, we'd be that much nearer Persia. There may be currents, too—going in the right direction, I mean."

He pulled on Dieudonné's jacket. The bunch of keys was digging into his palm.

Relax, don't hold them so tight.

He glanced at the Caspian.

"Candido . . ."

He made the mistake of looking at her.

Don't, or you'll crack.

"Oh Candido, what have they done to you? You're different . . ."

She was crying. Crying as if she would never stop.

He walked back to the house.

He removed the handkerchief that held the piece of soap in Kirilenko's mouth, then the piece of soap itself.

"I'm going to leave this noose around your neck," he said in Russian. "Your wrists will remain bound and your feet hobbled."

"Please don't kill me," said Kirilenko.

"I will if you so much as blink without my permission, and I've got three ways of doing it: the blowgun, the revolver in my belt and this knife. I've cut plenty of throats before now—one more won't matter. Come on!"

He yanked Kirilenko to his feet and helped him downstairs with Samantha looking on. She was still crying a little.

They reached the telegraph room.

"Sit down. Hands flat on the table and don't move."

He made sure there was no gun in the drawer. Then he wrote down the text of the message.

"Oh, my God!" Samantha was leaning over his shoulder. "Candido, don't! For my sake, if you ever loved me . . . For our daughter's sake . . ."

Don't listen, shut her out. Don't even consider the possibility that, in trying to dissuade you, she's trying to protect Him.

You really have turned vicious, Jaguar.

"Send this, Kirilenko."

"I can't," Kirilenko said in a choking voice.

Candido relaxed his pressure on the noose.

"Now you can. Send it exactly as it stands and I may not kill you after all."

TO A M ALEKHIN STOP JAGUAR REQUESTS A TÊTE-À-TÊTE STOP
SOONEST

Once Kirilenko had sent the telegram, Candido locked him up in a cellar with a stout door and a barred skylight. Annoyed with himself for being so lenient, he sat the Russian on a chair and tied his wrists to a ring in the wall.

"You might at least give him something to drink," Samantha said in a subdued voice.

"As you wish," he replied, genuinely indifferent.

The floor of another cellar was stacked with big slabs of ice, and above them, suspended from hooks in the ceiling, hung some sides of beef. Taking the kitchen knife, which he'd been careful never to put down since returning from the creek, he cut himself a two-pound steak and got the kitchen stove going.

"Let's take that boat and get out of here, Candido. Please. What can I say to make you listen to me?"

"You've already said all there is to say."

She hadn't stopped talking, weeping, imploring, threatening.

Don't listen. You can't hear a thing.

"Like some of my steak?"

"He won't come," she said.

"Don't say 'He.' His name is Aliochka Mikhailovich Alekhin, remember?"

I'm going to eat it nice and rare.

Glowing embers had formed in the wood-burning stove. He searched the cupboards for some salt.

"He'll come, Samantha. He won't send his private army, either. He'll come alone, and for three good reasons. In the first place, he can't want too many comrades to know that he's done up this house for his own personal use. Secondly, he couldn't bear to admit, even to himself, that the invincible Aliochka Mikhailovich Alekhin had been defeated by a pipsqueak like me. . . ."

There, it's done enough: almost charred on both sides and bloody in the middle.

He dumped the meat on a plate and settled himself at the table.

"And thirdly, if he brought someone with him, it would mean he's scared of me."

He cut up the meat with the knife and proceeded to eat with his fingers.

Mm, good. I was starving.

"He'll come, sure enough. He'll come with his hands in his pockets, ready to crush me between his thumb and forefinger."

Not enough salt. He added some.

That's better.

"You can have the keys, Samantha. You shouldn't find it too hard to start up and cast off. There's nothing to stop you leaving. If you want to, of course."

He removed the keys from the ring and tossed them on the table. She turned on her heel and walked out. He heard her going upstairs to her room.

Pleased with yourself? Was that last bit really necessary?

I don't care. I'm falling ever faster down a well with black velvet sides as slippery as glass.

Will I be clearheaded enough tomorrow?

Yes, never fear.

Samantha's scared of you, did you notice? Scared of you and your knife.

I don't want to think about her, only Him. He'll be here by tomorrow evening. Or night. Or dawn the next day.

I need to make preparations.

He was sitting on the floor at the end of the ballroom when she came to ask him a favor. She'd prepared some food for the servants and Kirilenko. Would he open up?

"As you wish."

He did the rounds with her and locked the doors again, shutting his ears to anything she said, then went for a stroll in the garden.

When night came he wrapped himself in a blanket taken from the guards' bunkhouse and camped outside in the bushes. He slept extremely well, too, except that on two occasions he was jolted awake by the certainty that He—a dark, gigantic figure—was looming over him.

Scared?

Not at all. Just impatient.

The morning dragged by. He hadn't seen Samantha since the previous day. He was sitting among the rocks south of the creek when, at about three in the afternoon, to judge by the sun, he heard the distant hum of a car beyond the pink perimeter wall. He took another nibble at his hunk of bread, then climbed the terraced garden to a pergola covered with the remains of a dying clematis planted by some gardener in the old days.

He sat down on a marble bench. The Caspian was visible for miles through a gap between the trees.

The sound of the car was quite distinct now. Samantha must have heard it too, because he saw a curtain twitch.

I'd sooner she stayed out of sight.

Why? It doesn't matter either way.

The car finally came into view at the end of the drive that resembled the Appian Way. It pulled up. Alekhin got out, strolled over to something lying on the ground—the corpse of a guard, no doubt—and knelt down beside it. After a while he rose, returned to the car and drove on at a walking pace. He reached the expanse of gravel in front of the house, circled it leisurely, and pulled up facing the pergola. He didn't switch off. Self-assured though he was, he obviously suspected a trap.

I was right. He came alone.

"You haven't changed a bit, Cavalcanti."

"Thanks. Neither have you."

They were twenty yards apart. Alekhin was still behind the wheel. Candido, seated on his bench with the hunk of coarse bread in one hand, was picking off little bits and popping them into his mouth.

No sign of Samantha.

Alekhin switched off at last, opened the door and got out with a revolver in his hand. He tossed it onto the seat and leaned against the car.

"Georges Albert Dieudonné, eh? One thing's certain: nobody followed you here, I saw to that. But for me, you'd never have known this house existed. I had you conveyed here as comfortably as possible. My agents made sure you didn't get lost en route."

"For a moment I thought you might have planned the whole thing."

Alekhin laughed.

"And now?"

"Now I think I managed to stay a step ahead of you for once."

"You found Matriona by chance?"

"Yes, thanks to Stepa's address book."

"Stepa?"

He's genuinely forgotten. It's just as I thought: as far as He's concerned, the Jaguar affair is a dead letter and has been for ages.

"Stepa Onegin," said Candido. "There was him, and Otto Krantz, and Matriona, and an even bigger thug than you—I christened him the Man Mountain."

"I knew them by different names."

"I can well imagine."

"Ah, now I remember. You say the addresses were in that notebook?"

"In code, but I cracked it."

"And Afonka?"

"Dead too—the Brazilian jungle was too much for him. He went on trying to kill me to the last. You mustn't blame him."

"You're a hard man to kill, it seems."

"I'm afraid so. You wouldn't think it to look at me, would you?"

"I remember sensing, while shadowing you in Berlin, that you had—how shall I put it?—unexploited potential."

"I've since exploited them in a big way," Candido said, "thanks to you. You've been a regular father to me. No one could have done more to help me mature. Mind if I ask you a couple of questions?"

"My train back to Moscow doesn't leave for another six hours."

"How are you doing these days?"

"Things couldn't be better. I haven't attained all my objectives yet, but I'm getting close. I know how to bide my time."

"You aim to become the boss of this country?"

Another laugh.

"That's one ambition I've never cherished. I'm perfectly satisfied with the man at the top."

"Are you in charge of his secret police?"

"No, I've created my own organization. The Soviet Union is like a castle under siege and will remain so for generations. I'm responsible for what happens outside the castle walls."

"Hard work, eh?"

"Very hard. I appreciate your interest."

"Am I wrong, or was the Jaguar business only a secondary operation?"

"Quite secondary. It was a sort of rehearsal carried out at a time when my proposals needed clarifying in one or two respects—a demonstration, if you will."

"Of how to foment revolution and assassinate people worldwide without being held responsible?"

"Among other things, but that was only a detail. My basic idea was to create something out of nothing, if you'll pardon the comparison. To manufacture an international terrorist who could never be caught because he didn't exist. The idea found favor. It will doubtless be employed again."

"When did you lose interest in the Jaguar?"

"I don't recall, to be frank—from Mongolia onward, or even a little before. After that I left you to Matriona and Stepa Onegin, as you call them, and concentrated on more important matters. Did you kill Grigory too?"

"Yes. And the servants, while I was at it."

"Where is she?"

Alekhin had stirred at last. He glanced back at the house, only to refocus his gaze on Candido an instant later. He also took two steps to one side.

He's making sure I don't have a gun hidden under the bench or elsewhere.

"Where is she, Cavalcanti?"

"In the house."

"Alive?"

Candido turned his head and looked at the sea.

"I don't believe you've killed her," said Alekhin's voice.

"Go inside and see. What happened to Herr Doktor?"

"Dead. A heart attack."

Gravel crunched under Alekhin's feet.

When his footsteps become almost inaudible, it'll mean he's reached the grass. In other words, he'll be about twelve yards away.

Now.

Candido went on picking at his hunk of bread.

He's stopped. Range? Five or six yards.

"That bread," said Alekhin. "I hardly see how it could conceal one of the darts you used on the guards."

Silence. Candido waited.

Alekhin removed his jacket and wrapped it around his left arm. He smiled.

"So that's it. I wondered what you had in mind. Of course, some friends of yours may have arrived by sea and be covering me from the house or the rocks, but that I don't believe. You foresaw I would come alone, and—"

Alekhin moved with phenomenal speed and agility, but Candido, his entire body uncoiling like a spring, launched himself into a forward roll. His momentum took him farther than he intended. He fetched up two terraces below and landed on a projecting stone. Pain transfixed his chest.

He regained his feet in an instant and stepped back, his thumb and forefinger still embedded in the bread.

"Amusing," said Alekhin. "So we're all on our own. Your hatred of me has got the better of you, Cavalcanti—it's blinded you to reality. Those months in solitary confinement may have left more of a mark on you than you realize, has it ever occurred to you? Yes, probably, but a madman doesn't know he's mad."

As nimbly as before, he jumped down and landed with the jacket-swathed arm held out in front of him.

"As for those darts, from what I saw of the one in the guard's neck they're too brittle to penetrate clothing. But of course, you've probably replaced the original dart with a needle from the house. What's on it? Curare? How melodramatic."

He was now only one terrace above.

"You're quick, but so am I. The little Jaguar, armed with his poisoned toothpick, versus the big, bad tiger armed with nothing but his own physical strength."

Candido stepped back quickly as Alekhin launched himself off the wall. The next drop was just behind him now.

"I've slept with her, Cavalcanti. She really does have a magnificent body, doesn't she? And how passionately she makes love. . . . Quite unforgettable. Have you noticed how she sometimes hollows her back and lies there with her arms above her head and her neck arched?"

He advanced with his left arm extended. Candido retreated until he felt the parapet beneath his feet, then jumped—and almost simultaneously leapt aside as Alekhin followed suit. The Russian's fingers brushed his shoulder. Their touch was fleeting but perceptible.

"That was close, Cavalcanti. Next time, perhaps. I notice you keep backing away. Are you trying to lead me on? Where to? The creek? The boat? Have you got something hidden there? A gun, maybe?"

Alekhin resumed his advance, as light on his feet as a boxer in perfect control of every muscle.

Candido tried an outflanking movement in the direction of the creek, but the Russian headed him off. He backed away still farther, withdrawing the needle from the bread as he did so.

"What about the fragrance of her body during the act of love, Cavalcanti? What about those plaintive little moans she gives?"

He's incredibly quick for a man his size—quicker than you expected. You underestimated him, didn't you?

Alekhin rushed him, seized and held him by the left wrist. Momentarily terrified, Candido essayed a lethal thrust with his right hand but found that immobilized too. He tore himself free and ran, only to be brought up short after ten yards. There were just rocks now—rocks and the sea a few feet away.

"You must have been very confident of your ability to kill me with a few pinpricks, Cavalcanti. Well, you're going to find it harder from now on. You're cornered, in case you hadn't noticed."

Another onslaught. The fist with the jacket around it dealt him a violent blow in the stomach. He managed by some miracle to escape, but the rocks lacerated his arm as he hurled himself sideways.

"First blood to me, Cavalcanti. It may have escaped you, but you wiped your absurd little toothpick on my jacket—there can't be any curare left. We're not more than six feet apart. Try climbing that rock face behind you, and I'll take pleasure in breaking your bones one by one. You were counting on my jealousy, weren't you? Well, you were right. It seems I'm not a perfect machine after all—not yet. I shall solve that minor problem by killing her too, in the end."

Candido was watching Alekhin's right hand. He darted aside a microsecond before the Russian struck, but there was insufficient room for maneuvering. Although he got his body out of the way and launched a last, despairing attack with the needle, his right wrist was promptly imprisoned in a vicelike grip of terrifying, irresistible strength.

"Drop it, little man. Drop it!"

Inexorably, his fingers opened. The needle slipped through them.

And then, a shot.

Alekhin gave a start. He didn't fall—the bullet only grazed his neck, plowing a bloody furrow just above his shirt collar—but the distraction was sufficient to make him relax his grip. Candido launched himself into a running dive. Two more shots rang out as he hit the icy water.

He swam straight down for at least thirty feet, clung to a rock on the bottom and instinctively started counting.

He looked up just in time. The sea was crystal clear, and through it he saw Alekhin forging his way down with a breaststroke so powerful it seemed to rend the water apart. He pushed off desperately with his arms and legs.

It was a near miss. Alekhin's fingers brushed his heel.

Twenty-six, twenty-seven, twenty-eight . . .

He swims as well as I do. I should have guessed.

Thirty-nine, forty, forty-one . . .

The pressure on his eardrums increased as he dived deeper.

Fifty feet down at least. All He has to do now is wait on the surface, quietly treading water till I come up for air. I'm not a fish, after all, and even in the water He could crack me like a nut. It won't be a pleasant death.

Fifty-five, fifty-six, fifty-seven . . .

The shore, a vertical wall bare of algae and marine plants, was getting nearer.

Why didn't I swim out to sea, for God's sake? I could have repeated the Afonka trick—lured Him so far out into the Caspian that not even He would have made it back to shore. The cold would have killed us both, but at least I'd have finished Him.

He shot upward and to the left. Alekhin's fingers brushed his ankle for the second time. A black hole appeared in the wall, a narrow, elongated cleft in the rock.

What kind of fish do they have in the Caspian? Moray eels? They're carnivorous, moray eels. The Roman emperors used to feed them slaves.

Seventy-nine, eighty, eighty-one, eighty-two . . .

He had to straighten out to squeeze through the opening, which was so narrow that he could only negotiate it sideways.

If I go in any farther I'll never get out again.

Alekhin appeared in the luminous blue mouth of the cleft. A little blood was oozing from his neck, his fair hair waved to and fro like the tentacles of a sea anemone. Smiling, he clung to the rock with one hand and extended the other. His fingers grasped a fold of Candido's shirt and grazed his skin. Candido retreated a few more inches.

Ninety-nine, a hundred, a hundred and one, a hundred and two . . .

Alekhin flattened himself against the rock, still hanging on with one hand, and reached out still farther.

A hundred and three, a hundred and four, a hundred and five . . .

I can't see his face any longer, just that hand getting nearer and nearer. Now!

He seized the mooring chain he had secured to the rock the day before, wrapped it swiftly around the enormous wrist and snapped the padlock shut.

How about that, Aliochka?

Alekhin's reaction was immediate. His face reappeared in the blue luminescence, smiling no longer, and the chain drew taut. The tension was extreme, the links scraped against the rock, chipping off flinty pieces as Alekhin pulled frantically at the chain that held him prisoner desperate.

Haul away, Aliochka.

A hundred and twenty, a hundred and twenty-one, a hundred and twenty-two, a hundred and twenty-three . . .

Bubbles were escaping from Alekhin's lips.

Even if I don't get out myself, He's definitely done for. Congratulations.

A hundred and seventy, a hundred and seventy-one, a hundred and seventy-two . . .

Three minutes.

The huge frame, sculptured by the blue waters of the Caspian, went limp. The free hand opened, the feet lost their purchase on the rock. Alekhin's body seesawed gently, gracefully.

Yes, Herr Doktor, I know. Any object immersed in liquid of a greater specific gravity will rise to the surface.

Discounting the arm still wedged in the cleft, the entrance was now unobstructed.

A hundred and ninety-one, a hundred and ninety-two, a hundred and ninety-three . . .

Get out of here.

I can't.

Try again.

Two hundred and three, two hundred and four . . .

I can't, I tell you. I'm stuck.

He pulled on the chain and Alekhin's body obediently drifted across the entrance again.

Two hundred and eight—or is it nine?

Panicking, eh? Thirty feet down and your air's running out.

Two hundred and eleven . . .

There must be a way. Don't give up.

Two hundred and sixteen . . .

How do you get a truck under a bridge a few inches too low for it?

Shut up, it's useless.

They deflate the tires. All right, try it: deflate your lungs.

He distinctly saw the bubbles of air expelled from his chest rise to the roof of the little cave and cluster there like frog's spawn.

A bit more. Let it all out.

Alekhin's legs and free arm seemed to be trying to hold him back. Another surge of panic.

He isn't dead. He was shamming!

His mouth opened, his throat relaxed. He could see the surface shimmering miles above. Vertigo.

I'm not rising, I'm sinking, I . . .

Something exploded inside his head.

A big hand was gripping his neck. He started to struggle.

"Don't, Candido, it's me!"

Samantha! What's she doing in the water?

She was swimming with her body against his and her arm beneath his chin. He was lying almost on top of her.

The Caspian. I remember now.

His fingers touched rock. He choked as a wave broke over his face, but Samantha, panting hard, caught him under the arms and hauled him out. She laid him down on his back and then, when he coughed and retched, rolled him over on his side.

"Are you all right?"

Fine, couldn't be better.

He opened his eyes, but his head was spinning.

That'll teach me to try breaking records.

"Are you all right, my love?"

The face above him swam into focus. It really was Samantha. In spite of her efforts to restrain him he turned on his stomach. Laboriously, he drew up one leg, pushed down hard on his arms, got to his feet. He was on the concrete landing stage to which the boat was moored—by one chain only now. He reeled sideways and saved himself just in time by grabbing the upright of the derrick used to sway the boat ashore in bad weather.

The sea was turning from indigo to black as the daylight faded, but the body was clearly visible four or five fathoms down. Alekhin might almost have been performing a balancing act on one arm, the arm that was still imprisoned by the chain.

Candido slowly subsided. He slid down the derrick and rested his cheek against it.

It's over.

It took him a moment to realize that he was crying.

◆　◆　◆

Samantha had managed to cast off and get the engine going. They were proceeding without lights. The only lights visible were those of Astrakhan, miles away to their right.

"How can I tell where south is?"

"There must be a compass somewhere."

Candido, slumped on the bench seat behind her, closed his eyes.

I'm a long way down that black velvet well, but now it's time to get out. I can't stay here for the rest of my life.

Really? Why not?

The silence gradually roused him from his lethargy. The engine had stopped and the boat was drifting. The only sound was a gentle hiss as the bow cut through the water.

"Have we broken down?"

"I just switched off. It's almost daybreak."

She climbed on the cabin roof and made her way forward carrying a boat hook. Almost simultaneously, there was a violent jolt.

"I couldn't avoid that pebble," she said. "Let's hope it didn't make a hole in the side."

She returned, and for the first time in ages he looked at her closely. Her face was pale and drawn, with dark smudges under the eyes.

"Hungry?"

He didn't answer.

"I bet you are. I am, anyway. There's a spirit stove. I'll make us some breakfast."

She disappeared into the cabin. They were in a narrow inlet surrounded by rocks. The sea was almost out of sight, the silence broken only by the splash of wavelets and the rhythmical thud of the hull colliding with Samantha's "pebble," a boulder the size of a house.

Candido got up, feeling pretty good apart from his recurrent spells of dizziness. In a kind of cupboard he found an anchor with a coil of rope attached to it. He threw it as far as he could toward the mouth of the cove. The anchor lodged in the rocky bottom, which was less than six feet down. The boat obeyed with surprising ease when he hauled on the rope and wound it around a cleat. The banging stopped.

It's true, I am *hungry.*

Samantha set out their breakfast on a folding table: a pot of scalding hot tea, a bottle of milk, some slices of bread and butter, a jar of gooseberry jelly from Fortnum & Mason and a mass of fried eggs.

"I did eight."

"What?"

"Eggs. I did eight. How many would you like?"

"We'll go halves."

She nodded. They ate in silence, sitting side by side on the bench seat in the stern but studiously avoiding each other's eyes.

"More tea?"

"Just milk, if you don't mind."

I prefer coffee to tea. I can't help being a Brazilian.

That black velvet well—I'm coming up fast.

Yes, but I'm not out yet.

"I'm going to get some sleep," she said.

"All right. I'll keep watch."

"We'll leave again as soon as it's dark. We're going to need some more gas. There are some cans in a locker up front."

He dozed on and off for the next few hours, listening with half an ear. Around mid-afternoon he got out the cans. The contents smelled more like oil than gasoline, but he emptied two of them and part of a third into what he took to be the fuel tank.

"Any idea where we are?"

He'd taken his turn at the stove and was scrambling some eggs with whatever additions he could find. Samantha's face was moist and flushed with sleep.

"Don't ask me," he said. "You did the steering last night."

"The compass said we were going south-southeast. I spotted some headlights once. There must be a road not far away."

"See any islands?"

"No."

The map showed some islands just before the Fort Tsevchenko promontory. Maybe she'd passed them without noticing.

Maybe.

"Ugh," she said. "This is revolting."

"I'm no cook."

"And I'm no sailor."

"You didn't seem surprised when I turned up the other evening."

The words just slipped out.

Well, that's that. You've done it now.

"So what?"

"You knew I was alive?"

"No, but I hoped so."

"Why?"

She bent her head for a moment, then looked him in the eye.

"Because I wanted you to be, that's all."

She continued to hold his gaze.

"Any more questions, Cavalcanti?"

Only a couple of million, not counting the ones that really matter—for instance, about her and Him. It's one thing or the other: either ask them now or bury them at the bottom of your black velvet well. Either way, you'll regret it for the rest of your life. I know you, though. Leave those questions unasked and you'll analyze every word, every silence, every tone of voice, and suspect her of lying even when she isn't.

"We can leave now," she said. "It's getting dark, and it's raining."

I hadn't noticed—must be dreaming.

Samantha took the wheel.

"Make yourself useful," she said. "Pull up that goddamned anchor, if it isn't too much to ask."

They headed south, or as nearly south as they could manage in the darkness and the teeming rain, which reduced visibility to zero.

If we should by some miracle reach Persia, she'll want to take Candida back to the States with her. It's her country, after all.

"I own Bragança Boa Vista, the house at Petrópolis and four or five million dollars. Plus a few knickknacks."

Samantha said she didn't give a damn.

They spent the second day hidden in another cove.

"Back in Brazil they all think I'm dead—or pretend to think so. No one would recognize me. Even if they did, none of them would show it. None of them except Ciccio, and João Pessoa, and Clovis, and the staff at the fazenda. And Villa-Lobos. I plan to make music with him till I die, because I won't leave Brazil in a hurry."

She said she couldn't care less.

She's angry—she's guessed your damnfool questions. You can still ask them, but I warn you, she's always had a foul temper. It's true you made love to Juliette in Paris—you enjoyed it, too, whatever the pretext—but that wasn't the same. It's different for a man.

Think so?

No. Anyway, what proof do I have that she and He . . . She's never said anything. You're obviously getting on her nerves, you and your suspicions.

It was still pouring. The third night they had to bail out the bilge with a bucket.

Besides, who fired at Him when He got His hands on you? Who, if it wasn't her?

But are you really sure it was Him she was aiming at? All right, so you were underwater when she fired again, and the fact that she missed proves nothing— she's as good with a rifle as you are with a saucepan. On the other hand . . .

That's enough. Switch off your head.

"Why did you stop the engine?"

"I didn't. We're out of gas."

She left the wheel and sat down on the stern seat, but not before giving it a violent kick.

Silence.

"We're drifting off course," he said.

"Very observant of you. It must feel wonderful to be so smart."

"I only said it for something to say."

"Then I'd sooner you kept your mouth shut."

It was their fifth night on the Caspian, and they hadn't the least idea of their position. Two violent storms had hit them since the previous

night, but the waves seemed to be subsiding. They were definitely drifting off course, whether she liked it or not.

"There's a boat coming," he announced.

"Stop talking for the sake of it, Cavalcanti."

"Not just one boat. There are three of them or even more. Six or
seven, maybe eight."

His keen ears had caught the hum of engines. The sound was coming
from everywhere at once, left and right, behind and ahead. It steadily
increased in volume.

"They're closing in, Samantha."

She said nothing, just sat there in her characteristic way, hugging her
long legs and staring into the darkness. They continued to drift in silence,
powerless to alter course. The mist that had appeared at nightfall was
even denser than it had been six hours ago. Visibility was down to twenty
yards.

"Did you hear what I said, Samantha?"

"Yes."

"They're looking for us. I bet they've been after us for days. They'd
have caught us a long time ago if it hadn't been for all that rain and mist."

*I won't let them take us alive. God knows what they'd do to her now that He's
dead—at least He protected her. The best thing is to jump in—we're far enough
from the coast and the water's like ice. She'll go under first. I'll swim down with
her—take her body as deep as possible and weight it down with stones. First her
and then myself, so we don't come up again. They'll never know where we went.*

"Samantha?"

He hardly dared look at her, wondering how to put it into words.

All at once she gave a funny little hiccup. She was weeping almost
dry-eyed, with terrible, inconsolable intensity.

"I'm sick of this," she sobbed. "I've had enough. I've wanted to kill
myself all these months. I nearly did it, too, more than once, but I kept
telling myself you couldn't be dead, no one could kill you—you'd manage to find me again the way you did in Mongolia. I love our little girl,
God knows, but you were the one I lived and waited for—you were the
only one I thought of when things were at their worst. I told him again
and again, the swine. 'You'll never stop him,' I said. 'You don't know
him like I do. He'll come after you and kill you, you bastard. . . .' And
now you're here and they're going to recapture us. It isn't fair, Candido!"

He stared at her transfixed. He wanted to take her in his arms, but a
kind of paralysis restrained him. Samantha saved him the trouble. She
clung to him, racked with sobs.

"I'm sorry I took so long, Samantha. It wasn't my fault—I did my best,
believe me. I love you."

"*Now* you tell me! About time, too!"

His jaw dropped.

"What do you mean, about time, too? When did *you* ever tell *me* you loved me? Not once!"

"It was obvious," she said. "Of *course* I love you."

Obvious? What a nerve! Honestly, she's incredible!

A peculiar frenzy of rage overcame him. He stood up on the seat, yelled at the top of his voice, told Alekhin's minions what he thought of them, swore at them in a dozen languages. The nearer the lights came, the louder he yelled.

I don't care if they try to shoot me. I don't care if they take Samantha alive. It won't be the end even then—I'll give them the slip and drown the whole of Russia in blood. I'll teach them to tangle with the Jaguar!

In fact, all the Persian fishermen wanted was, first, to induce him to stop yelling because he was scaring the fish, and, second, to extricate his confounded boat from their nets.

About the Author

LOUP DURAND began his career as a novelist at the age of forty-two. Pseudonymously, he has written a number of French best-sellers that have won prizes and have been translated into twenty different languages. Under his own name, he is the author of the international best-seller *Daddy*. Mr. Durand lives in Italy.